Strangers Below

Strangers Below

PRIMITIVE BAPTISTS AND
AMERICAN CULTURE

Joshua Guthman

The University of North Carolina Press
CHAPEL HILL

Publication of this book was supported in part by a generous gift from Florence and James Peacock.

© 2015 The University of North Carolina Press
All rights reserved
Set in Miller by codeMantra
Manufactured in the United States of America

The paper in this book meets the guidelines for permanence and durability of the Committee on Production Guidelines for Book Longevity of the Council on Library Resources. The University of North Carolina Press has been a member of the Green Press Initiative since 2003.

Cover illustration: Members of the Primitive Baptist Church in Morehead, Kentucky, 1940; photograph by Marion Post Wolcott (Library of Congress, Prints & Photographs Division, LC-USF34-055314-D), with stock-art border added

Library of Congress Cataloging-in-Publication Data
Guthman, Joshua.
Strangers below : Primitive Baptists and American culture / Joshua Guthman.
　pages cm
Includes bibliographical references and index.
ISBN 978-1-4696-2486-0 (pbk : alk. paper) —
ISBN 978-1-4696-2487-7 (ebook)
1. Primitive Baptists—United States—History. 2. Primitive Baptists—
United States—Influence. I. Title.
BX6383.G88 2015
286'.4—dc23
2015018762

A portion of this book originated in Joshua Guthman, "'Doubts still assail me': Uncertainty and the Making of the Primitive Baptist Self in the Antebellum United States," *Religion and American Culture: A Journal of Interpretation* 23, no. 1 (Winter 2013): 75–100. Used with permission.

THIS BOOK WAS DIGITALLY PRINTED.

For August

Thus saith the Lord, Stand ye in the ways, and see, and ask for the old paths, where is the good way, and walk therein, and ye shall find rest for your souls. But they said, We will not walk therein.
—Jeremiah 6:16

Contents

Introduction: Strangers Below, 1

1 Who Are the Primitive Baptists?, 21
2 Doubts Still Assail Me, 46
3 Filthy Lucre, Hired Nurses, and the Suckling Preacher, 66
4 Rocking Daniel, 87
5 The Lonesome Sound, 116
  Epilogue: The Subterranean River, 147

Notes, 153
Bibliography, 187
Acknowledgments, 209
Index, 213

Illustrations

The St. Bartley's baptisms at the Big Spring, ca. 1895, 96

Postcard of "Negro Baptizing, Huntsville, Alabama", 97

The Primitives' African Baptist Church seen from a bird's-eye view of Huntsville, 1871, 98

Roscoe Holcomb as talisman, 122

Bud Fields and his family at home, 123

Roscoe Holcomb and the Stanley Brothers singing the old hymns, 132

Ralph Stanley and the Clinch Mountain Boys, ca. 1967, 135

Ralph Stanley as preacher and the Clinch Mountain Boys as his band of pilgrims, 136

Ralph Stanley outside and inside the old mountain church, 137

Ralph Stanley in front of his own grave, 138

Strangers Below

Introduction
Strangers Below

This book tells an unlikely story, but it is a vital one, an American one. It opens in 1803 in a rain-soaked North Carolina churchyard, moves across the long nineteenth century—to a rude settlement along Tennessee's Little Pigeon River, to a debt-ridden merchant's counting room, to an everlasting spring in the center of Huntsville, Alabama—and ends, improbably enough, onstage in Los Angeles, California, at the 2002 Grammy Awards, as an elderly bluegrass musician chanted out a deathbed dirge before a television audience of millions. It is the story of a people and a mood, and it unfolds in its own admittedly idiosyncratic way by following the peregrinations of a little-known religious sect, the Primitive Baptists, whose adherents and spiritual descendants have stood for two centuries at the center of wide-ranging battles over religious doctrine, cultural authority, and social class in a changing American South. This contrarian sect shaped two seminal moments in American history—the Second Great Awakening of the early nineteenth century and the post–World War II folk music revival—while mounting what members saw as a defense of Calvinism, the nation's oldest Protestant creed, from the forces of evangelical greed and enthusiasm. I tell that story through the often turbulent lives of black and white Primitive Baptists, lives that reveal the fractious origins of the southern Bible Belt and allow us to trace a key strain of Calvinist experience across the nineteenth century, where it was reshaped by newly emancipated African American believers, and into the twentieth, where, unmoored from its original theological underpinnings, it emerged in southern roots music as an enigmatic lonesome sound that appealed to popular audiences searching for meaning in the drift of postwar American life and the shaky days after September 11, 2001.

For me, at least, this all began where this book ends: with a sound, a keening voice begging God for deliverance, a sound that possessed me and puzzled me and would not let me go; but the story itself, the story about the Primitive Baptists' unusual journey and surprising legacy, only began to take shape for me on a road in central North Carolina several years later. There, outside the city of High Point and its thicket of furniture stores, beyond the cul-de-sacs of its residential neighborhoods, a two-lane blacktop led me for miles past neat patches of bright leaf tobacco and the occasional house and graying barn to a white-steepled, red-brick building that stood primly over the surrounding countryside. Inside, stained glass windows floated from just above the floor up close to the vaulted ceiling. Beside the building, visitors sat in a manicured garden with stone statues and a fountain. A tidy asphalt parking lot wrapped itself around the building's grounds like a cummerbund. From there, green lawns rolled down to meet the road where drivers like me, approaching from either side, could not miss a large columnar sign made out of the same red brick that read in white capitals "ABBOTTS CREEK MISSIONARY BAPTIST CHURCH."

Across the road lay another brick building—this one small, plain, low-slung, a homely cousin to the looming church. At first glance, it could be a parsonage or a recreation hall. Drivers whipping by are liable to miss it entirely. No one was there when I found it that first time, a June Sunday when the weather was silent—no clouds, no wind, no rain, no sounds at all but an occasional car on the road and, in the distance, a family, running late that day, piling out of a minivan and into the big church across the way. But on the first and third Sundays of every month, a handful of cars pull onto the gravel path running alongside this modest building and leading eventually to a cemetery studded with graves dating back to the late eighteenth century. These biweekly visitors are Primitive Baptists—believers who, as their name indicates, prize their order's antiquity—and they meet in that small, plain building, the Abbott's Creek Primitive Baptist Church, which is to say they worship in the shadow of the missionary Baptists across the road.

In this same spot nearly two hundred years ago, things, as I eventually learned, were much different. There was, as late as 1831, only one church, and its members, as they had been doing for more than seventy years, called themselves simply the Baptist Church at Abbott's Creek. When the church broke apart in 1832, the majority excommunicated a small, unruly faction—twelve in all: seven women and five men—who insisted in their petitions that they "stood on the old ground," were "orthodox in their principles," and were "clearly the old Abbots Creek Church." This defiant minority found themselves hustled out of the meetinghouse, the doors nailed shut against them as if they were vandals and the church itself a citadel built to thwart their depredations. The exiles told themselves that they had *not* been excommunicated; that, in fact, they had *chosen* to leave; that all they had done was heed the command of the apostle Paul to "withdraw yourselves from every brother that walketh disorderly"; that though they now strained under "a burden too intolerable for us to bear," they would learn to endure it, for God, they reminded one another, "rides on the storm and commands a calm at his pleasure."[1]

But God's peace never made its stately arrival at Abbott's Creek. The factions of 1832 remain with us. The commanding majority who seized possession of the church house and the little band of exiles who insisted on their own antiquity of course vanished long ago, but their ancestors endure, lodged in buildings on opposite sides of the road like pale heirs to an uncertain truce.

It is at first both confusing and a measure of the gulf between our own day and the time of the Abbott's Creek fight to realize that in 1832 it was the soon-to-be Primitives whose superior numbers earned them control of the church house and the soon-to-be missionary Baptists—people who would shortly join the evangelical Protestant vanguard, people whose descendants at today's Abbotts Creek Missionary Baptist Church now belong to the Southern Baptist Convention, a denomination more than sixteen million strong—who were shut out of the church, standing "on the old ground," carrying a burden too much to bear.

I had come to Abbott's Creek because I was fascinated and puzzled by that confusing gulf between past and present. I had been trapped in the assumptions of the archive, assumptions I had unwittingly made my own. The sources thundered with a vitriolic insistence that missionary and Primitive Baptists were but nineteenth-century manifestations of two utterly distinct peoples whose lineages could be followed like a sounding line back even to Jesus's day. I was a novice but not a fool. I knew that archival sources were perilous stuff, that the past was a baffling pageant, and that many-headed ideologies, such as Baptist successionism, were not to be confused with historical facts. Still, the angry rhetoric in the archives had me hunting for its origins in some generative event—certainly something prior to the acrimony that broke out across the pages of the church record books in 1832. I wanted to begin with the beginning. I wanted a story that was stable and linear—where effect would follow cause with a rhythmic order and the origins of the early nineteenth-century Baptist schism would reveal themselves with a pleasing finality—and I hoped, naively, that my trip to Abbott's Creek might dislodge something, that the tangible present might gift me with new powers of discernment. Nothing like that happened, not then, nor during subsequent visits, when I slowly realized that I had been circling around a historical blankness. There would be no unsullied starting point to the rippling anger in the old record books, and present-day believers, however kind and wise, had more pressing concerns than the historical questions that bedeviled me.

But what remained proved useful. The angry rhetoric, I eventually learned, told its own story in its own historic moment. And I could still catch the traces of that first sound I had heard, the sound of men and women pouring out their souls' complaints before the Lord:

> Guide me, O thou great Jehovah
> Pilgrim through this barren land
> I am weak, but thou art mighty
> Hold me with thy powerful hand.[2]

When I listened to that Primitive hymn and when I sang it with congregations gracious enough to welcome me, I heard in its bent and slowly sliding melody a lonesome sound, an unmistakable sorrow tinged with a hope of God's grace. And, finally, those two Abbott's Creek church buildings: when set against the counterpoint of the archival record, they spoke of a reversal in circumstances, of a time in the Carolina piedmont and elsewhere across the South and the western frontier when the Primitives held sway. In the old South during the years of the rolling Baptist schism, a host of aspirant creeds competed for the American soul, and nothing as taut and unfaltering as a "Bible Belt" had fastened itself upon the land. In that vertiginous religious landscape, the Primitives' message—their anger and sorrow and their fragile hope of God's grace—echoed loud and clear.

Asking for the Old Paths

That Primitive message was sounded loudest and sharpest about two hundred miles east of Abbott's Creek when, in 1827, the Baptist churches of the Kehukee Association voted to "discard all Missionary Societies, Bible Societies and Theological Seminaries, and the practices heretofore resorted to for their support, in begging money from the public . . . believing these societies and institutions to be the inventions of men, and not warranted from the word of God." The Kehukee churches belonged to one of the oldest Baptist associations in the land, and their broadside against the emergent Benevolent Empire circulated widely. "We do most sincerely believe that it is the missionary proceedings and beggars that have come among us that have been the principal cause of our distresses," the Kehukee churches announced. These "emissaries and agents of Anti-Christ"—these "traveling beggars" with their "modern schemes" and "worldly principles"—sought honor and profit, while they, the humble

Baptist churches of the Kehukee Association, styled themselves defenders of the "the simplicity and purity of the religion of Jesus Christ."[3]

Similar resolutions poured out of churches across the Republic. Well before the Kehukee declaration—as early as 1818, in fact—Baptists in the southwestern corner of the Indiana Territory questioned whether the operations of the new Baptist Board of Foreign Missions were "agreeable to gospel order." These Baptists answered themselves in the negative a year later. Nearly fifteen years after that, the majority at Abbott's Creek decided similarly. They resolved to "unfellowship" the then-new missionary societies and theological schools and anyone who aligned with them, such as that nettlesome faction they had been forced to excommunicate. These new things, they wrote, were "repugnant to the word of God."[4]

By the 1840s, tens of thousands of Baptists in churches from Florida's swamplands to Illinois's prairie had arrived at the same dire conclusions that had roused those Indiana Baptists in 1818, the Kehukee-ites in North Carolina in 1827, and the majority at Abbott's Creek in 1832. The new ecclesiastical organizations chained to new theologies, new money-raising schemes, and new means of conversion formed, as these outraged Baptists put it, a "monstrous combination" whose Christian trappings only served to disguise its worldly lusts. The American Bible Society, founded in 1816 and dedicated to placing the Holy Scriptures in every American home; the American Sunday School Union, which had worked since its inception in 1817 to strengthen religious instruction on the Lord's Day; various tract societies that papered the land with pamphlets about the virtues of temperance and the evils of Unitarianism; sectarian colleges that conferred divinity degrees upon new pastors; missionary societies, which delivered the gospel to the heathen both at home and abroad—these were not worthy organizations ushering in a new Christian millennium but the arms of an ecumenical machine that, in the name of power and efficiency, threatened to trample small Baptist churches, strangle liberty of conscience, and scrap the old, hard doctrine of predestination in favor of some cheery creed that flattered human pretensions rather than broke them.[5]

All around them these Baptist skeptics witnessed the rise of what they called "the mechanical art of revival and convert making": a kind of sinister religious theater in which unscrupulous preachers deployed "stratagems to mesmerize, galvanise, electrify, and steam the deluded . . . into full compliance with all the terms and conditions of a worldly religion"—a religion that relied on "human systems instead of God's revealed truth, human ceremonies instead of God's ordinances, and human schemes instead of that order and plan which God has established in His word."

The men and women who refused to be mesmerized pleaded with their fellow Baptists—and with Methodists and Presbyterians, too—to disenthrall themselves from these new institutions, theologies, and means of worship that they had devised, supposedly, to further Christian causes. With a sour clarity, these Baptist skeptics could see that an age of religious subterfuge—what they called "priestcraft"—loomed. Everyone else seemed so sweetly blind.[6]

What, though, to call these unusual believers? Early on, some dubbed themselves "Reformed Baptists." Others preferred to see themselves as "Old Fashioned Baptists," as "Baptists of the Old Stamp," or, most often, as members of the "Old School" stubbornly refusing to cede the clear warrant of the past to the hordes of missionary upstarts and pulpit innovators. (Their foes lit upon that stubbornness: "Hardshells" or "Straight Jackets" seemed a suitable moniker, they said. "Ignoramuses" would also do.) By the mid-1830s, the faction that insisted that all Baptists—all Christians—needed to "ask for the old paths, where is the good way" settled on the appellation "Primitive" in order to signify their direct descent from the primitive church—that is, the church gathered around Jesus nearly two thousand years earlier. They would look back in order to go forward.[7]

That Baptists of any stripe would denounce missionary work as ungodly, that they would, in fact, describe its underpinnings—the seminaries and Sunday schools; the various Christian publishing enterprises; the white-hot tent revivals; the money-raising operations, both modest and monumental—as a monstrous "system of cheating" and missionaries themselves as "hungry mosquetoes" ("Knock them off, and they will at you again, and again, until they suck your money," explained one of those Kehukee-ites), can seem baffling and peculiar, especially when glimpsed from our own historical moment where an evangelical culture of entrepreneurialism, activism, and missionary outreach stretches from the Bible Belt to the Sun Belt. But in the antebellum South, that modern evangelical ethos—organizationally sophisticated, theologically pragmatic, politically adroit—was only just being born. Many Baptists hoped its life would not last long.[8]

Until then, Baptist history had been a cramped affair. Baptists' numbers were paltry: a mere 80,000 members scattered across the entire nation by 1800. Their organizational efforts were perpetually hamstrung, the seemingly inevitable result of trying to coordinate a denomination that was allergic to church hierarchies. And in some regions, such as Virginia and New England, they were subject to persecution from official church establishments. But Baptists were hardly the only Christian denomination that struggled across the eighteenth century. Other evangelicals also fared poorly, and prospects in the South were especially bleak. "By the most generous estimate," writes the historian Christine Leigh Heyrman, "less than one-fifth of all southern whites over the age of sixteen and fewer than one-tenth of all African Americans had joined Baptist, Methodist, or Presbyterian churches by the 1810s." If, as they say, God could always count on Dixie, he certainly got off to a rough start.[9]

But between the 1810s and 1840s, membership in Baptist and other evangelical churches grew swiftly, and each denomination fashioned new organizations and tactics that were both cause and effect of the evangelical transformation of southern society. The once-tiny evangelical sects, which in their eighteenth-century youth had reached out to the region's dispossessed—the poor, women, slaves—learned by the early nineteenth century to successfully recruit new, more powerful adherents: white men, patriarchs, slaveholders. These decades also witnessed the beginnings of all those things that the Primitive Baptists loathed: orchestrated revival strategies, popular Arminianized theologies that told sinners that they could play an active part in their own salvation, national missionary societies, state and regional denominational conventions, a network of Sunday schools and divinity colleges, and the proliferation of mite societies that asked for money for everything from caring for the infirm neighbor up the road to posting preachers to foreign lands thick with "Hindoos," "Musselmans," and sundry other idolaters. As Heyrman has succinctly explained, southern evangelicalism was "being reinvented during the very decades that it took root in that region."[10]

For evangelicals, these were years of flux, and for several decades, it seemed in certain places that the Primitives might carry the day. As far north as Ohio, Baptist churches, which had raised more than five hundred dollars for foreign missions in 1820, ceased raising money at all between 1821 and 1828. In 1829 and 1830, the state's Baptists found a total of fifteen dollars for missionary causes. At the same time in Tennessee, "the cause of missions was for a long time paralyzed," noted a frustrated missionary Baptist chronicler. By 1845, "not a man [in Tennessee] ventured to open his mouth in favor of any benevolent enterprise or action," lamented another missionary. "The missionary societies were dissolved, and the associations rescinded all their resolutions by which they were in any way connected with these measures, and in this respect, the stillness of death rested upon the whole people!" In the meantime, the Primitives had carried their success farther south where, by the 1830s, "the churches of north Alabama almost without exception became anti-missionary." In

Mississippi, they destroyed the Baptist state convention. In Virginia, more than a third of the state's Baptist associations had moved into the Primitive column by 1845. And in the Wiregrass Country of southern Georgia and the Florida panhandle, Primitives, many of them migrants from eastern North Carolina and Georgia, flourished through the 1840s.[11]

Primitive Baptists in the antebellum South struggled not only with missionary adversaries but with an austere set of beliefs that put them at odds both with their fellow evangelicals and with their own fraught consciences. As uncompromising believers who, as one historian put it, were "more Calvinistic . . . than Calvin himself," the Primitive Baptists held two core beliefs from which flowed all other matters of worldly and otherworldly affairs.[12] They knew that God had decided, even before the foundation of the world, who among the planet's later inhabitants would be saved and who would be damned. They knew as well that not only could they never know or understand God's decision, they could do nothing to alter it. This put them far indeed from the more optimistic strains of evangelical Protestantism sweeping the early Republic. For the Primitives, God's grace, the only possible succor in a fallen world, remained a mystery. When Primitive Baptists sang the words of their old hymn "I Am a Stranger Here Below"—"I am a stranger here below / And what I am 'tis hard to know"—they sang from personal experience.[13]

Those plangent lines distilled a quintessentially Primitive disposition of estrangement, uncertainty, and longing. Even after their conversions, Primitives suspected themselves to be aliens to God and strangers to his grace. Divine assurance did not entirely elude them, but those warm comforts, which enfolded legions of American Protestants across the nineteenth century, were for the Primitives always imperfect and fleeting. A Primitive woman, for instance, might in quick succession sense God's mercy, question her ability to discern God's will, beg him to guide her doubting footsteps, and conclude finally that she was, in the hymn's words, "so vile, so prone to sin / I fear that I'm not born again." To read Primitives' writing is to trace that harrowing journey again and again. The uncertainty was unrelenting. Yet to be a Primitive Baptist was not to be utterly desolate and paralyzed. To be a stranger below was to hang on to the expectancy of a better world above. Hope flickered against the looming walls of self-abhorrence and fear. "All feeling sense seems to be gone / Which makes me fear that I am wrong," the Primitives sang. But in that whirling confusion, the lonely Primitive pilgrim learned the lesson announced in the "I Am a Stranger Here Below" hymn's last line: "Without free grace, I know I'm lost." There was a deep loneliness in that kind of knowledge. One's own ability and desire earned one nothing. But for Primitive Baptists, there was, too, a peculiar comfort: though God's will might be inscrutable, his majesty was infinite, his power was inextinguishable, and his saving grace alone carried redemption's promise.

Primitive Baptists in the Telling of American Religious History

Scholars have attempted to explain these dissenters from any number of directions—as products of a particular regional culture, as heirs to a centuries-long tradition of Calvinistic theology, as disaffected subsistence farmers, as exemplars of a widespread primitivist cultural impulse. We have, on the one hand, studies that locate the Primitives' revolt in theological controversy. In this model, rows over doctrinal matters, such as unconditional election and salvation by grace alone, pushed the Primitives' dissent. Ideas became the key motivating factor.[14] Other scholars, however, seize upon the Primitives' rural roots, their apparent provincialism, their contempt for paper money, and their fear of bureaucracy as signs that the anti-missions controversy was caused by worldly affairs: economics, social class, cultural revolt, even politics.[15] This second model shows how even religious rebellions are caused by larger social forces. The debate here is no doubt familiar, although the particulars, here as elsewhere, may at first be alien. Why do religions exist? What functions do they serve? Do they legitimate social hierarchies or destabilize them? Indeed, the argument over causation in the Primitive Baptist case parallels similar disputes between historians of the antebellum market revolution and religious awakenings, where scholars have tended to stress either evangelicalism's liberatory potential or its social conformity.[16] The questions are at once invigorating and enervating, for though the quality of debate has been high, the discussion remains deadlocked. There has been, of course, a third response to the Primitives—namely, to avoid them. Many histories do not reference them at all or mention them only in passing or treat them as unproblematic members of a larger Baptist denomination or evangelical movement. Such avoidance is troubling, though often understandable given both the immense diversity of American Protestantism and Primitives' comparatively small numbers. But the upshot of this "approach" is that southern evangelicalism begins by implication to resemble the united front of some evangelicals' imaginations—an inevitable, unstoppable force—rather than a movement or movements rife with divisions.[17]

For a generation now, scholars of religion have been working their way through and around and beyond theoretical and historiographic impasses like these. Indeed, hardened distinctions between intellectual and social history (or between ideas and social class, or theology and culture) of the kind limned above can seem quaint when viewed in the light of scholarship on what we now call "lived religion," an approach that locates religion *in* culture rather than in some realm—call it "belief" or "inner experience" or "the transcendent"—set apart from the day-to-day workings of power, habit, and ideology. To study lived religion is to examine, as the historian Robert Orsi explains in a foundational essay, "how particular people, in particular places and times, live in, with, through, and against the religious idioms available to them in culture—*all* the idioms, including (often enough) those not explicitly their 'own.'" This is the study of religion as something more palpable than naked belief, more mundane than rarefied doctrine. But to study lived religion is not to dispense with belief and doctrine or to dismiss them as mere social constructs. It is instead to find belief and doctrine—and much else that we deem religious—in, as Orsi puts it, "the unfolding interplay of religious idiom and immediate circumstance that constantly reconfigures both."[18]

To capture something of this "unfolding interplay," scholars have increasingly relied upon the theoretical concept of practice, a sweeping term that encompasses not only those typical things religious people do, such as praying and meditating, reading holy texts and singing sacred music, but also how such things and other far more mundane activities and dispositions—say, one's gait and posture or a culture's codes of hospitality and its manner of dress—embody everyday habitual expressions of religion's power and authority. By turning toward the study of practice, by analyzing what people do with their religious worlds even as those religious worlds structure what they do, scholars have materialized the study of something—religion—that their intellectual forebears long understood as essentially ethereal, spiritual, and transcendent. While the results of this theoretical shift have hardly escaped the serial wrangling over terminology that marks any attempt to define religion, scholars have nonetheless crafted a range of studies that have gone a long way toward closing what Orsi has described has "the otiose boundary between 'inner' experience and 'outer' environment that so bedevils scholarship in religious studies."[19]

Running parallel to this materialist turn in religious studies—this turn toward the study of lived religion and practice—has been a concurrent emotional turn in scholarship across the humanities and social sciences. (So many turns! One becomes dizzy.) Here, too, scholars have sought to dissolve artificial boundaries between mind and body and to retheorize something—in this case, feelings, moods, passions, sentiments—that generations of Western common sense had deemed natural, involuntary, internal, irrational, and universal. Anthropologists and even some psychologists have demonstrated the local, cultural, and social origins of emotional expression. In many non-Western cultures, for example, the line between "emotion" and "thought" is not drawn so sharply, and emotions themselves are understood as products of social exchange rather than as innate "inner" essences buried within the self. Based on findings such as these, many ethnographers have concluded that emotions, instead of being biologically based, are culturally constructed discursive phenomena that mask the workings of power. Or, as the anthropologist Catherine Lutz explains in her classic ethnography of emotions on a Pacific atoll, "emotional experience is not precultural but pre*eminently* cultural."[20] Although historians of emotion have not, in general, abandoned the idea that emotions may have some biological basis, they have embraced theoretical approaches akin to Lutz's that emphasize emotions' cultural plasticity. Doing so has allowed historians to recover and explain personal experiences and changes in emotional standards without resorting to the often ahistorical, sexist, and ethnocentric methods of psychohistory or psychobiography.[21]

Much of the recent historical scholarship on emotion contends that the navigation of feeling—the struggle to control or manage emotional expression—constitutes the central drama of human social life. In his synthesis of emotions scholarship in cognitive psychology, anthropology, and history, William Reddy concludes that "a normative style of emotional management is a fundamental element of every political regime, of every cultural hegemony." Those who master that normative emotional style gain and maintain political and cultural power, while "those who fail to conform may be marginalized or severely sanctioned." Like Reddy, other leading historians of emotion, such as John Corrigan, Nicole Eustace, and Barbara Rosenwein, have focused on how different social groups (families, neighborhoods, churches, denominations, and so forth), groups Rosenwein describes as "emotional communities," exercise power by summoning, shaping, tolerating, and deploring various forms of emotional expression.[22]

In the case of nineteenth-century American evangelicalism, Corrigan has persuasively argued that "the Protestant construction of the emotional profile of other groups ... functioned as a *primary* means by which to distinguish themselves from such groups. Emotionality, just as importantly as skin color, national origin, language, or social class, served as a marker of difference for the Protestant middle class." Even within Protestantism, revivalist Christianity—the kind of Christianity that so disturbed the Primitives—fostered what the historian Richard Rabinowitz has termed "a new cognitive style" that took the freedom of the human will as a kind of emotional and religious common sense.[23]

To study American evangelicalism is, then, to study emotion. A history of religion that is attuned to changes in emotional expression and alterations in emotional norms—a history aware of the contest between multiple and overlapping emotional communities and of how individuals within those communities navigate life—promises to help us grasp more fully the sweeping changes in nineteenth-century American religious life. "Belief has much to do with feeling," Rosenwein writes. "If I believe that my anger should be 'let out,' I cultivate it. . . . People train themselves to have feelings that are based on their beliefs. At the same time, feelings help to create, validate, and maintain belief systems." There, in the gap between belief and emotional expression, between doctrine and experience, religion is felt and lived.[24]

Strangers Below leans on the scholarship of both lived religion and emotion to tell the Primitives' story. In practice, this means that this book sees the birth and flowering of the Primitive Baptist movement between the 1820s and 1850s as a kind of religious improvisation worked out by certain betwixt-and-between evangelicals in response to dramatic shifts in Protestant church life, emotional norms, theology, gender roles, and the further intrusion of the capitalist marketplace. Or, to put all of this somewhat involutedly in the terms of the foregoing discussion, to become a Primitive Baptist in, say, 1835, was to call upon and reconfigure, consciously and unconsciously, particular religious and emotional idioms— for instance, one's tentative experience of God's grace, one's abiding sense of guilt, one's uncertainty about one's own reliability as an interpreter of the state of one's soul, *and* the conventional discursive structures one used to tell about these things to oneself and to others—while many of those around such believers, including their neighbors, friends, and even, perhaps, members of their own family, did likewise but reached different conclusions or yielded to different feelings, to feelings that, say, spoke to their assurance of the Holy Spirit's touch, their certainty of salvation, and their knowledge that in a time after time they would, as the camp meeting hymn put it, meet on Canaan's happy shore. Primitive Baptists felt differently than other Baptists, than other Christians. Or, at the very least, their records—their diaries and letters, published and unpublished conversion narratives, polemics and sermons—demonstrate that they expressed, meditated upon, cultivated, and discouraged certain emotions in ways strikingly different from other Christians in the young nation.

If there is an answer to the Primitives' rise, we must begin here with this experiential difference. It is not enough to describe the Primitives as anti-missionaries. Nor is it sufficient to dub them "Calvinists," opponents of "new measures" revivalism, or exemplars of a restorationist impulse. They were anti-missionaries because they feared the certitude of the missionary crusade. They were Calvinistic because they lived lives assailed by doubt. They opposed revivalism because the camp meeting's sweaty haste left them cold, bereft, and, as they put it, "alone in every sense of the word" despite prodigious efforts to make it not so. The Primitives' movement was birthed in these feelings of fear, doubt, and loneliness—and the anger that quenched and fueled them all at once.

When we conceive of the Primitive Baptist movement as a kind of religious improvisation worked out by people in crisis, we see a way to yoke together the various prior explanations of the Primitives' rise. It is true, of course, that Primitives were strict Calvinists who dissented from Arminian theology. And it is true, too, that their dissent was steeped in the kind of customary republicanism that plain folk used to savage elites. But these theological and social postures were inhabited by people roiled by personal crisis. There is no good way to separate, say, the Primitives' persistent worrying about the status of their own souls, and indeed their persistent worrying about whether or not they could know anything at all about the status of their own souls, from their formal predestinarianism and their place in what they experienced as the uncertain capitalist marketplace. When we see the Primitives' emotional experiences as their embodied or lived theology, we find a way to understand their movement without pigeon-holing it as an instance of cultural revolt or theological dissent. We discover in Primitive Baptists' lived experiences a better explanation of who they were and why they came to be. But that is not all we learn.

The Primitive Baptists are exacting tutors; their history compels us to revisit and reassess many of the key developments in American religious history. Early nineteenth-century Primitives, for instance, stood within and against the great religious movement of their time: the surge of evangelical Protestant revivals and institution building that scholars refer to as the Second Great Awakening. The Primitives, too, had been forged in the fires of religious awakening, but they quickly found their identity as bitter opponents of missionaries, benevolent enterprises, Bible tract societies, Sunday schools, and the other accoutrements of evangelical Protestantism.[25]

The rise of the Primitive Baptists in the early decades of the nineteenth century marked a crisis within the bounds of American evangelicalism. Because the Primitives broke with evangelicalism in a number of ways—against missions, against revivals, against the blandishments of an Arminianized theology—one is tempted to understand them as a distinctly *anti*-evangelical phenomenon. But like their evangelical adversaries, the Primitives believed in the necessity of the new birth, understood the Bible as God's inerrant word, knew the importance of an individual's relationship with God, and preached about the enduring urgency of Christ's sacrifice on the cross. And, of course, that first generation of Primitives and their bitterest enemies, the missionary Baptists, shared church pews and much else right up until the point at which the schism, like a creeping plague, came upon their particular church or church association.

The Primitives' peculiar status as both children and adversaries of evangelicalism allows us to rethink the origins of the Bible Belt as a fight, not between the churched and the unchurched or between insurgent evangelicals and a curdled Anglican establishment, but between different factions of evangelicals over the future of American Protestantism. The Primitive Baptists—a people beset by doubt, a community of believers engaged in constant anguished discussion about their own minds—provide an especially compelling case study of emotion's power to call communities of belief together and stir them to action. The Primitives' story shows that antebellum fights over the fate of American Protestantism were catalyzed not so much by the organized structures of denomination, social class, and ideology as by believers' unpredictable emotional experiences. To know, then, about the Primitives' faith, their crises of belief, their organizational life, and their struggles with their former brethren will be to gauge the stakes of the Second Great Awakening. And to gauge these stakes is to learn why and how the Protestant temperament changed in the early decades of the nineteenth century.

The Primitives, to be sure, were not alone in revolting against missionary operations, the rise of "new measures" revivalism, or the drift toward an Arminianized faith. In antebellum America, one could find anti-missionary Baptists bearing a variety of theologies, including ones that were directly at odds with the Primitives' Calvinism. Nor were the Baptists the only evangelical denomination riven by theological and political differences. Presbyterians, for instance, also split into Old School and New School camps, though their divisions do not map neatly onto the issues that drove the Baptist schism. (To take but one example,

Old School Presbyterians, though they castigated their New School foes for going wobbly on the doctrine of original sin, continued to support foreign and domestic missions.) And a desire to return to first things, to be guided by the canonized bones of a pure past—well, many other American Christians, including the Mormons, the Shakers, the Disciples of Christ, and, by the 1850s, the Landmark Baptists, also felt that longing. But no antebellum Christian group combined these traits or did so in such potent fashion as did the Primitive Baptists, and so to study these Old School Baptists is to examine in full the fault lines of antebellum Protestantism.[26]

Dwelling on the Primitives also demands that we revisit the scenes of another American epic: the rise and fall of Calvinism, the nation's oldest Protestant creed. There is a story that historians tell about the long decline of Calvinism in the West: that its militant rigidities, which had served it so well during the Reformation, were out of place in an increasingly cosmopolitan world; that Enlightenment rationality pushed it aside; and that various strains of Protestantism either more moderate or pliant came to warm the Christian soul. It is a true story, and though its details often change depending upon each particular historian's predispositions, the essential fact that Calvinist orthodoxies exert less influence than they once did is incontrovertible. The American scenes of this saga always seem to play out in Massachusetts, but there is no good reason to exclude action in the South, the Appalachians, and along the western frontier, where the Primitive Baptists made their stand.[27]

Now, one could argue with some justification that the Primitives' efflorescence was merely a sign of their irrelevance—that their fulminations against Arminianism were just the last violent shudderings of a dying beast. And perhaps that is their role in the story. Consult the numbers. Haul out the church and association records. They tell the familiar tale of decline, for even at their peak—approximately 138,000 members and 3,700 churches in 1906—Primitive Baptists' ranks remained modest.[28] By the turn of the twenty-first century, only about 72,000 members were left.[29] Look more closely and watch an always-fractious sect turn upon itself, splitting into ever-more discrete units even as its overall numbers plunged. Even that 1906 high-water mark disguised intra-Primitive fissures that formed in the late nineteenth century before rupturing in the twentieth. Divisions arose between so-called absoluters (those who believed that God predestined every act) and the vast majority of Primitives who held that God's predestinary powers applied only to the selection of the elect. In 1907, African American believers, who had established their own churches after emancipation, cleaved in two after a breakaway faction met in Huntsville, Alabama, to form the National Primitive Baptist Convention, which, as its name suggests, embraced organizational practices, such as the founding of seminaries and Sunday schools, more commonly associated with missionary Baptists. As with black Primitives, so too with their white counterparts, some of whom began in 1909 to identify themselves as Progressive Primitive Baptists because they incorporated instrumental music into worship, paid a salary to their elders, and established Sunday schools. Two decades later, a clutch of central Appalachian churches married their Calvinist heritage to the doctrines of Universalism. (An unlikely match, to be sure.) Told from an "authentic" Primitive point of view, this story reads like a nightmare of fragmentation and disintegration, as small blocks of the true church began worshipping in ways increasingly similar to other Protestants. Even if we expand our circle to include the Primitives' religious siblings, the collection of Appalachian churches that contemporary scholars call the "Old-Time Baptists"—the Regulars and Old Regulars, the Separates and Uniteds—the story remains largely the same.[30] Like the Separate Baptists, these factions either shed Calvinistic doctrines long ago or, like the Old Regulars, retained both their Calvinistic roots and small church memberships as the twentieth century wore on. It is hard to escape the confines of the declension narrative.

Strangers Below, however, tells a different story about both the Primitive Baptists and their Old-Time Baptist brethren, and it is a story, strangely enough, about reinvention and influence, about how black Primitives in the decades after the Civil War rehabilitated Calvinism's withered frame and about how something like an Old Baptist spirit—what W. J. Cash called, in a different context, a "thoroughgoing Calvinism in feeling"—seeped into American popular culture during the twentieth century even as the influence of orthodox Calvinist doctrines waned. We have been so busy tracking and, in some cases, celebrating Calvinism's decline that we have sometimes overlooked its strange persistence and startling transformations. We also know much about how a formal theology changes over time, but we still know too little about how formal theologies escape their ecclesiastical bounds to lead altered lives in the imaginative culture of people bewilderingly disconnected from those theologies' originating circumstances. By understanding religion as a changing set of embodied practices and moods—and not just a network of beliefs—we can tell a different story about American Calvinism. Following the turns of the Primitives' old paths in the modern world will take us there.[31]

The Shape of This Book

This is an idiosyncratic book. It seeks to tell something of the Primitives' history, but it does not offer anything like a comprehensive chronicle of the Primitives' movement. It draws on recent theoretical advances in religious studies and history, but it does not systematically apply any of those elegant theories of human action and emotional expression. In its essayistic structure and chronological leaps, and especially in its insistence or, as some might put it, its intuition that the Primitives reveal something essential about the American story, it owes a lot to new and old ways of doing American studies. But enough with preambles. Here is the book's map:

Chapter 1 explores the construction of competing stereotypes of the Baptist self in the historical memory of Primitive Baptists and their missionary Baptist adversaries. By reading denominational, associational, and church histories as imaginative documents, the chapter shows how these works crafted and sustained the two clashing group identities—one missionary, the other primitive or anti-missionary—that lay at the center of the nineteenth-century Baptist schism. Each side drew its idealized self-portrait against a backdrop teeming with invidious caricatures of its opponent. These stereotyped notions of self and other lived in such perfect symbiosis that for Baptists on either side of the schism it often seemed unimaginable that such different groups of believers had shared church pews only years earlier. Here, in the emotional construction of self and other, lay the schism's origins and durability.

Chapter 2 considers the making of the Primitive Baptist self at the level of the individual. This chapter uses a series of individual portraits to argue that the Primitive Baptist self was fundamentally an uncertain one, that such uncertainty manifested itself in a variety of ways, that such manifestations were first of all emotional experiences that could be linked to—but were not identical with—Calvinist theology, and that such emotional experiences catalyzed the Primitive Baptist movement both by binding Primitives to each other and by serving as the raw material that Primitives projected onto their missionary enemies. Primitives—both before and after their conversions—tried but failed to cultivate the normative emotional style associated with Protestant evangelicalism. That style was characterized by what historians have long recognized as some of evangelical Protestantism's distinctive features: the pursuit of a direct, personal relationship with God; the necessity of the new birth, in which the Holy Spirit regenerated a corrupt heart and outward emotional expression—tears, shouting, fainting—signified piety; and an increased emphasis on the role of the human will in aiding the conversion process. This was an emotional style that prized sincerity and promoted instrumentality. It was, as we know, a style whose rapid growth in popularity mirrored the rapid growth of evangelical Protestantism across the early decades of the nineteenth century. The public testimonies and private papers of people who became Primitive Baptists show that, despite prodigious efforts, they failed to conform to evangelical Protestantism's emotional habits and that there were enormous consequences for that failure. For Primitive Baptists, it was their questioning—especially their experience of persistent doubt—that set them apart from their evangelical brethren. But the uncertainty that colored Primitive Baptist selfhood motivated believers rather than paralyzed them. It propelled them toward a community of like-minded souls, and it stirred those souls to action as a more ardent brand of evangelical Protestantism crowded church pews. In their uncertain selves, in lives assailed by doubt, we find the most compelling explanation of their movement's unlikely rise.

Chapter 3 uses two extended case studies to show how uncertain Primitive Baptist selves—the merchant and elder C. B. Hassell and the polemicist Joshua Lawrence—navigated the currents of the antebellum marketplace and the rapids of antebellum gender relations. In the Primitive Baptist imagination, missionaries were deceivers, and their sordid calling was greed. These well-heeled mercenaries roamed the land carrying a corrupt "do and live" gospel in saddlebags stuffed with silver. Primitives studied them well. In Tarboro, North Carolina, in 1830, a Primitive church clerk dutifully noted that missionaries arrived in town "with an intent to deceive the Simple & get the money from the poor & ignorant under pretence of grat piety & ardent zeal—to prey upon them." In Tennessee at the same time, a group of Old School Baptists summed up their sect's opponents like so: "The advocates of modern missions are (with a few exceptions) men of style and fashion, pictures of elegance and pride, and are for the most part rolling in luxury and ease at the expenses of the laboring class of the community." When Primitives were not summoning the republican-inflected rhetoric of poverty to advance their cause, they drew on the related language of technology and the marketplace. Their evangelical opponents, they said, devised a "steam system of religion," "built a piece of Arminian machinery," and "have factories to manufacture preachers." Many historians, in turn, have interpreted such bombast as a sure sign of the Primitives' poverty or plain-folk status and, therefore, have concluded that class resentment lay beneath the Primitives' apparently religious concerns. This chapter, by contrast, argues that for Primitives the antebellum marketplace, its terminology, and its attendant phenomena—panics, commodity shortages, currency crises, techniques of merchandizing—are best understood as cultural resources, though ones the Primitives were not always conscious of mining. The Primitives' gendered rhetoric reveals a similar complexity. Because Primitive elders sneered at dandified missionaries and the "silly women" who were their quarry, the Primitive movement seems, at first blush, to be either a patriarchal reaction against the forces of a burgeoning, feminized evangelicalism or yet another example of how erstwhile religious insurgents adopted the South's dominant social mores—its patriarchy, especially—in order to gain converts. But, as this chapter shows, the Primitives' patriarchy was deeply compromised, ambivalent, streaked with doubt, and only partially conscious.[32]

Chapter 4 follows African American Primitives from emancipation through the founding of the National Primitive Baptist Convention in 1907. It is a journey that has almost entirely escaped notice, even though its burdens and aspirations tell us something new about African Americans, Calvinism's complex fate, and the religious reconstruction of the post–Civil War South. It has long been a given among historians of religion in the slave South that Calvinism had little, if any, purchase among the enslaved; that slaves may have employed Calvinistic language but were in practice Arminian; that Primitive Baptist worship, in particular, was simply too reserved to appeal to African Americans; and that the doctrines of predestination were invariably arms of the status quo. Many historians have thought that a sin-obsessed Calvinism was inimical to the emancipationist energies coursing through black America in the decades after the Civil War.[33] The post-emancipatory founding of black Primitive Baptist churches would seem at the very least to complicate these assumptions. But black Primitives did more than merely exist. In the decades after the Civil War, they built an education movement grounded in what they described as their "hard-shell" Calvinist identity: rugged yet flexible, durable yet capable of adaptation. These black Primitives floated a new kind of Primitive-ness, a new kind of American Calvinism—born in slavery, reborn in freedom, and then reconceived in the twilight between Reconstruction and Jim Crow as an educational movement that moved nimbly between black Calvinist sectarianism and optimistic ecumenism. And in their dramatic public baptisms and private "Rocking Daniel" ring shouts, we find evidence of how they drew from the deep well of Afro-Baptist ritual to sustain a black Calvinism that was at once organizationally dynamic and theologically orthodox. Their story is a crucial and until now overlooked chapter in the reinvention of black religious life during the late nineteenth and early twentieth centuries.

Chapter 5 leaps ahead to the mid-twentieth century and falls back to the seventeenth. An Old Baptist feeling, or "lonesome sound," rooted in the folkways of dissenting Protestantism and in the nineteenth-century Primitive revolt seeped into modern American culture through the singing of old-time musician Roscoe Holcomb (an Old Regular Baptist) and bluegrass legend Ralph Stanley (a Primitive Baptist). Holcomb's emergence during the postwar folk revival and Stanley's long career as well as his more recent stardom mark the strange eruption in the nation's popular culture of a distinctly Calvinist presence that had, by all rights, been buried at least a century before. But outside the confines of church, sect, and denomination, religion can have a second life ruled by mood and metaphor, where believer and nonbeliever alike reconfigure an old faith to meet their current needs. In Holcomb's and Stanley's music, we hear Calvinism's second, altered life sung into being. No longer hardened doctrine or the subject of contention in a fight over evangelicalism's future, Calvinism was free to become a feeling, a mood—a lonesome sound whose echoes connected audiences to the past even while signaling their distance from it.

I end my study here, in the early twenty-first century, with a brief conclusion that explains how I came to meet the Primitive Baptists and why their presence has been so fleeting in the stories we tell about America's religious past. The sounds that captured me so many years ago still won't let me go. They fascinate and confound me and lead me back, always, to an unlikely journey along the old paths.

1 Who Are the Primitive Baptists?

Lemuel Burkitt preached while the rain fell. The hot August sky had cracked open, drenching the thousands gathered in the churchyard to hear Burkitt's sermon and feel "the powerful effect," the "uncommon effect," that only Christ's grace could bring. The effects that day were obvious. Men and women sobbed, collapsed to the ground as if dropped by a bullet, begged their fellows to pray for them, and cried out to God, "What must I do to be saved?" Others stood frozen in the hot rain, transfixed by Burkitt's words, the holy company, and the legacy of two years of revival. For in North Carolina in 1803, God worked wonders. He sobered drunks and reformed liars, he made enemies into friends and friends into converts, he stamped out jealousy and led the wayward home. And in a rain-soaked churchyard, his spirit moved.[1]

For decades, Burkitt and his fellow Baptists had waited and worked for times like these. When, at last, the revival arrived and meetinghouses overflowed, they praised God for his mercy, testified to his power, and beseeched him for a future filled with such glad tidings. "After a long and tedious night," wrote Burkitt in the midst of the revival, "the sable curtains are withdrawn, the day has dawned, and the sun of righteousness has risen with healing on his wings." Burkitt's Baptists in North Carolina and Virginia, like so many Protestants in the young nation, read the signs: the revivals burning across America at the century's beginning were, they believed, marks of spiritual progress and harbingers, they hoped, of a Christian millennium. Wrote Burkitt: "O! that He would continue his work until the whole world is brought into subjection to the peaceable reign of Christ."[2]

Within a generation, however, enthusiasm turned to skepticism. For many Baptists in the churches stoked by Burkitt's preaching, the once-familiar flames of revival looked now like strange fire. Calm reflection, a gift of time's passage, revealed different truths and exposed grievous errors. By the mid-1820s, skeptics viewed the 1802–3 revival and others like it with alarm. Obscured within the blessed multitude who joined the visible church during those heady days were those who were, as the skeptics explained, "deceived and [who] deceive[d] others." The revivalists' zeal, they wrote, had excited base passions of those gathered to hear the gospel. Led by such frantic guides, prospective converts lost their way: "human means" and religious "machinery" supplanted the Holy Spirit's healing touch. In the revival's cauldron, would-be Christians "imbibed the notion that the Holy Ghost is somehow so the creature of human feelings that he is led to regenerate persons by our getting their animal feelings excited; and therefore that in the same proportion as we can by any measure get the feelings of the people aroused, there will be a revival of religion." For the latter-day doubters, the revivalistic excesses during the earliest years of the nineteenth century beckoned the wholesale religious treachery of their own day. What Lemuel Burkitt had described as progress, these later Baptist skeptics interpreted as the beginnings of decline. What Burkitt once assumed to be fidelity to God's word was now seen as a step toward heresy.[3]

Baptist skeptics had dotted the ranks of the faithful for years, but they only crystallized into a movement by the late 1820s. During those years, they began referring to themselves as "Reformed" or "Old School" or "Primitive" Baptists, and as their various monikers indicate, they disavowed much of what passed for recent Baptist history. These Old School Baptists insisted on their own antiquity and chastised fellow Baptists for elevating the edicts of modern benevolent and missionary organizations above the authority of local churches and for adopting the "new measures" of the day, a term friend and foe alike used to describe the techniques of emotional excitement deployed by modern revivalists.[4] While the Primitives railed against an array of Protestants, they engaged most often with their opponents within Baptist ranks. Primitives described these people in sweeping terms as "new school" or "missionary" Baptists, labels that did not correspond to a particular sect but rather evoked those believers' association with what Primitives considered the objectionable traits of modern evangelicalism, namely, its innovations in doctrine and its devotion to organized benevolent causes, such as the emergent missions movement.[5]

In the wake of the schism, each group of Baptists produced preacher-historians who turned to the past for all the usual reasons: for comfort, for justification, for curiosity, for the preservation of memories that might serve as a guides to the present. Among the many functions of the accounts crafted by these preacher-historians was creation of a story of origins for each side in this intradenominational dispute. Believers could read these accounts and learn something of how their group came to be. These rather different missionary and Primitive chronicles appeared around midcentury—several decades after the schism—but each side's writers drew from a shared Baptist past. That shared past was most carefully reconstructed in a third set of histories, written in the early 1800s by chroniclers poised on the cusp of two different eras in Baptist history. These early nineteenth-century chroniclers wrote during the series of revivals that were the most dramatic sign of Baptists' changing fortunes. While these books reflected that era's newfound confidence, the writers dwelled extensively on the lean times of the eighteenth century, when persecution and disorder reigned. This shared past of both persecution and incipient triumph offered missionary and Primitive chroniclers the raw materials for their own distinct tales of Baptists' deep history and their more recent conflicts.

What is most remarkable about the early nineteenth-century Baptist histories is their optimism. Within the world conjured up by these works, there is a consistent movement from confusion to certainty, from chaos to order, from fragmentation to unity, from darkness to light. To be sure, the journey charted by the early Baptist historians never comes across as a leisurely tour though an uncomplicated landscape. Hardship, deprivation, persecution, and doubt litter the way, but these trials were mere prelude. Writing in the midst of the early nineteenth-century revivals, writers such as William Fristoe, Lemuel Burkitt, and Jesse Read interpreted their ancestors' struggles as signs of providence. They brandished their ancestors' scars, for the old wounds symbolically bound them to their Savior, who, too, had suffered before rising. The prior struggle only confirmed the present triumph.

The confidence that had seeped into the early nineteenth-century accounts soon flooded Baptist discourse. In histories of the sect written in midcentury, missionary Baptist writers displayed their faith in progress and their devotion to a God who matched their aspirations. These were romantic tales where a Baptist phalanx conquered adversity and subdued chaos. Baptists' recent history—their growth in numbers, their benevolent efforts, their initiatives to formally educate the laity and the ministry, and especially their foreign and domestic missionary work—became the logical consequence of a divine plan to save the world. To these forward-looking missionary Baptists, their Primitive brethren, who opposed all that they held dear, were an obstinate people whose objections to progress could stem only from ignorance and a small-minded fear of the future.

Surveying the same historical landscape as their missionary brethren, Primitive Baptists spied deception and error where others had found glory and progress. Works by Primitive Baptist writers took a tragic and, in some cases, bitterly sarcastic turn. Primitive chroniclers often mocked the missionary Baptists' optimism and what they saw as their insouciant certainty of salvation. When mockery would not suffice, Primitives accused missionary Baptists of betraying their faith for reasons of pride, envy, or greed. Old heroes also populated Primitives' tales of the Baptist past, but these men persevered rather than triumphed. And in those lonely luminaries of days gone by, the Primitives discovered themselves: yet another generation of Baptists, stretching back even to the apostolic church, called to shepherd the true faith through a benighted land. What made such tales particularly tragic and instructive was that the worst deceivers now emerged from Baptist meetinghouses, not from the Catholic Church, the Anglican establishment, or other familiar bastions of treachery.

We recognize these plots. They are conventional, trite even, and, therefore, we may be tempted to dismiss them as cloudy narrative strategies that obscure our view of the past as it really was. But such conventions should not frustrate us. The poetics of these seemingly bland accounts have much to tell us. The church and denominational histories that nineteenth-century Baptists wrote were at once factual reports and symbolic narratives. Anyone who has perused these or similar texts—their pages blanketed with baptismal tallies, lists of preachers' names, and bare summaries of church meetings—can confirm the former description. But even these seemingly tedious details find themselves part of a larger whole whose thematic qualities are revealing. Even the driest of these histories is a record of a people's self-understanding: who they were, how they came to be, what they believed, where they were headed. If, then, we consider Baptists' church, associational, and denominational histories as imaginative documents, if we read them not only for what their authors wrote but for the ways in which they wrote, then we can begin to understand the two very different group identities—one missionary, the other "primitive" or anti-missionary—at the center of the nineteenth-century Baptist schism. We will see how these identities came to be, how they were sustained in the histories each side crafted, and how their competing notions of self and other lived in such perfect symbiosis that it often seemed unimaginable that such different groups of believers had shared church pews only years earlier.

The Shared Past

In the colonial South, Baptists found themselves estranged from the rituals of plantation society and persecuted by colonial authorities. Outsiders noticed appearances first. In Virginia's piedmont and tidewater, Baptists with "cut off" hair dressed plainly, refusing to don the powdered wigs or ruffled finery that filled the gentry's armoires. Baptist churches were rudely constructed outposts or, just as often, members' homes—a stark contrast to the more elaborate Anglican houses of worship that drew the allegiance of each parish's most powerful families. Even more than appearances, Baptists' rituals and beliefs set them apart from other colonial Christians. They insisted that their central rite be full-water immersion (no sprinkling allowed); that only adults were allowed to descend and then arise from this watery grave (no baptism for babies); and, finally, that all baptisms needed to be preceded by the convert's experience of the saving grace of Jesus Christ (without such an encounter one remained outside the beloved community).[6]

Anglicans exacted a steep price from Baptist dissenters. Like all colonists in Virginia, Maryland, and the Carolinas, Baptists were required to attend and pay taxes to support the "established" Church of England. For noncompliance, Baptists faced fines, jailings, whippings, and beatings. Throughout the 1700s, Baptists' numbers remained small, but their presence nevertheless betokened a radical rupture in the region's gentry-dominated social life. By 1760, Baptists in colonial Virginia, at least, constituted what the historian Rhys Isaac memorably describes as an "evangelical counterculture," revolting against both the Anglican religious establishment and the time-honored pastimes—hunting, drinking, horse racing, music making—of the planter society.[7]

Even as they fended off Anglicans and pleasure-seeking planters, eighteenth-century Baptists found their own ranks splintering. Consider North Carolina, where three different Baptist sects sparred over matters profound and petty. The General Baptists, many of them settlers from England, arrived first. They preached a generous doctrine of general atonement, which held that Christ's death made salvation possible for everyone and not just for a limited number of predestined souls. Nor did these General Baptists require prospective members to publicly relate their conversion experience or submit to full-water immersion. A second Baptist sect called Regulars also traced its roots to England, but members espoused a "particular" rather than a "general" atonement. That is, in Calvinist fashion, they believed that Christ's atonement on the cross did not make salvation available to all but instead saved only a predestined elect. The growth of Regular Baptist churches in North Carolina soon outpaced the halting progress made by the General Baptists, and by the 1760s Regular Baptist churches in New Jersey had dispatched preachers to the South on a successful campaign to reorganize many once-General churches along the Regulars' Calvinist scheme. Meanwhile, a third clique of Baptists, the Separates, entered the fray. The notoriously spartan Separates scorned the Regular

Baptists' "superfluity of apparel." They deemed the Regulars lax in doctrinal matters, too, objecting to what they considered the Regulars' willingness to admit converts without requiring a relation of their conversion experience. For their part, the Regulars suspected the Separates of unreasonably hiding their true beliefs.[8]

For Baptists who had drifted into the rolling hills of Virginia and Carolina in the mid-1700s, it was not an auspicious start. Certainly, that is what the nineteenth-century descendants of these Baptist pioneers believed. Whether they were writing during the heady days of the Great Revival or during the fractious years following the denomination's split, nineteenth-century Baptist chroniclers of all stripes recalled their ancestors' struggles with a mix of horror, disappointment, and awe.

In Baptist histories and memoirs of those early years, tales of persecution abound. At times, the books read like catalogs of abuse. Verbal ridicule and threats of violence were standard fare. Interlopers shouted down Baptist preachers in midsermon. Dogs were cast into the river to interrupt baptisms. Such ridicule easily turned to violence. Colonial authorities ripped Baptist elders from the stand and carried them to prison for preaching without licenses. Elder John Tanner received a thigh full of buckshot for baptizing a woman whose husband disapproved of the upstart sect. Club-wielding mobs lay siege to churches, a miscreant brandished a gun at a preacher, and another mob rushed a meetinghouse, beating worshippers "so that the floor shone with sprinkled blood." And so it went. The examples were legion, and Baptist chroniclers took them down with a bookkeeper's efficiency.[9]

When nineteenth-century Baptists recounted this violent past, they poured their ancestors' experiences into a familiar mold. The persecuted were to be admired because in their suffering they resembled Christ, and their injuries were to be carefully chronicled because the wounds formed a record—they were proof—that the current revivals were real and, in some sense, prophesied. Writing in 1808, William Fristoe, for instance, concluded that the early Baptists' persecution was, in fact, responsible for their growth. Just as stories of Christ's patient torment on the cross attracted converts, the early American Baptists' trials must have earned them new followers, or so Fristoe surmised. Lemuel Burkitt and his coauthor Jesse Read also availed themselves of this enduring Christian model. Writing at roughly the same time as Fristoe, they praised the aforementioned Tanner for refusing to seek restitution, and they pointedly noted that instead of feeling angry or fearful when he was shot, Tanner "submitted to it patiently as *persecution* for Christ's sake." Primitive Baptists, too, patterned the Baptist past this way, declaring themselves startled, but happily so, that the endemic suffering of Baptists was "precisely the same in the modern eighteenth century as in the ancient first century."[10]

While the nineteenth-century chroniclers easily apprehended and admired the Christlike suffering of their ancestors, they found the intradenominational chaos and strife that plagued these same people to be a more difficult interpretive challenge. When the first wave of antebellum Baptist chroniclers gazed backward, they either downplayed their denomination's recent history of factionalism or admitted the disharmony only to the extent necessary to shoehorn it into a grand narrative of Christian progress. Such denial seems a corollary of the newfound unity born of the revivals. Even for the notoriously fractious Baptists, disagreement and division were nearly impossible to countenance during the years immediately surrounding the Great Revival. This shift in both story and mood marked a significant departure from what had traditionally been the conventional Baptist narrative, a narrative featuring bloodied and imprisoned preachers, struggling but holy churches, and ruthless oppressors. Baptists with particularly keen historical imaginations traced their denominational roots well past a familiar figure like Roger Williams, connecting themselves instead to a series of little-known sects—the Waldenses, the Petrobrusians, the Hussites—that, they claimed, also practiced believers' baptism and were, therefore, Baptists in everything but name. But during the years of revival, this story of suffering and hiddenness lost some of its relevance. To make it comport with their present reality, the early nineteenth-century chroniclers downplayed it. These writers reduced the old narrative of persecution into an unfortunate, if necessary, prelude to their joyous present and smoothed the pitted surface of intra-Baptist conflict to reflect the harmony of their own era.

Perhaps our best sense of this narrative strategy comes from Burkitt and Read, the two preachers mentioned above who in 1803 cowrote a history of their particular Baptist association, the Kehukee—the same association that a little more than two decades later would spearhead the Primitive Baptist revolt. Though primarily a catalog of minutes, church enrollment figures, and doctrinal resolutions, Burkitt and Read's book tells us much about how turn-of-the-century Baptists understood their past and envisioned their future. A collection of minutiae, the book also works to situate the Kehukee Association's Baptists in the middle of a symbolic story about Christendom. The coauthors were themselves living testimony to the spirit of unity that pervaded the Kehukee and many other Baptist associations in the South beginning in the late 1700s. Both Burkitt and Read found their calling as preachers, but they first tended to flocks on different sides of the Baptist divide. Lemuel Burkitt, a Regular Baptist preacher, had led the movement to effect a union with Read's Separate Baptists. To do this, Burkitt turned out from his churches anyone who had been baptized without first having a conversion experience. Satisfied that the churches under Burkitt's care were now sufficiently rigorous in their membership standards, the Separates joined with them and, in the spirit of unity, decided to rename the new conglomeration the "United Baptists." This union of 1787 had itself been preceded by what Burkitt and Read called, with a sense of historical significance, "the Reformation." The reformers, in this case, hailed from Philadelphia rather than Wittenberg or Geneva. Part of several waves of northern Baptists seeking common cause with their brethren in the southern colonies, the Philadelphia Baptists organized matters on "the Calvinist scheme." By 1765, they had convinced many Baptists in the South to do likewise. Across stretches of Virginia and North Carolina, these newly Calvinist churches called themselves the Kehukee Association. After the "Reformation" of 1765 and the union of 1787, old differences over doctrine and dress and the very means of salvation—differences that had divided southern Baptists into the ranks of Separates, Regulars, and General Baptists—were now seen simply as "imaginary conjectures" or, at worst, ecclesiastical gimcracks swept mercifully away by time's tide. Soon "all the churches were united again," wrote Burkitt and Read, "and the names *Regular* and *Separate* buried in oblivion." "And blessed be God," they continued, "the distinction at this time has become obsolete, and the different names lost throughout the United States, and we hope throughout the world."[11]

Burkitt and Read's portentousness (they were writing about a new Reformation, after all) clashed with their simultaneous effort to paint such momentous events as ordinary (those old differences were simply "imaginary"). That thematic discord was the precipitate left behind as Burkitt and Read dissolved Baptists' bleak past into the emergent logic of evangelical millennialism. Within a generation, Primitive Baptists would find such logic dubious. Even then, however, missionary Baptists, along with a growing phalanx of other evangelicals, found such logic irresistible, as natural as the new dawn Lemuel Burkitt had seen rising over the Carolina piedmont back in 1803.

A New Ethos

Burkitt's Baptists were not alone. A similar spirit of optimism prevailed in evangelical precincts across America and the wider Atlantic world. In Baptist and Methodist and Presbyterian churches, more and more sinners felt the Holy Spirit descend upon them. Just as their hearts were changed by God's touch, they believed that the world, too, might soon witness startling changes, among them the return of their Savior. There were the portents they knew: the rolling fires of revival, the suddenly swollen church rolls, the cataclysm of political revolution. And beneath these were the tectonic social and economic shifts that only later generations came to catalog: increasing immigration, rapid westward expansion, the beginnings of a market revolution, the explosive growth of cities. Millennialism and, in particular, the belief that the Kingdom of God might soon be at hand flourished in the soils watered by such torrents of change.[12]

The hothouse of revival seemed to ensure the continued growth of millennial hope. With glee, evangelicals tallied up the additions to God's flock. But the numbers, astounding as they were, told only part of the story. It was the intensity of the gatherings that drew the most attention: the weeping and groaning, the convulsions (the "jerks," as they were called), the dramatic testimonies that revealed moments of instantaneous transformation. More than one convert recalled his days at a revival by comparing himself to a burning coal whose fire would not go out. There were other surprises as well, the child converts not least among them. Their piety commanded crowds and bespoke the dawning of a time of wonders.[13]

These experiences of regeneration along with a pervasive sense of optimism became the emotional analogues to the theological changes that were both cause and effect of the awakenings. A new ethos stressing a keen hope for salvation and an incipient belief in the power of the human will to help bring about such change worked to push aside the old Calvinist emphasis on doubt and the fallenness of man. In the heat of revival, the "old starched" Calvinists, as the revivalist Peter Cartwright described them, simply wilted: "Illiterate Methodist preachers actually set the world on fire, (the American world at least,) while they [the Calvinists] were lighting their matches!" Eventually, the laggards relented. "They, almost to a man, gave up these points of high Calvinism, and preached a free salvation to mankind," Cartwright wrote. With the doddering Calvinists dispatched, the gales of optimism blew unimpeded. As Cartwright's comments indicate, a Christianized common sense that celebrated individual moral agency blossomed in evangelical circles. Anything seemed possible, and the souls awakened by the revivals' heart religion showed the way: "Private perfectionism would produce social improvement." That, according to the historian John Boles, was the corollary to the theology of individual conversion that dominated the revivals and became evangelicalism's hallmark. Though evangelicals were careful to maintain some distance between their beloved community and the workaday world, millennial thought was no respecter of boundaries. Capacious and protean, it escaped the churches and camp meetings and happily ratified popular optimism in the wake of America's successful revolution. "Such unrivaled success in preaching, such remarkable scenes of mass conversion, infused the faithful with a buoyant optimism," Boles writes. "Expansive revival success had set free millenarian imaginations. The image of the awakening now transcended mere numerical growth; it now pointed toward the final justification of history."[14]

Nevertheless, the hope generated by millennialist expectations might have faded away had it not found concrete expression in evangelicals' fervent intent to sacralize the world.[15] As if to hasten Christ's return, evangelicals found new ways to yoke heaven to earth, and of all the reform movements to which antebellum Baptists attached themselves, none figured so prominently as the foreign and domestic missions cause. Missionary work channeled the revivals' enthusiasm outward, directing it first toward the frontier, where eager itinerants sought out Native Americans and unchurched whites, and then toward foreign lands, where the heathen masses might finally be delivered from their misery. Missions galvanized the Baptist faithful in all sections of the young nation. Because the work was so momentous and the task so daunting, Baptist churches, which were notoriously jealous of their autonomy, even consented to the creation of the denomination's first large-scale, extra-church bureaucracies. It was these new missionary societies that would transform weekly donations by the laity into a massive effort to save mankind in preparation for Christ's return. With only slight exaggeration, it can be said that the foreign and domestic missions cause was responsible for organizing Baptists as a denomination. The bureaucracy that sprang up to support their missionary work offered Baptists their first formal state- and nationwide networks of communication and association. The novelty of this Baptist bureaucracy and the speed with which it was erected caused Baptists to look upon it with either admiration or dread.

From our vantage point, this missionary enthusiasm seems unremarkable. Evangelicals seek converts; it is their nature. But for the first wave of missionary Baptist chroniclers—men like David Benedict and Robert Howell who came of age in the early 1800s just as Baptists' denominational and institutional growth surged—the missions cause was a new one, and they interpreted it as a sign that their denomination had finally found its calling. In 1814, when American Baptists organized a national board to direct their missionary operations, the denomination found itself in the midst of a series of remarkable events. The late eighteenth-century union had ushered in an era of intrasect harmony where acrimony had once reigned. And the early nineteenth-century revivals had quickened seemingly barren churches and swollen the denomination's once-modest numbers.

Missionary Baptist chroniclers insisted that it was the worldwide missions crusade that secured these victories. As David Benedict told the story, it was in the nineteenth century's second decade when Baptists' nascent missionary efforts finally awakened "the dormant energies of our denomination." By 1820, "the foreign missions cause stood very high in the estimation of the American Baptists as a body," Benedict wrote. "The whole denomination, North and South, acted in concert, so far as it was aroused to any benevolent action in supporting this then favorite undertaking." Indeed, by midcentury, it seemed clear to the first generation of missionary Baptist historians that their denomination's missionary efforts surpassed all successes enjoyed by Baptists in a history they often traced back to Jesus's day. A sustained, organized missionary enterprise, they argued, allowed Baptists to finally carry out Jesus's ancient instruction that his followers should "go . . . into all the world, and preach the gospel to every creature" and "teach all nations." "The missionary spirit of the Baptist denomination is its greatest strength, and its missionary record its greatest glory," wrote George Hervey. Since the start of Baptist missionary societies just a few decades earlier, "missions have rapidly multiplied, gifts have vastly increased, great numbers of men and women have gone forth, into nearly all the tongues of heathen and Mahometan nations the Bible has been translated. Schools, colleges and seminaries have been planted in all these fields, and many hundreds of thousands of idolaters have forsaken their gods and embraced the religion of Jesus." When missionary Baptist chroniclers gazed into the Baptist past, they realized that however noble their ancestors had been, however unjust their suffering and righteous their cause, those old Baptists' ability to carry out Christ's Great Commission had been hampered. "The work to be done, before Christ's sway shall have been made complete, demands yet broader purposes, bolder hands and braver hearts," Hervey wrote. "Efforts commensurate with the greatness of the task can only come with a largeness of view and an intenseness of devotion begotten by the thought that 'The field is the world.'" A small sect subjected to persecution and stubbornly insistent on church autonomy could imitate Jesus's suffering but never effectively spread his gospel. Only a denomination able to shed such a past could emerge to share Christ's gospel in the most effective way possible. Only a denomination like theirs had recently become could transform instruction into action, creed into deed. That old Baptist past of persecution and hiddenness was becoming a dim memory.[16]

The new missionary work required the establishment of a sturdy bureaucracy (modern missions needed "more *system*," as the Baptist preacher Adiel Sherwood put it), but missionary Baptists typically framed their depiction of these corporate actions as a study in heroic individualism. The familiar account, which appeared in any number of missionary Baptist publications, went something like this: In 1812, the American Board of Commissioners for Foreign Missions dispatched two Congregational ministers to India. During their voyage, the two men experienced conversions of a kind and adopted Baptists' creed and rituals. After several months on the subcontinent, one of these men, Luther Rice, returned to America. Like a latter-day Paul, Rice roamed the land urging stubbornly independent Baptist churches to band together to form a tiered network of local, state, and national missionary societies. In Richmond and Philadelphia and Fredericksburg and countless towns and hamlets in between, Rice's efforts bore fruit. By the spring of 1814, the General Convention of the Baptist Denomination, a meeting with representatives from churches across the nation, endorsed Rice's plans. The account nestled Rice inside a Pauline mold that Christians often used to shape their hagiographies. Here he was: a lonely individual sojourning in strange lands (either India or the American backcountry); a traveler who, like Paul on the road to Damascus, experienced a startling conversion; an evangelist and a correspondent on an errand that succeeded despite overwhelming odds. Charismatic, eloquent, and tireless, the "young apostle" convinced American Baptists that his mission was one that they ought to endorse.[17]

Rice's heroism did not last long. In the accounts crafted by the first wave of missionary Baptist historians, Rice quickly became a transitional figure, an individual who birthed a far-flung missionary network but who, ultimately, was not suited for the new bureaucratic era that he single-handedly ushered in. In the typical hagiographic mode Baptist writers had long used for their ministerial portraits, a story like Rice's would end either in a conventional triumph like, say, the founding of a church or in martyrdom, which, after all, was simply a different kind of Christian victory. But with Rice's story, Baptist chroniclers deployed a new narrative arc. Consider, for example, David Benedict's treatment of Rice. Benedict refused to allow Rice to bask in the glow of his missionary triumphs, and he gave his death only a glancing notice. Instead, Rice's story reached a sad denouement as the doughty missionary became a failed bureaucrat. We learn that soon after the denomination adopted his ambitious plans, Rice was beset by a series of "pecuniary embarrassments." He misappropriated funds. He ran a seminary into debt. Benedict lamented Rice's missteps, but he concluded with a kind of literary sigh that "this was the way things were managed in those [that is, past] times." Benedict's account described the emergence of an era of Baptist bureaucracy, where traditionally heroic figures such as Rice were easily subsumed beneath the denomination's new organizational machinery. Other chroniclers treated Rice in similar fashion, blaming him for "his lack of business sagacity" even as they honored his missionary efforts.[18]

As the once-heroic Rice sank into financial ignominy, missionary Baptist chroniclers trained their gaze on the new institutions—benevolent societies, missionary societies, Sunday schools, and the like—that folk heroes such as Rice helped bring into being. Describing the era of institution building—the "golden age" of Baptist history, as its admirers called it—required new character types and tropes. The preacher-heroes of yore no longer dominated the narratives of this new era. Writers might laud them, but they did not flinch from also chastising them for an assortment of managerial misdeeds. Indeed, the men—most of them preachers—running these institutions were, like Rice, subject to criticism their eighteenth-century forebears would not have recognized. Like grumpy managers, missionary Baptist chroniclers issued constant complaints about the disorganization and waste endemic to the new bureaucratic structures. They blamed the problems on a few "inside managers" who, like vain executives, droned on during meetings and drew too much money from the groups' coffers.[19]

The institutions themselves, at least as embodied in their motivating ideas, remained unscathed. Missionary Baptist writers invariably framed the institutions as the embodiment of righteousness and the logical expression of Baptists' calling. Instead of the noble but sporadic efforts of earlier itinerants, the modern, permanent missionary organizations unleashed permanent transformations. In "modern foreign evangelization," wrote one especially enthusiastic chronicler, Baptists were experiencing "successes, yes, Pentecosts as wonderful as Paul and Peter ever knew!" Even apparent setbacks became new triumphs. When northern and southern factions in the denomination acrimoniously split apart over the question of slavery, the foreign missions cause only grew stronger, according to the missionary Baptist chroniclers. Just as they had downplayed the significance of the cleavages that rent their denomination in the 1700s, they learned to finesse the cataclysmic regional split of the denomination into a "very quietly effected" move that increased organizational efficiency. Though he regretted the split over slavery, David Benedict nonetheless concluded that his proslavery brethren in the newly formed Southern Baptist Convention would "do much more for the support of all benevolent objects under management of their own men, whose names were familiar to them, than they had hitherto accomplished." In this way, the chroniclers cataloged various nuisances and even instances of malfeasance, yet they attributed these problems to the failings of individual men rather than to any weakness in the causes or institutions they served. The result was a new portrait of the denomination where individual Baptists were consistently eclipsed by the institutions they inhabited.[20]

If, to us, that result seems like the unsurprising consequence of both an evangelical understanding of sin and the natural growth of bureaucracy, it held far more significance to the people who came to call themselves Primitive Baptists. In the missionary Baptists' narrative of progress, Primitives saw a betrayal of the Baptist past.

A New Dark Age

As one reads Primitive Baptist histories, conversion narratives, polemics, and theological tracts, it becomes clear that, for the Primitives, the darkness of the Baptist past never receded. A perpetual gloom shrouds these works. If all antebellum Baptists acknowledged their ancestors' eighteenth-century persecution, Primitives remained the Baptist sect most engrossed with the subject.

Primitive Baptists insisted that the persecution of the faithful persisted into the nineteenth century not simply because its eighteenth-century incarnations had never been vanquished but because persecution of the faithful had, as they explained, "shown itself in every age" and had "always been the case."[21] Suffering was law. The chief error of most modern Baptists, the Primitives argued, was their desire to escape a constant condition of suffering that God, if he had not ordained it, had, in some sense, allowed to occur.[22] To seek to alleviate Baptists' suffering by, for instance, increasing the denomination's numbers or raising its esteem among fellow Christians was a mistake. Even to aspire to such things—to hope to rinse the stink of the "dunghill" off his Baptist brothers and sisters, as the missionary and theologian Andrew Fuller colorfully put it—was to sink further into the sloughs of error and sin.[23] "The truth is," wrote a leading Primitive writer in response to Fuller's ambitions, "the Baptists never could endure prosperity to any great extent, without, like Israel of old, running into idolatry."[24] Precisely because, following Fuller's lead, many nineteenth-century Baptists had sought in various ways to remove themselves from the mire, Primitives considered the century to be the darkest one yet. The story that Primitive Baptists told themselves unfolded in this darkness. While they insistently traced their history in an unbroken line back to the apostolic age, the Primitives, like their missionary foes, realized that the recent past could tell them even more about who they were and how they came to be. After all, Primitives knew that it was only recently, in the opening decades of the 1800s, that Baptists, indeed Christendom itself, had taken its most precipitous plunge.

The Primitives' origin story was simple and compelling. It straightened the coils of theological exegesis and hauled the older, familiar Baptist narrative of persecution into the Primitives' present experiences. As did the missionary Baptists, the Primitives viewed the turn-of-the-century revivals as a significant turning point in Baptists' recent past. The revivals, Primitives argued, trembled with excitement, and excitement was the handmaiden to sin. Excitement disturbed the senses, induced good people to admit the unsaved into the church, and encouraged sinners to believe that they, rather than God, had an active role in their apparent salvation. Under the spell of such enchantment, once-humble Baptists concocted man-made schemes that purported to save the heathen but, in fact, enriched the self-appointed saviors.

Primitive Baptist writers populated their origin stories with characters drawn from the realm of stereotype. Here the missionary Baptist played the villain. Underhanded, prideful, aristocratic, the missionary Baptist either willfully or foolishly mistook his good fortune for a sign of God's favor, sought to consolidate power in his own hands by building Byzantine money-making schemes disguised as benevolent institutions, and chided those who refused to abide his plans as pigheaded, backward fatalists. Primitive Baptists of course wrote themselves into their story, although the process always seemed to them more like self-discovery than self-generation. When the Primitives surveyed their past, they saw themselves walking the old paths, lonely truth-bearers in a fallen world, guardians of the doctrine of election, and hard-working husbandmen whose labor preserved Jefferson's Republic against encroaching aristocracy.

No work told this story more thoroughly than *History of the Church of God*, a sprawling account regarded since its publication in the late 1880s as the definitive history of Primitive Baptists. As indicated by the book's serpentine subtitle—*From the Creation to A.D. 1885; Including Especially the History of the Kehukee Primitive Baptist Association*—it sought to place the Primitives within a grand cosmology, to see them as heirs to an epic history rather than as isolated malcontents dappled across the South and the western frontier. At the same time, the coauthors—Cushing Biggs Hassell and his son Sylvester, both of them long-serving Primitive Baptist elders—consciously designed the book as a revision and extension of two earlier and decidedly more small-scale histories of the Baptists in the Kehukee Association.[25] But the Hassells' book was the one that Primitives inside and outside of the Kehukee Association quickly called their own. Written toward century's end, long after the schismatic years of the 1820s and 1830s, the book reflected more than fifty years of Primitive Baptist wisdom and conjecture. When Primitives turned to the *History of the Church of God*, they found snippets of argument and streams of thought that they had encountered in other texts, in conversations, or perhaps during a preacher's sermon. The Hassells gave this miscellany a solid form. Their book told Primitive Baptists—and told them in encyclopedic detail in a way no pamphlet or sermon could and told them forcefully in a way their predestinarian theology formally discouraged—that they lived during a new dark age but could be reassured that they were at the center of God's plan.

If any single thing ushered in that new dark age, it was the revivals—their ubiquity, their innovations in preaching and worship, and the consuming passion they generated in attendees. The revivals at the century's beginning burned so brightly that Lemuel Burkitt's Baptists in North Carolina and Virginia compared them to the brilliance of a new dawn. Observing those same events, the Hassells saw instead "Heavens [filled] with clouds of inky blackness." What caused such a dramatic change in perspective? Who or what had turned day into night? The Hassells could rattle off a list of malefactors: rationalists, materialists, Roman Catholics, socialists, and a host of "isms" ranging from anarchism and atheism to "Presumptuousism" and "Atrocicism."[26] But the Hassells channeled most of their ire toward their fellow Baptists, and the enduring theme of their account was that the new dawn celebrated in camp meetings and church houses had, in fact, never arrived. It was an illusion conjured up out of the revivals' inevitable farrago of hope, ardor, faith, and self-deception.

The revival of 1803, the Hassells explained, was only a "revival, so called." Yes, more than 1,500 souls were added to church rolls in the Kehukee Association within two years. But upon closer examination, the revival seemed a chimera, its effects either muted or, because of their unreality, deleterious. Were all those souls truly saved? The Hassells could conclude that it only "seemed" that way, that if one were to observe the electrified crowds in Lemuel Burkitt's churchyard, it once again "seemed" that the preacher's enthusiastic testimony had encouraged the gathered to beg for mercy, which they quickly received from a gracious God. But it was not so much grace abounding as it was the appearance of grace. The seeming had supplanted the real. Witnesses observed all the outward signs of salvation among the crowds: despair, conviction, conversion, and rejoicing. Such stirring displays, said the Primitives, amounted to a kind of emotional theater so convincing that even its participants mistook performance for reality.[27]

Outright fraud lurked at the edges of the scene like a half-seen stage manager calling cues in a theater's darkened wings, yet the revivals' emotional drama was most often not so consciously crafted. In the camp meeting's hothouse atmosphere, zeal—a term the Hassells and other Primitives returned to time and again when discussing revivals—became it own object. Since "self-styled sincerity . . . is all that is necessary for salvation," the Hassells lamented, the revivals were "transforming religion from a saving inward reality into a vainglorious outward show." The anxious seat and the mourner's bench were only the rudest props in the revivals' emotional theater. These "new measures," as they were known, worked like public cauldrons in which potential converts were brought to a boil from the combined heat of a congregation's stare, a preacher's exhortations, and their own burning consciences, all of them stoked by the divine bellows of the Holy Spirit.[28]

But the revivals' machinery did not need to be so conspicuous. In the Primitives' diagnosis, much of the work was carried on silently by men and women who sincerely believed they were experiencing the work of the Holy Spirit. But sincerity itself was the problem. The revivalists' belief in their own sincerity became their warrant for upheaval. Since an impassioned yet apparently sincere display signaled the Holy Spirit's touch, it was no wonder that revivalists learned to cultivate such experiences. In the camp meetings, emotion usurped reason and a feeling of grace replaced the thing itself. "Men dream," the Hassells wrote, "and then assert that their visions are truth."[29]

From the vantage point of Primitive Baptist writers like the Hassells, it was clear that the revivals during the early 1800s ushered in a new era in Baptist history. In their telling, a newfound exuberance had replaced judicious Calvinist restraint, and a preoccupation with surface appearances had crowded out Baptists' traditional inward gaze. Because the excitement stirred up at revival meetings blunted rational thought, it was axiomatic that "errors in practice would creep in" during "this exciting time." The process was simple, if pernicious: revivals generated false hope and false hope led to false conversions, which, in turn, fostered more false hope. The emotional logic was self-sustaining, which is what made it so insidious to the Primitive Baptists. The zeal that propelled preachers and congregants alike encouraged them to seek out ways that they might sustain the wonder-working effect of the Holy Spirit's touch. This quest, even if conducted unconsciously, meant that Baptists began relying on what the Hassells, following generations of Primitive Baptist usage, referred to as "human means," rather than divine grace, for the conversion of sinners. And to open that door—to, for example, put sinners onstage on an anxious bench in order to cultivate the cries and tears that were the outside signs of conversion—was to deign to overthrow an omnipotent and omniscient God who would save whom he wanted when he wanted. The drift toward "human means" in the conversion drama was, therefore, a theological betrayal, another breach in the Calvinist defenses through which their longtime Arminian antagonists would surge.[30]

Bedrock issues of emotion and perception propelled the Hassells' story forward. Though the Hassells relished theological debate, their narrative and, indeed, the larger Primitive Baptist historical imagination turned on issues both more mundane and fundamental. Theological transgressions entered through church doors first flung open by excited crowds. It was no wonder, then, that the question of missions, the issue that would eventually cleave the Baptist denomination in two, was first raised in this heated atmosphere. Only in the wake of the revival—only "at a time when the zeal and credulity of many hundreds of new converts were at their height," the Hassells explained—could Kehukee's faithful Baptists even have contemplated the missions question. "But for the revival, so called," they wrote, "this new measure and great departure from the custom of the fathers would, probably, have received no favorable consideration among the staid old members of the Association." By the time the Hassells wrote, verdicts like theirs had become Primitive Baptist commonplaces. The new missionary organizations, theological schools, and benevolent agencies needed money, after all. How else to slake their thirst? "To fill up these costly and splendid edifices with paying converts, something more attractive to the world than the preaching of Christ and him crucified was deemed necessary," was the conclusion drawn by another prominent Primitive writer. "Protracted meetings, anxious benches, exciting appeals to the carnal passions of men, women and children were regarded as the most effective agencies, and hence they were brought into requisition." Everything fit so neatly together. For all the sweating evangelists, "just three things are now needed," as the Hassells acidly noted: "more prayers, more tears, and more money."[31]

While the early nineteenth-century revivals seeded Baptist ranks with deceivers and the deceived, some of those "staid old members" clung to the true vine. At the time, of course, there were no Primitive Baptists. The rolling schism of the 1820s and 1830s lay a generation ahead. But the Hassells and their fellow Primitives had learned to locate their ancestors in the chaotic past. If they looked closely, they glimpsed the "few faithful soldiers of Christ" who dared oppose the excited revivalists and budding missionaries. That the Hassells' faithful few failed to prevent the introduction of missionary plans into the Kehukee Association made them no less heroic to their would-be descendants in the Primitive Baptist movement. The spurned truth-bearer, that durable model of the Savior, was precisely the type Christians had long used to describe their fallen heroes. It was missionary Baptists brightened by their newfound prosperity who found that reliable Christian type less useful in their chronicles of the recent past. Meanwhile, the Hassells marched through the past following their faithful few, reminding readers that in each epoch true Christians found themselves an outnumbered lot warding off enemies from without and deceivers from within. Theirs was a continuation, albeit a heightened one, of the older Baptist narrative, the story Baptists had shared before the schism. Primitive Baptist chroniclers clung to that old story just as their fellow Baptists were abandoning it.

This tale of resilience and deception only intensified when the Hassells and other Primitive Baptist writers turned their attentions to the missions cause. The Kehukee Baptists' initial interest in missions was sparked, as we have seen, by the buoyant mood surrounding the early nineteenth-century revivals. Are we not called, they asked in 1803, "to step forward in support of that missionary spirit which the great God is so wonderfully reviving amongst the different denominations of good men in various parts of the world?" Their answer was an assured "yes," a response that, as their query indicated, was shared by evangelicals across America who were posing similar questions. That their "Mother Kehukee" entertained the missionary cause for roughly two decades could be excused, the Hassells argued, because missions, like the revivalistic zeal that animated them, represented a form of deception. But unlike the self-deception that inevitably flowed from the revivals' "animal excitements," the missionary cause thrived on conscious acts of betrayal. And so the early proponents of missions came to be described as "adulterers and adulteresses" who had "gotten [their] bantling born" during a shadowy liaison in an eastern North Carolina church house. Or they were "wire-workers" manipulating their fellow Baptists like a puppeteer pulling a marionette's strings. The Hassells hinted that missionaries might be tied to a Masonic plot or that they were in the grips of Catholic "priestcraft."[32]

This is the language of conspiracy: sinister enemies, dark dealings, betrayal, and a people dispossessed. When crafting the tale of their origins, this was the Primitives' chosen lexicon. They operated in what Richard Hofstadter famously describes as "the paranoid style," a cultural posture at once warped and buttressed by the fantastical claims and overheated rhetoric that are its hallmarks.[33] But the Primitives' story of their origins was nothing if not coherent, its grand narrative proceeding with a relentless consistency from the betrayal at Gethsemane to the religious treachery of their own time. With clearly delineated characters, it was easy to tell good from evil even as the story implied how difficult such a task was in day-to-day life. In fact, it is easy to see how such a story might bandage the wounds of uncertainty inflicted by the Primitives' Calvinism. And if the reliable narrative and exaggerated types failed their instructional work, there were always the imposing drifts of evidence that accumulated at the reader's door. To cite just one such example, we learn from the Hassells that the Primitive Baptists' proportion of the population in the United States was the same as the proportion of nonidolaters among the ancient Israelites during Ahab's reign.[34]

The Rhetorical Origins of a Primitive Sect

In the Hassells' *History*, as in all Primitives' writing about their own origins, the missionary loomed, powerful and brazen like an autocrat, and second in importance only to God. The missionary was emotionally out of control and hitched to a new strain of Protestantism that was, depending upon the writer's mood, either lax or reminiscent of Catholic authoritarianism. The missionary descended from the North, a "New England rat" sniffed out as early as 1820 by a Kentucky anti-missionary preacher named John Taylor. The missionary arrived wealthy and yet begged for money, an itinerant grandee—"stiff, glove-handed, school polished"—who pilfered the plain folks' meager resources out of a sheer lust for power. If left unchecked, missionaries, who were "verging close on an aristocracy," would undermine "Baptist Republican government" and, therefore, send both church and state to ruin.[35]

Beside this insidious portrait of their enemies, the Primitives' cast a monument to themselves that shone like polished steel. Rather than power-hungry upstarts, they were an ancient and humble people. Broken glimpses of the past revealed their existence in spirit long before they took their denominational name. "Their origin was hid in the remote depths of antiquity," wrote the Primitive Baptist historian Benjamin Griffin in 1853 about the beginnings of his people. Like God's chosen ones throughout all time, they found themselves subjected to persecution, yet they persevered. In the current age, they knew themselves to be simple hardworking folk—the "farmers and mechanicks of our country," as the members of the Primitive Baptist church in Tarboro, North Carolina, described themselves—the very backbone of Jefferson's agrarian Republic. Their Calvinism, moreover, made them particularly effective guardians of both civil and religious liberty. "Predestinarianism," as the Hassells explained, "develops the power of self-government and a manly spirit of independence, which fears no man, though seated on a throne, because it fears God, the only real sovereign."[36]

Missionary Baptists were hardly immune to this sort of inflated rhetoric. They, too, steadied themselves against the sturdy railings of a Manichaean worldview. Missionaries packed their journals and correspondence with unflattering portraits of anti-missionary Baptists, whom they considered backwards, ignorant, unschooled, poor, and rude. Wandering in Missouri in 1818, the early missionary John Mason Peck bragged that his fund-raising efforts received enthusiastic responses even in hardscrabble settlements where money was scarce. But when Peck encountered frontier Baptists who refused his entreaties, he quickly concluded that they were "under the influence of the Evil One. Like the persecutors of Christ, they were blinded and knew not what they did." Nearly forty years later, a colporteur traveling in eastern North Carolina on behalf of the American Tract Society grumbled about the "hardshell" Baptists who "were opposed to books[,] Prayer & in a word to all good." The salesman spilled his frustrations across the pages of his journal: Primitive Baptists, he wrote, "were aided [by] a host of Ignorant & ungodly preachers who are worst than the people themselves ... these preachers finding that [an] increase of knowledge & higher Standard of moral is not favorable to them, they do all in their power to arrest its progress & though not posessed with common faith yet gifted & strong in opposing all good hence we find them so successful among their dark & ignorant class as to find them equiped to oppose every effort made to instruct them." Inflamed observations like these congealed into conventional wisdom as the century wore on. Primitive Baptists were stingy, opposed to "progress," fatalistic, and, by their stubborn refusal to aid evangelicals' missionary and benevolent efforts, determined to "lay the axe at the root of Christianity itself." That the Primitives' opposition to missions and benevolent organizations "was the result of a want of enlightenment—that is to say, of ignorance and prejudice," wrote the missionary Baptist clergyman and historian Samuel Boykin, "is but too painfully apparent." Missionary Baptists knew themselves to be Christianity's guardians against the Primitives' antediluvian fancies. In this undertaking, they relied upon a new generation of clergy drawn to what the historian Nathan Hatch has called "the allure of respectability," a centripetal force that pulled insurgent evangelicalism back "toward learning, decorum, professionalism, and social standing." To see this force in action, all one had to do was stroll the halls at a meeting of the missions-supporting Southern Baptist Convention: the movement's leaders were not the persecuted outcasts of yesteryear but instead, as one observer noted, "governors, judges, congressmen, and other functionaries of the highest dignity."[37]

In the Baptist schism, stereotype and the reality it supposedly represented became difficult to distinguish. There is the obvious: in this case, as in others, stereotype's imposing scale shadowed whatever cultural life took root beneath its ample boughs. In stereotype's crepuscular light, individual differences grow faint and the eye can make out only the broad outlines of the group. As the Baptist schism opened up across the early decades of the nineteenth century, Baptists of all stripes learned to spot themselves and their counterparts in this compromised landscape. And it was as if their eyes never quite adjusted to the gray light, as if their enfeebled vision came to seem natural. Certainly in their public pronouncements—the deliberately constructed histories examined here, or even the headlong polemics splashed across the pages of denominational periodicals—combatants on each side resorted to stereotype so regularly it suggests these caricatures were not simply, or even primarily, carefully placed framing devices but became instead embedded, like cataracts, into each side's way of seeing the world.

In this way, stereotype itself became the schism's most enduring legacy, for long after the social conditions that sparked the conflict died down, stereotype remained. Its fictions became the birthright of new generations of Baptists on both sides of the divide; its longevity and durability increased its purchase on reality. Not only did these types shape each side's historical imagination in the nineteenth century, but modern-day Baptists, both Primitive and missionary, continue to work in this broad-brush style.[38]

The competing sets of stereotypes colluded in this process of cultural infiltration. Inside the caricatures they constructed of their rivals, members of each group secreted the idealized portraits they had drawn of themselves. And these idealized self-portraits were themselves burnished opposites of the caricatures their opponents had constructed of them. So if the Primitives saw the missionaries as money-grubbing East Coast elitists, the missionaries saw themselves as earnest, respectable, well-educated Christian soldiers charitably seeking to help both the heathen and their less-enlightened Baptist brethren. Meanwhile, because missionaries painted the Primitives as uncouth, close-minded "hardshells," the Primitives conceived of themselves as humble "mechanicks," a simple folk defending God and country from encroaching aristocracy. While these types are easily cast as eternal enemies engaged in perpetual warfare, we might more accurately understand them as opposites that nevertheless fed each other on difference. The very intensity of the conflict sustained it.[39]

But stereotype's foothold in the Baptist historical imagination never was entirely secure, and the process by which it lodged itself in the public memory of the schism raises just as many questions as answers. Now, stereotype's omnipresence in the schism's historical record would seem to belie this contention. Often it seems that the types discussed here sprang to life, Athena-like, at some pivotal but still-obscure point in time. One leafs through church record books, discovers the passage of an anti-missions declaration, and searches in vain for a record of debate or discussion. At times like these, it can seem that Baptists slipped quietly over a border never to look back, occupants of a new country where everything—words, faith, history—no longer held their old meanings. At other times, it is clear that newly declared Primitive Baptists clutched older Baptist tropes, such as the idea of a persecuted remnant church, and fastened them to republican idioms in order to make sense of their novel circumstances. Because stereotype so quickly and deeply embedded itself in the public record of the schism, the process by which it did so has become obscured.

But if we leave behind the official histories each side crafted, we might glimpse something of this process—a process of identity formation and erasure—in the relationship between Gilbert Beebe and Zelotes Grenell, two Baptist preachers tending to churches perched along the western edge of New York's Hudson Valley. If nothing else, we can, in Beebe and Grenell's relationship, begin to reckon with the toll that public memory exacted from private experience.

Born in 1800, Beebe was licensed to preach at the age of eighteen, spent five years as an itinerant, and was formally ordained five years later. In the 1830s Beebe established himself as one of the nation's leading Primitive Baptist polemicists, a man who regularly took to the pages of the publication he edited, *Signs of the Times*, to lambaste missionary Baptists' teachings as "vain, delusive, fabulous fictions" and compare missionary Baptists themselves to whores.[40]

When Beebe more calmly observed in 1862 that "these two kinds of Baptists have become so distinct that neither claim any relationship to the other," he merely stated a commonplace. By then, a shared Baptist past seemed a curiosity, if not an impossibility. Beebe himself seemed to have forgotten his fondness for Zelotes Grenell, a fellow elder who had endorsed missions just as Beebe rose to prominence in the anti-missionary cause. As young preachers in the 1820s, Beebe and Grenell lived near each other, were each friendly with the other's families, and together attended meetings of the Hudson River Association and the Orange County Baptist Society, where they often sat next to one another. In 1830, as the churches they pastored began choosing sides in the growing intra-Baptist dispute over missions, benevolent societies, theological schools, and the like, Beebe reached out to Grenell in obvious distress. "I have never found a minister of the gospel for whom I felt so much nearness, christian love and fellowship, as yourself," Beebe wrote. "There are but probably few to be found who are, generally speaking, more united in the doctrine of salvation by grace. I do not know that we differ essentially in regard to the doctrine, discipline, or the ordinances of the House of God. In christian experience, I believe we have both drank of the same fountain. Our difference of views is wholly of a different nature." Beebe's gentle tone, his search for compromise (in his letter he proposed a system of voluntary contributions to support "poor itinerant preachers"), and his stress on the many points of agreement he and Grenell shared reveal a different kind of history than the kind written in the official chronicles that came to dominate each side's historical imagination. Alas, we do not know if as he grew older Beebe forgot his friendship with Grenell, if he purposely ignored it, or if he unconsciously repressed it. But we sense here the fraternity that preceded the split, the ambivalence that accompanied it, and the pain that followed in its wake. Stereotype, embodied in the histories crafted by each side's preacher-historians, obscured such ties in favor of drawing coherent, durable group identities.[41]

Indeed, the exaggerated group identities birthed during those years have proven far more durable than the social and theological differences that first gave rise to them. Those identities propelled the split in its early years and preserved it as the nineteenth century wore on. In our own time, these two contrary group identities, laden with stereotype and encrusted with more than a century's worth of unexamined assumptions, still color our interpretations of this crucial moment in Baptist history. They have snared even our best historians. William McLoughlin describes the Baptist story in ways that those jubilant mid-nineteenth-century missionary Baptist chroniclers would have recognized. "The history of the Baptists," he writes, "is a paradigm of the American success myth: from rags to riches, from outcast to respectability, from pariah to pillar, from heresy to orthodoxy, from criminal deviant to authoritarian standard-bearer." Sydney Ahlstrom, in his classic *A Religious History of the American People*, asserts that anti-missionary activity appealed to "the poorest and least educated . . . who felt threatened by eastern money-raising organizations and their relatively well-educated emissaries." And Bertram Wyatt-Brown, like a grizzled member of Old School cause, rhapsodizes about how the Primitive Baptists endure as representatives of "the persistent Southern struggle to preserve old values in an alien, changing, and often self-righteous world." The earlier era's invective has dissipated, but those two sturdy and exaggerated group portraits remain.[42]

The split itself was no fiction. From the 1820s through the 1840s, Baptist churches cracked apart over the question of missions and other benevolent enterprises. The dividing line between Beebe's Primitives and Grenell's missionaries was real, but stereotype's legacy was to make what was for years an open doorway, an easily scaled fence, a hastily drawn line in the sand, into a chasm. And all of this was cradled by the early historical narratives crafted by each side. Those histories told the story of the schism, widening the gulf even as they chronicled it.

2 Doubts Still Assail Me

In 1794, twenty-seven-year-old Thomas Hill dug the butt of his rifle into the earth and buried its muzzle in his chin. For years Hill had felt himself to be "a stranger in a strange place," a man "standing on a narrow point of time" whose next step threatened to plunge him into eternal ruin. After a sleepless night, he finally determined to "end his mortal existence." As Hill walked to the place where he would take his life, the devil walked with him, goading him on. "God and me never could live together," Hill thought, "and the sooner that I was dead and damned the better." Hill did not pull the trigger that day. He waited, instead, for what he knew would be God's swift judgment. But Thomas Hill's travails were not fleeting. Hill's near-suicide was only the most dramatic moment in his years-long journey from unbelief to devotion and back again, from Methodist meetinghouses to the Primitive Baptist order where he at last found a home. Like the devil on that awful day, turmoil stalked Hill all through these years. While collecting firewood one day, Hill heard a voice urging him to kill his newborn child. Months later Hill found himself paralyzed by the thought that nature itself would rise up against him: tree limbs would become menacing snakes, trees trunks would explode, and neighbors' dogs would tear him to pieces. Even during his baptism, Hill remained convinced that the muddy river would send a piece of driftwood to pierce him through. Hill's spiritual tempests occasionally slackened, replaced either by periods of calm or even delight in those moments when he felt God's grace. More frequently, however, Hill lived with a gnawing uncertainty about both his ultimate fate and a persistent frustration with what he described as his insincerity or hypocrisy. During his odyssey, Hill tried at various times to square his heart with his mind, his soul with God, and his feelings with social expectations. In nearly all of these efforts, Hill failed.[1]

The arc of Thomas Hill's spiritual journey was familiar to evangelicals in the old South. And in our own time, scholars also have become well acquainted with evangelical conversion narratives, discovering in them a basic morphology that guides the convert's welter of experience like a system of canals and sluices harnesses a raging river. Seen from a distance, Hill and other converts flowed from one stage of the process to the next, from conviction (the process by which God made Hill and others like him aware of their abiding sinfulness) to conversion to assurance (the point at which the convert believes he or she is saved). A Primitive Baptist like Hill followed the same basic path as a missionary Baptist, and the journeys described by both types of Baptists hit landmarks passed by members of other evangelical denominations during their spiritual progress. There were the frivolities of youth, such as horse racing, gambling, and dancing; the pungent discovery of one's sinful nature; the subsequent fear of eternal condemnation; a frightening struggle with Satan or one of his wily representatives; and finally an awesome encounter with God's grace. All of this was deeply patterned, which has made the conversion narrative an attractive source for scholarly investigation.[2]

Seen from a closer vantage point, the rough patterns that matched Primitive Baptists with evangelical Protestants remain, but their precise symmetries appear crippled. For instance, there is good reason to believe that for Primitive Baptists, the period of conviction lasted longer, was more convoluted, and was perhaps more acutely felt.[3] In particular, a feeling of uncertainty dominated Primitive life. These doubts appear to be the unmistakable offspring of the Primitives' Calvinist theology, but in practice they coexisted with an array of inquiries with much looser theological moorings. Questions about perception itself, about the relationship between subjective experience and objective truth, and about the possibilities and limits of self-knowledge strode alongside potential converts and full-fledged church members during their religious odysseys.

Primitives—both before and after their conversions—tried to banish such doubts, but they failed. They tried to mimic the ardent sentimentality kicking up dust at camp meetings. They schooled themselves on the sincere religion of the heart flowering in evangelical circles nationwide. But their keen feelings died, their attempts to revive them faltered, and the whole effort seemed like an appalling religious masquerade. Doubt crept across their lives like a blooming mold.

In scholarly terms, the people who would become Primitives tried but failed to cultivate what historians have long recognized as the normative emotional style of evangelical Protestantism. This was an emotional style that prized sincerity and promoted instrumentality. Believers pursued a direct, personal relationship with God; yearned for the new birth, in which the Holy Spirit regenerated a corrupt heart and outward emotional expression—tears, shouting, fainting—signified piety; and emphasized the role of the human will in aiding the conversion process. In the emotional precincts of early nineteenth-century evangelicalism, believers sought and found a congruence between avowal and actual feeling.[4] Indeed, that congruence was the mark of the sincere covert. But while legions of the converted felt this harmony between intention and experience, others, such as the people who later learned to call themselves Primitives, fell into a yawning gap of uncertainty. They ached for God's grace, sensed it like a blur at the edge of sight, and felt it vanish. Had God, in that fleeting moment, granted them eternal reprieve, or would they forever remain strangers to his grace?

This uncertainty that dominated Primitive Baptists' lives also catalyzed their movement's rise and fueled their strident opposition to the theological and organizational changes shaping churches across the country. For Primitive Baptists, it was their questioning—especially their experience of persistent doubt—that set them apart from their evangelical brethren. But the uncertainty that colored Primitive Baptist selfhood motivated believers rather than paralyzed them. It propelled them toward a community of like-minded souls, and it stirred those souls to action as a more ardent brand of evangelical Protestantism crowded church pews. In their uncertain selves, in lives assailed by doubt—not in their formal theology or in their socioeconomic condition—we find the most compelling explanation of their movement's unlikely rise.

The Uncertain Self, Part 1: Watched but Uncontrollable

Sarah Ann Hollister felt in need of supervision. Only a year earlier her church had broken apart over the question of missions, and like a running wound, the pain of the division refused to subside. Hollister watched as parents turned against their children and neighbor against neighbor. "Perilous times have come," she thought. That the division arrived on the heels of a season of revival, a time when God's spirit had regenerated the hearts of so many sinners, including Hollister herself, only sharpened the pain. In the split's aftermath, Hollister worried that she, too, might be tempted to leave the church. "O I find need of watching, to see whether I am 'in the faith,'" she wrote. "We need to watch and pray daily." Hollister believed that self-scrutiny might stave off sin's siren song and perhaps help her discern whether her recent vision of Jesus floating in the clouds above her farm was a divine visitation or just further evidence of her frothy imagination.[5]

Hollister's plea for "watching" was a reminder to herself of right thought and a signal to her church of right behavior. It was a common enough injunction among Primitive Baptists, who often heard preachers tell their flocks that the "true believer" had "'a witness in himself.'" Primitive congregations carried on the social surveillance typical of Protestant churches, describing new members as being under the church's "watch care" and sanctioning or even excommunicating members whose behavior slipped beyond the bounds of decency. Yet Hollister's words recall the extent to which surveillance became an internal occupation. This was not prayer per se but rather a companion practice. One petitioned God, as Hollister did, and then one turned inward. Watching was a search. Primitives like Hollister scanned themselves for evidence, for "a hope," as they put it, that they were true believers counted among God's elect. The search often ended quickly and with a happy enough result.[6]

But watching was an unstable practice, and it often cultivated the very doubts it was designed, in part, to police. By watching herself closely, the diligent believer, like Hollister, might catch herself before sinning. And in case she did sin, her watchfulness allowed her to spot her error and then correct it. But here is where Hollister and her fellow Primitive Baptists ran into an intractable dilemma, where the believer's internal vigilance led unintentionally but inexorably to creeping uncertainty. Now, Primitive Baptists knew they were sinners, that sinning was inevitable, and that trespass hardly vanished from life after baptism. As a practical matter, however, doctrinal truths like these failed to assuage a day-to-day guilt among Primitives that we might dismiss as mere angst if its consequences for the afflicted were not so momentous. It was not just that by watching themselves for transgressions Primitives inevitably discovered what they hoped not to find. In deed if not in creed, many Old School Baptists shared the sentiments of one of their frontier preachers who, during a sermon on "watch-care," insisted that just as "a cracked jar never afterwards rang clear; so with the Christian who gives over to the flesh and falls a victim to false doctrine or bad habit. While they may see their error and turn from it, yet full confidence is seldom, if ever, restored."[7]

Under conditions like these, confidence, let alone "full confidence," suffered grievously. At its most sinister, the process seemingly suggested that as Primitives understood themselves more and more, they ought to trust themselves less and less. Certainly, the elder Joshua Lawrence found himself trapped in this situation. "The more I study and think of my state, the more I doubt," he wrote, "until I doubt almost every thing, and can believe nothing concerning myself, but what is bad." Still, Primitives watched, internal eyes peeled, knowing they would see their sin uncoiling before them and knowing, too, that their efforts to right themselves would at some point fail. That awful sight, of all things, was a certainty.[8]

Under the pressure of that relentless gaze, is it any wonder that Primitive Baptists like Hollister learned to doubt themselves? Hollister, for example, often remembered her vision of Jesus in the clouds above her family farm. Each time she recalled the vision, skepticism, like an overeager valet, followed in tow. Had she seen her Savior and did she, therefore, have a hope? Or had she let her sight be claimed by Satan? She cried out in frustration, "Is this the Lord or no?" Hollister did not know who or what to trust. With no resolution in sight, she vowed to try to keep the memories out of her mind entirely, depriving herself of the beautiful vision and sparing herself, she hoped, from fears that she had been deceived.[9]

"Who can fathom or control the human mind?" asked Rebecca Phillips. "I cannot." Phillips posed her question in her spiritual autobiography, which she titled, appropriately enough, *Led by a Way I Knew Not*. And if her account proved more didactic and less circuitous than its title implied, that did not prevent Phillips's story from becoming one of the more popular in its genre. Born in 1832 to Primitive Baptist parents, Rebecca Phillips nonetheless spent the first eight years after her baptism within the embrace of missionary Baptist churches before returning, prodigal-like, to the Primitive fold. Her first published explanation for this turn of events appeared in pamphlet form in 1875. Some twenty-five years later, she finally "yielded to solicitations" and expanded her earlier work into a book-length narrative. With chapters denouncing Sunday schools and theological seminaries, *Led by a Way I Knew Not* was very much another volley in the ongoing war between Primitive and missionary Baptists.[10]

But in its brief summation of the vicissitudes of its author's emotional life, Phillips's book succinctly captured one of the essential experiences of Primitive Baptist life, namely failure. This was not a record of failure in life's conventional pursuits, the kinds of things that dot most any biography—finding a mate, earning a livelihood, raising a family, and so on. There is ample evidence that Primitive Baptists, men and women, did just fine in that regard, and in the South, there is a record of slaveholding that belies Primitives' reputation as hardscrabble backcountry folk. Rather, Primitives failed most often and spectacularly in their interior lives, in their efforts to manage—to control, as Rebecca Phillips put it—their thoughts and feelings. These failures were not entirely atypical. Placed within the bounds of a broader evangelical culture, which, at least among southern whites, often had the effect of breaking down the sinner before building him or her back up again, the Primitive Baptist experience, at first blush, hardly appears unusual. But for Primitive Baptists, that process of reconstruction was never complete and always crumbling.[11]

There was, for example, Mary Beckley Bristow, who, in the fall of 1832 in a northern Kentucky hamlet just south of the Ohio River, thought she might lose her mind. An unbidden gloom had recently engulfed Bristow, and it seemed now only to grow darker. She felt guilty of something she could not name. She strove "to get rid of these feelings, fearing as there seemed to be no cause for them, if indulged [they] would produce insanity." She "resolved to go more into company, to be as gay as the gayest and have all those gloomy phantoms chased away." But the feelings of misery never left. She listened to preachers from the Disciples of Christ but found their talk "all nonsense." A memory from childhood kept rising in her mind like a melancholy chorus: an old Baptist man talking to Bristow's mother about religion as Bristow, just a young girl then, drifted through the room. "I heard him say he had no power to control his own thoughts. Thinks I to myself, 'What an old fool you are.'" But now the adult Bristow wondered if she, too, had lost control.[12]

Emotional Effort and Failure

As their minds swirled and their doubts mounted, would-be Primitive Baptists, such as Mary Bristow, redoubled their efforts to master their feelings; more often than not, those efforts failed. These same rhythms of emotional effort and failure sound over and over again in Primitive Baptist conversion narratives, spiritual autobiographies, and private correspondence.[13]

Thomas Hill's case is exemplary. At about twenty years of age, Hill left his native Virginia for a fresh start in the mountains of what would later become eastern Tennessee. During childhood he had flirted with Methodist and Baptist churches, but soon after his move, Hill's frustration with hypocritical Presbyterian neighbors as well as a stint as a soldier on the western frontier, "where the bullets flew thick" and landed indiscriminately, convinced him "that there was no reality in religion." In time, however, Hill's thoughts turned back toward religious contemplation. He worried that his dismissal of the religious life would leave him "in a bad fix" should heaven and hell prove, in fact, to be real. Less than a year after marrying, Hill abruptly left his pregnant wife to travel three hundred miles on a religious errand. He intended to bury his skepticism once and for all by observing his father, a Christian, for any signs of doubt or lapses in behavior. "All the way I went, I thought I would watch him," Hill wrote. "If I could see any thing through his conduct that I did not think was a Christian, then the matter would be decided." What Hill watched awed him. His father's rectitude convinced him of God's existence. Hill quickly set about matching his father's behavior, but within a few days he was left with only broken promises and a renewed skepticism. Hill ran into similar difficulties when he turned his attentions inward. His mind wandered during prayer, and despite prodigious efforts to bend his feelings to God's will, he found himself continually unable to do so. "My heart seemed to me that it could not be sincere," he wrote. "I wanted to be sorry, but I could not." Hill's failure of will left him despondent. It was this consuming sense of his own impotence that drove him one morning to the brink of suicide. Hill suffered alone that morning, but the rough pattern of his life—the labored and unsuccessful efforts to navigate the treacherous waters of feeling—became one of the defining features of the Primitive Baptist self.[14]

Like Hill, many Primitives strove to cultivate the sense of guilt they believed they deserved, a sense of guilt they craved (however unwilling they may have been to admit it) because such guilt, they knew, inevitably accompanied the Holy Spirit's efforts to regenerate a corrupt soul. And so in Frankfort, Kentucky, a young merchant already feeling the first pangs of conviction taught himself to draw pictures of hell in his mind's eye while imagining the "torments of the damned" echoing inside his skull. He sought out preachers who shouted about hell and damnation, fire and brimstone, because that was, he said, "the sort of preacher I ought to hear." For two years, this young man carried on his mental exercises and churchly excursions until, alone in bed one night, he decided that he was damned, that his initial experiences of conviction must have been a mirage, because all that fervid preaching, all that time spent diligently reconstructing hell's agonies, left his heart unmoved.[15]

Still others worked to turn their minds toward thoughts more serene. A young Joshua Lawrence, for example, immersed himself in thrice-daily devotions and, like a manic monk, would at various times each day chant "bless God, bless God, as fast as I could speak, perhaps for half an hour." No matter. For each blessing he recited, a companion curse echoed inside him: Curse God and die, curse God and die. "It was constant in my mind," Lawrence wrote. "It came as fast as I could have thoughts, curse God and die.... And the misery I felt in my mind my pen can't write." The internal rumblings menaced him for more than three years, during which time he faithfully attended church meetings and intensified his devotions, the result of which, more often than not, was a hardening despair. If only to rid himself of these unbidden thoughts, Lawrence wished he could somehow be transformed into one of the unthinking animals grazing in his fields or stalking the nearby forest. Well after his conversion, Lawrence continued to find himself pushed and pulled by cosmic forces much stronger than himself. Neighbors described seeing him darting aimlessly through the woods for several days at a time before winding up rolling around on the ground wailing. "The devil had got me and gone off with me," Lawrence offered by way of explanation. At other times God's spirit possessed him, and he had nothing to do but to hold open his mouth as words of supplication poured out for an hour straight without interruption.[16]

The Uncertain Self, Part 2: Deceived and Deceiver

Even while casually leafing through Primitive writings, one quickly notices how often the phrase "if I be not deceived" (or some close variation) hitches itself to the end of sentences. So ubiquitous is its presence in Primitive Baptist discourse that the phrase, which initially calls attention to itself, soon fades into the surrounding text the way that once-novel landmarks, after one has lived near them for some time, eventually melt into the landscape. The utterance seems to be a Calvinist reflex; antebellum Primitive Baptists found the phrase useful even in conveying uncertainty about seemingly banal issues. In 1837, a believer named Arthur Bolch devoured the first several issues of a new Primitive periodical. He wrote to the editors to applaud their efforts. Bolch reckoned that Old School Baptists had found in the *Christian Doctrinal Advocate and Spiritual Monitor* a much-needed champion of their cause—that is, he added, "if I am not deceived."[17]

But it was in the discussion of obviously consequential matters, such as conversion, where this Calvinistic reflex was most often triggered. Joshua Lawrence, for example, asked readers of his autobiography to "tell me what you think of it? Does it [his conversion experience] amount to being born again, or not? For I yet am afraid I am deceived." Eyewitnesses reported that on his deathbed more than forty years later, Lawrence shuddered with similar fears.[18]

Or consider J. H. Purifoy, a doctor from Snow Hill, Alabama, who endured the travails of conviction for ten years before experiencing in a moment, after a spring morning spent plowing his field, the fullness of God's grace only to be seared hours later by withering self-doubt. "What is all this about?" he asked himself later that afternoon. It would be the first question in a self-interrogation that lasted the rest of his life. "You think this is religion, but it is a mistake," Purifoy said to himself. "It is nothing but the mere imagination of your own mind." He worried that the regeneration of his soul had been a delusion. "I may be deceived," he thought. He begged God, "Undeccive me if I [am] deceived." So uncertain was Purifoy that he refused to tell anyone about his seeming moment of pardon or his subsequent doubts. For two years, Purifoy struggled to make sense of what had happened to him. "I was deceived sure enough," he finally concluded. Soon, though, an irresistible longing to be baptized possessed him. Uncertain and confused, but desperate for relief, Purifoy yielded to his desire, related the exercises of his mind to his church, and was baptized.[19]

Baptism, as Purifoy knew, was a moment of great joy and fellowship. It was the central rite of his church. His baptism linked him to his Savior and to the men and women of his beloved community who stood on the riverbank as their preacher lowered him into the watery grave and lifted him up. By accepting him as a member of their church, they had ratified, as much as mere men and women could, Purifoy's experience of grace. For two years, Purifoy had wondered whether he had been deceived. His church answered, "No." But instead of relief, Purifoy felt "oppressed and burdened with some inexpressible something." It would be bad enough if he had deceived himself, but the thought that he also may have deceived others left him anguished. After the baptism, he fled the meetinghouse for the nearby woods, where he buried his face in the earth and begged God once again to undeceive him if he had been deceived. God remained silent. "Many are the times that I have prayed that prayer," Purifoy explained thirty years later, "and I cannot say now that I have ever received a positive answer to it. . . . So from the day of my baptism on I have not been free from burdens. . . . Doubts still assail me."[20]

Behind worries about deception lay a companion concern, an obsession even, with the problem of sincerity. Purifoy described himself as a "miserable hypocrite." Thomas Hill, as we have seen, wondered why he could not be sincere. The stoic Kentucky merchant, who found himself unable to repent, decided that his prayers were counterfeit. And in 1900, in a kind of coda to a century's worth of Primitive Baptist contemplation and self-condemnation, an elderly preacher, bedridden for nearly a month, prayed for God's mercy, and then interrogated himself: "Am I sincere even in that?"[21]

The Primitives as Emotional Exiles

Brief Primitive Baptist conversion narratives as well as longer spiritual autobiographies brim with trials like those outlined here. Evidence of these lost struggles for control of the human mind and, at times, body is strewn all about the pitted landscape of conviction. Indeed, in most

Primitive Baptist narratives, the bulk of the action pulsates to the familiar cadence of struggle and failure. And, as in the cases examined here, such turmoil often continued well past the Primitive Baptist's period of conviction. Satan might play his part, but these men and women found themselves preoccupied by their own deceptions, their own hypocrisy. Why had they turned on themselves?

That question and its answer might make more sense if we tended to them while rooted in the sensorium of the evangelical world, for, like internal exiles, Primitives found themselves both of this world and estranged from it. It is a truism that evangelicalism, especially as embodied in the Second Great Awakening, narrowed the gap between the human and the divine, between the believer and his or her God. This was not just the case in the realm of formal theology, where John Wesley could argue, for example, that believers might attain "Christian Perfection"—that is, they could find "deliverance from inward as well as outward sin." In church pews, along the slat benches of the camp meeting, and in the privacy of their own homes, American evangelicals were living, by the early nineteenth century, in a world where the whispers of the Holy Ghost and visions of Jesus were commonplace.[22]

In this world—the world of popular belief and practice—emotional expression, because it was so intimately connected with the divine, was prized, seen as natural and good, a force for personal and even, perhaps, political change. Prayer was an intimate conversation with God the Father or, more often, with his Son. And it was these experiential connections that were so assiduously cultivated, consciously and unconsciously, by evangelicals during prayer, revival, conversations, and even sleep. There was, as the historian Leigh Eric Schmidt has argued, an evangelical "metaphysics of the senses" centered around cultivating an intimate relationship with Jesus specifically by educating the bodily senses to become spiritual ones. "But always the head followed the heart's lead," writes Christine Leigh Heyrman about antebellum southern evangelicals. "What led men and women to accept that proposition as a stark truth were not the reflections of the dispassionate mind but the inclinations of the engaged emotions." Nowhere were evangelicals' emotions engaged so systematically and intensely as during a revival. But revivals simply condensed what had become a distinct evangelical emotional style—one in which fervent exhortation led to sudden conversion, where tears of sadness erupted into shouts of joy, where transports of love became signs of a direct link to the Holy Spirit. A revival was a way to enhance normative evangelical emotions and experiences, to work them to an ever-higher pitch. Perhaps John Corrigan puts it best: "The pursuit of revival, a virtually constant theme in nineteenth-century Protestantism, was part of a larger cultural phenomenon, the pursuit of feeling."[23]

Primitive Baptists bathed in feeling, but they largely disdained its pursuit. Quite often the Primitives' critique of evangelicals' emotive culture closely tracked the assessments proffered by Enlightenment-influenced skeptics: by Deists, who dismissed the possibility of evangelicals' running conversation with God, and by rationalists, who reduced the dramas of revival to something quite like what modern-day sociologists term peer pressure. But the Primitives had more in common with the evangelicals with whom they had recently split than with these apostles of the Enlightenment. Instead, the Primitive Baptist critique of evangelicals' emotive culture sprang from a deep well of Calvinist restraint that simultaneously acknowledged frequent and authentic experiences of the divine and cautioned against mistaking enthusiasm for genuine religious affections. They chastised evangelicals for "firing . . . the natural passions" and indulging in manipulative preaching that veered from the treacly to the alarmist. Can it be, wondered a group of Maryland Primitive Baptists in 1832, "that the Holy Ghost is somehow so the creature of human feelings that he is led to regenerate persons by our getting their animal feelings excited?" When the theologian Edward Beecher (brother of Harriet, Henry, and Catharine; son of Lyman; and, as such, a member of the nation's Calvinist elite) pleaded with Christians to embrace a higher standard of personal holiness because God wanted "his holy kingdom to feel on this subject as he does," Primitive Baptists recoiled. "The sensations and emotions of the Deity [are an] unsearchable mystery," thundered Mark Bennett, a Primitive Baptist from Tarboro, North Carolina, who would have been at best bemused at the Calvinist credentials held by Edward or any of his more famous relations.[24]

More immediate, though, than their theological heritage were Primitives' persistent frustrations during private and public devotions, frustrations that left them feeling estranged from man and God alike. Many of these episodes—the near-suicides, the visitations by the devil, and so on—are so tangibly described that they reach beyond the didactic and reveal something more primal. Similarly, these are, of course, Calvinist narratives, yet they speak to an experience often apart from, and prior to, doctrine. "I was as ignorant of the doctrine and order of the church as a negro," one believer starkly and typically put it about his familiarity, both before and immediately following baptism, with the intricacies of Primitive Baptist theology.[25]

Thomas Hill and others like him knew full well what it meant to be estranged from man and God alike. The broken link between outward appearances and inward reality rattled their lives. A young man in South Carolina, Joseph Lewis, had, as he described it, "rambled and blundered along for some time" in life. As the revivals burned through his stretch of country, he drifted between Baptist churches and Methodist meetings before abandoning them both. "I could not tell what I was," Lewis wrote. "I read the scriptures, but instead of getting better, I got worse. . . . I went to hear preaching, it done me no good. . . . When I tried to pray, my thoughts of other things stared me in the face." He promised God he would try harder, but he only met with despair: "I had made so many promises to God, and I had broken or violated all." Years of failed efforts like these took their toll. "I could see hell open ready to receive me," he recalled. "This brought me in such distress, that at times I lost my common reason." Thomas Hill, too, had spent years attending church meetings, offering prayers to God, repenting of his sins, and bringing his behavior in line with Christian expectations. His efforts also largely proved futile. If he occasionally felt the joy other believers described, it inevitably dissolved several days or even hours later. On the eve of his brush with suicide, Hill watched from afar as his neighbors in the small settlement along the Little Pigeon River testified publicly about their private ecstasy: "Though at that time there was great excitement amongst the people," he wrote, "and many going forward to be prayed for, I never did, thinking it may be would wear off, as I had had so many shocks and I hated to appear as a hypocrite."[26]

Experiences like Lewis's and Hill's were common among the first generation of Primitive Baptists. These were people who, like Lewis and Hill, stood inside evangelicals' emotional world but struggled to cultivate that world's normative emotional and spiritual experiences. And so they saw themselves as hypocrites, as insincere, as impostors—people who went through the motions of prayer and revival and whatever else passed for Christian behavior but whose pursuit of feeling, to use John Corrigan's apt phrase, felt to them perpetually stymied.

Primitive Baptists would go on to develop a thoroughgoing critique of evangelicalism that tied its theological betrayals to its emotional demands. And they would, too, more firmly plot out the loneliness of their plight even as they forged bonds of fellowship with others who felt like they did. To be a Primitive Baptist was, as they told themselves, to experience "many lonesome hours and hard trials," to "hobble through lonesome valleys," to be "strangers and pilgrims in this world of trouble." But those critiques of evangelicalism and those patterned descriptions of loneliness would come later, in the 1820s and 1830s. First came experience itself. In their youth, during the 1790s and early 1800s, the first generation of Primitive Baptists lived through the great upsurge of evangelical sects in the young Republic. They were, it is true, children of the revival. But as they described it—as they felt it—they were the Second Great Awakening's orphans, watching alone from the edge of the scene, like Thomas Hill, as their brothers and sisters in Christ celebrated a connection they failed to make.[27]

Refuges and Battlements

Thomas Hill's exile eventually ended. After years of torment, he walked one day into a meeting of Old Baptists near his home in the foothills of the Smoky Mountains: "I told them that I was in distress, and I hoped that they were the people of God and would deal faithful with my soul." After Hill related his hope of grace, "the old deacon, Spencer Clack, raised up his head and said, who can forbid water, that these may not be baptised who have received the Holy Ghost as well as we?" When they raised him from the muddy river the next morning, Hill felt heaven and earth knit together. "My soul seemed to join the saints above, with them that were singing around us," he wrote.[28]

That Primitive Baptists such as Hill testified abundantly to their faith's beauty and comfort left their critics flummoxed, if not incensed. These critics equated the Primitives' predestinarianism with abject fatalism and considered the Old Baptists' belief in particular election (the idea that God had preordained the salvation of only a select portion of humanity) to be nothing but obeisance to a God who was, in Charles Finney's words, "an infinite tyrant." It is not difficult to see how Finney and the others came to their conclusions. For when they were not lashing out at missionaries, individual Primitive Baptists spent a good portion of their time—in print, at least—sighing over mankind's depravity and, especially, their own personal fallenness. And this is surely why so many outsiders considered their faith bleak.[29]

But those depths were labyrinthine, offering the Primitive Baptist believer various routes of spiritual progress, many of them, at least to those outside the faith, unlikely. One finds, for instance, that Primitives regularly referred to themselves as worms, a self-description that is painful to read even at this great distance. But that self-abnegating, if not self-loathing, comparison is revealing, for the same words were spoken by the psalmist who declared, "I am a worm, and no man." And it is the first line of this same psalm—Psalm 22—that Jesus cried out while bleeding on the cross: "My God, my God, why hast thou forsaken me?" So when Wilson Thompson or Joshua Lawrence or other Primitive Baptists described themselves as worms, they were, at once, demonstrating their distance and closeness to God. They were debasing themselves even as they connected themselves to God by adopting their Savior's voice. For Primitive Baptists, these two seemingly opposite emotional vectors—one of estrangement, the other of affinity—traveled hand in hand.[30]

Doubt, too, could be strangely comforting. It had brought many of them together, after all. Among other Christians, they felt isolated, "alone in every sense of the word," as a man named Lee Hanks put it. "They told me they had no doubts and fears," Hanks wrote about the people he later learned to call Arminians. "But I never could get to the place where I had no doubts and fears." An anxious Hanks shared his concerns with his employer, a Methodist with whom he often discussed religious issues. Hanks told the Methodist man that he felt an instant kinship with the local Primitive Baptists whom he had just met. The Methodist man shrugged. Primitives were "demoralizing," he said. But for Hanks and people like him, the affinity they felt for Primitive Baptists was not only immediate but uplifting. Hanks reported that the first Old Baptists he met "told my experience better than I could . . . they could tell my feelings so well." "Like one alone I seem to be / Oh! is there any one like me?" they sang, in a hymn directed not at God but at each other. And in the surging cadences of their fellow saints, they heard an affirmative sound. "Thus filled with doubts, I ask to know / Come, tell me, is it thus with you?" Questions sung in unison: this was what Lee Hanks had searched for.[31]

The uncertain self found a home in Primitive Baptist meetinghouses, but varieties of dualistic thinking took shelter there too. Even the same doubt-saturated believers who lived in an uncertain world could, especially in moments of crisis, pipe their ambiguous experience into two opposing categories. This quotidian dualism was everywhere: in hymns and poems, diaries and autobiographies. But the epitome of such thinking might be found in Joshua Lawrence, the Primitive Baptist elder and polemicist who after years of spiritual and emotional uncertainty finally discovered that, as he put it, there were "two armies" inside him, "a contrariety of passions, and spirits in me . . . warring one against the other . . . by day and night." Lawrence ended his autobiography with a mammoth catalog of these contending forces, arrayed on the page in two columns like so:

The devil	Christ
Angels of the devil	The angels of Christ
Unbelief	Faith
Despair	Hope
The desire of the flesh	The desire of the soul
Lying	Truth
Strife	Fellowship
Fornication	Lawfulness

Lawrence identified ninety pairs of warring principles inside himself. He said their combat was eternal and irreconcilable.[32]

Many Primitive Baptists waged identical wars within themselves. They were, as they put it, "half saint, and sinner half." For many, eternal conflict became a sign of a renewed heart, the struggle an indication that at least Satan found himself having to fight for one's soul rather than being able to easily claim it. That hardly meant the tumult would end or that those torn by strife would earn a respite. Those who found themselves at ease were, in fact, considered suspect. "The christian's life abounds with contrarieties," wrote John Watson, who, like Lawrence, cataloged a list of opposing forces. "There is no . . . escape from these conflicts in this life." There are echoes here of the *complexio oppositorum*—a binding together of logical and metaphysical opposites—that some theologians have used to characterize Calvin's thought, but we should take Lawrence and his fellow Primitives at their word: passions warred inside them, the conflict rattled their bodies and souls, and any unity of opposites vibrated ominously. None of this, of course, escaped the Primitives' penchant for skepticism. Each side "may be so nicely counterfeited," warned one believer, "that the fraud shall hardly be detected." While there is abundant evidence that such spiritual combat could lead to despair and stalemate, there is, too, the sense that in the split subjectivity of the ordinary Primitive Baptist, one side or the other often had the upper hand at any one moment. In this way, the Primitive Baptist could and did avoid stalemate and would not wallow in open-ended doubt.[33]

Any sense of nuance, though, disappeared in the thinking of Daniel Parker, who espoused a "Two-Seeds" doctrine that seemed to make Satan and God coequals. Parker had come of age along the Georgia frontier, where he witnessed the aftershocks of the Great Revival and, in 1802, at the age of twenty-one, was baptized. In subsequent years, Parker found work, variously, as a preacher, a farmer, a land speculator, and a politician. But the pulpit was his calling. Contemporaries described him as an archetypal frontiersman: rough-hewn, a man "of the gipsy type," poorly educated, and possessed of coarse manners and an indomitable will. That obstinacy sometimes seemed in need of enemies, and Parker soon found them in the horseback Methodist circuit riders who preached an Arminian doctrine at odds with Parker's predestinarianism. By the 1820s, Parker had escalated his battle against Arminianism. Not only Methodists but all those who supported missionary schemes drew his ire. Two-Seedism became Parker's attempt to justify his anti-missionary Calvinism and explain the growing presence of "devil sent" missionaries among the Old Baptist faithful.[34]

Two-Seedism held that God had implanted the divine seed of Christ in Adam while Satan had implanted his seed in Eve. Adam's descendants, therefore, composed the true church, which had existed since the Creation. They were the elect. The non-elect, meanwhile, were the literal children of Satan. After their time on earth, the descendants of each seed would meet with their respective makers. As theology, Two-Seedism was, to say the least, glib. But it did grapple, however ham-fistedly, with a problem faced by many religions, namely how to reconcile a benevolent God with the presence of evil in the world. Parker's solution to this hoary dilemma was to explain that all evil emanated not from God but from the devil, who was God's eternal opposite. The point was to separate God somehow from responsibility for evil and for the creation of the damned.[35]

Two-Seedism attracted scads of critics, not least among them many of Parker's fellow Primitive Baptists who worried that he was making a mockery of their predestinarianism. Parker's own church fractured over Two-Seedism, and quite a few Primitive Baptist polemicists, momentarily tired of lambasting missionaries, directed their ire toward "the author of American Manichaeanism." Critics quickly latched onto the fact that Parker's scheme elevated Satan from one of God's fallen angels to a coeternal and seemingly coequal presence. Many Primitive Baptists were particularly bothered by Two-Seedism's apparent disavowal of Adam's original sin. If Adam had not fallen, then man's desperate need to have his corrupt soul regenerated by the Holy Spirit seemed to have passed by the wayside. This was "nonsense in the extreme," fumed one Old School Baptist elder, while another wondered if Parker might be compelled to remove himself to the Rockies where he "could scatter [his] two seeds among the Mustangs and wild Ass."[36]

Yet denunciations like these failed to prevent a string of churches—many in Parker's stronghold of southern Illinois but still others in Indiana, Kentucky, Tennessee, Mississippi, Louisiana, and Texas—from embracing "Parkerism," as the homespun theology came to be called. Meanwhile, the memberships of many other Old Baptist churches, without explicitly adopting Two-Seedism, had no difficulty identifying Parkerism and its adherents as kin. Parker's Old Baptists along the frontier were, after all, Calvinists engaged in the fight against missions and other assorted ills afflicting modern-day Baptists.

Over time, Two-Seeds-in-the-Spirit Baptists became little more than a curiosity. By the late nineteenth century, the vast majority of Primitive Baptist churches had disavowed Parkerism. Modern-day Primitive Baptists, if they address Two-Seedism at all, consider it something of an embarrassment, a moment of doctrinal inconsistency and exuberance that emerged from an otherwise estimable Baptist elder. Meanwhile, missionary Baptists have been inclined to tar all Primitive Baptists with Parker's stain. In their eyes, Two-Seedism was nothing but a more candid version of the Primitives' "hyper-Calvinism," a theology they already considered absurd.[37]

In these somewhat abstruse theological debates, the cultural context surrounding the birth and early growth of Two-Seedism has been neglected. If it remained a distinctly minority taste, Two-Seedism nonetheless distilled a strain of popular theology scattered among Old School Baptists along the frontier. Parker freely admitted he did not invent the theology but rather had heard it circulating in his churches as early as 1812. For theologians, it may be worthwhile to label Two-Seedism a heresy, but for cultural and religious historians, it may be more useful to see Two-Seedism as part of a continuum of dualistic thought that flourished among Primitive Baptists. The eternal war raging in Joshua Lawrence's soul found external expression in Daniel Parker's homegrown theology. In Parker's world, it became especially clear who were the children of God and who were Satan's offspring. Primitive Baptists like Parker and his followers claimed descent from the apostolic church, and they explained that all other Christian sects had gone astray somewhere along the line. In Parker's glib theology, it was but a short step from this claim to an even more explosive one: that the saints in Two-Seed churches were the elect and their opponents—missionaries, Methodists, Arminians of all stripes—were literally children of the devil. American Manichaeanism such as Parker's or Lawrence's shadowed the uncertain Primitive Baptist self, offering it in moments of crisis or weakness a sturdy defense from the doubts that might otherwise bedevil it.[38]

Emotional Uncertainty and the Missionary Enemy

But even Primitive Baptists suffused with doubt found their spiritual tempests ranging into the day-to-day world. They did not set out to subdue evil in the world as did missionary Baptists and other evangelicals fired by millennialism. Temperance seemed an imposition, sabbatarianism a threat, masonry a conspiracy, and abolition a pure menace. No, instead of reforming drunkards or working earnestly to deliver the gospel to the heathens or doing any of the other things that came to be identified with evangelical Protestantism before the Civil War, Primitive Baptists channeled their energies into fighting missionaries, the churches that aided them, and the revivals that buoyed them. And it has been the Primitives' anti-missionism that scholars have been determined to explain by reference either to the Primitives' "anti-means" Calvinism or to their supposedly marginal place in the antebellum market.

The history of Primitive men and women such as those examined here has long been overshadowed by the searing rhetoric Primitive Baptists used to attack missionaries. As a result, many historians have interpreted the Primitives' vitriolic attacks on "effort" Baptists and "man-made" Christians as essentially Calvinist ripostes to a rising tide of Arminianism. Other historians, however, have seen the Primitives' disdain for evangelicals' "taste for money" as a sure sign of the Primitives' poverty and, therefore, evidence of the economic origins of an apparently religious movement. Yet examined within the emotional framework proposed here, the Primitives' anti-missionary activity looks different: less antique, less clearly theological in nature, less driven by economic deprivation. Theological and economic concerns do not disappear here. Instead, they are felt and understood always through the emotional uncertainty that shadowed the Primitive Baptist self.

Consider for a moment how the Primitives' dogged anti-missionism could, in fact, be rooted in their uncertain selves. As the Primitives described them, missionaries were frauds, impostors, wolves in sheep's clothing, spies, spiders spinning webs of entrapment, men of style costumed as mendicants, mountebanks hiding, as it were, "behind the curtain."[39] Missionaries came to catch banknotes rather than souls. That, at least, was Joshua Lawrence's verdict. "I have seen the missionary preacher stretch every nerve of eloquence, and bear hard on every pathetic string to affect his audience in favor of missions," Lawrence said. "It has always appeared to me that when I see a minister after preaching a missionary moneyed sermon come down out of the pulpit, singing and shaking hands to whet up the passions and press upon young ladies to form a missionary society and give their money, that the preaching, the singing, and the shaking of hands of the minister were but the craft of the preacher to have access to the purse."[40] Here, according to one particularly caustic Primitive believer, was the step-by-step missionary method: "First, preach to please the people—then affect their human sympathies and passions—then persuade them that they are converted—then prevail on them to join the church (as they call it)—then pick their pockets by begging them for their hard earnings under pretense of supporting the gospel."[41] It was religious deceit conducted on a grand stage.

Of course, all of these descriptions—the emotional fraudulence, the deceit, the insincerity, the temptation to confuse emotional outpourings with God's grace—of missionaries, revivalists, and evangelicals were descriptions Primitives had provided about themselves. Like Thomas Hill, they knew themselves to be incapable of sincerity. Like Joshua Lawrence and J. H. Purifoy, they wondered if they were both the deceiver and the deceived. And like Mary Bristow and Rebecca Phillips, they doubted their ability to control their own minds. The Primitives' inner turmoil had provided them with a built-in vocabulary for describing and categorizing the outside world, including the missionaries they found so loathsome. They projected their uncertain selves onto their enemies.

Here, in the welter of experience and emotion, we begin to discover what catalyzed the Primitives' movement. It was not the high theology of John Calvin. Nor was it anything as sturdy as a denominational identity. As so many of them pointed out, they knew little, if anything, of Calvinist doctrine. Nor were they members of the church when doubt entered their lives and refused to leave. Instead, these men and women found themselves perched precariously on the boundaries of evangelical Protestantism's emotional community. They tried to join that emotional community, but what happened when the pursuit of feeling failed? When a young woman's public display of emotion did not match her private feelings? When her friends responded to the revival preacher's pathetic words while her heart, despite prodigious efforts, remained unmoved? When scenes like these played out over and over again in her life? Would she turn on herself, declare herself damned? Or might she wonder whether her friends, her neighbors, the people she saw in the meetinghouse—might she conclude that it was they who were the real sinners, that it was they who were, perhaps, too easily excited by the preacher's words, too tempted by the offers of quick salvation, too comfortable with the new ways, too eager to leave "the old paths, where is the good way"?

These men and women found emotional refuges in Primitive Baptist churches, where others, too, grappled with their uncertain fates while fighting a protean enemy—an enemy that was, at one moment, Arminianism, broadly construed, and at another, the Methodist circuit rider or the neighbor who fed him. It could be the seminary-trained preacher, the missionary dispatched to India, the woman who told the church "that she had been letting her light shine in a dark place . . . and that it made no difference where a person belonged if they were Christian for there was nothing in the name."[42] It could be as close as one's own clerk or as distant as the Bank of the United States. But, above all, the guilty party was oneself—a sinner, a hypocrite, a deceiver and the deceived, someone in need of constant watching. An uncertain self, a stranger below surrounded by enemies and in need of God's grace.

3   Filthy Lucre, Hired Nurses, and the Suckling Preacher

On September 24, 1834, C. B. Hassell, a merchant in Williamston, North Carolina, saw that supplies were running low. On that early fall day, the hard-to-come-by item was something at once more ephemeral and more substantive than Hassell's usual stock of dry goods. Christianity, the merchant noted, was "scarce in market and in little demand if we may use the terms."[1]

Hassell need not have bothered with the politesse; for years, he and his fellow Primitive Baptists had been using the language of the marketplace to discuss their religious affairs. The metaphors arrived easily enough. Centuries' worth of English usage linked money and salvation; in the language of the King James Bible, God had "bought" the souls of those he saved, and Christ had come "to give his life a ransom for many." Those old usages took on added freight and gained new companions as the antebellum market revolution, panics and all, pushed Jefferson's agrarian Republic into the modern age. That ragged birth bequeathed to generations of Americans a new vocabulary for making sense of their circumstances, economic and otherwise. From their pulpits, preachers encouraged thrift and industry before thundering against mammon, whose evil influence sometimes seemed to spread as rapidly as the new networks of canals and turnpikes crawling along the nation's skin.[2]

For the Primitive Baptists, the market—its sprawling lines of communication and the capital that coursed through them like blood—triggered an acute crisis. Money, in some broad sense, had brought them into being. Money had pushed them out of their familiar Baptist churches and into new meetinghouses that they adorned with old-time names. They loathed the missionaries—the beggars, as they called them—the young men scouring the countryside for funds, the Bible-toting thieves who, they said, "had the same taste for money that the horse leech has for blood." In the 1810s and 1820s, when Baptist churches began soliciting these "beggars" and choosing to collect money for their new missionary and benevolent crusades, the people who would become Primitives decided that greed had corrupted their companions and that the boards, conventions, societies, and organizations that controlled the missionaries would enslave them, too, if they did not soon leave. It was in this sense, then, that money created and re-created the Primitive Baptists, for the issue never did go away. In 1835, for instance, when the editors of the *Primitive Baptist*, an epistolary biweekly devoted to the Primitives' cause, included in their inaugural issue a table listing by name and amount what they saw as the exorbitant salaries paid to evangelical missionaries, the list so inflamed the already partisan readership that the next issue featured an editorial plea to readers to please refrain from outright ridicule and abuse when writing letters exposing missionaries' errors. Appeals like this had little, if any, effect. Denunciations of missionaries' avarice and celebrations of Primitive Baptists' self-abnegation were staples of the early nineteenth-century Old School Baptist cause.[3]

Yet Primitive Baptist meetinghouses were not filled with paupers and ascetics. There were believers like C. B. Hassell, men of little means who had become men of middling means who, eventually, became men of wealth; men buffeted by the economy's sudden swings; and men in the South, certainly, who presided over a family both black and white. Indeed, the only study to attempt anything like a systematic investigation of the socioeconomic profiles of Baptists involved in the missionary schism found that, in the North Carolina piedmont at least, members on each side of the conflict possessed similar demographic profiles. If anything, the regional anti-missionary faction tended to be somewhat older and to own slightly more slaves. The numbers remained similarly aligned at the smaller congregational level, where the fight over missions played out most dramatically. Census, marriage, and estate records show, for instance, that members of the pro-missionary and anti-missionary factions in the Tarboro Baptist Church—the flash point of the schism in North Carolina—were economically comparable. A majority on either side of the divide appear to have been members of yeoman households— that is, households headed by self-working farmers who sometimes owned slaves.[4]

The history of Primitive men and women such as these, and the larger history of the sect's relationship to the antebellum marketplace, has long been overshadowed by the searing rhetoric Primitive Baptists used to attack missionaries. As a result, historians have interpreted the Primitives' disdain for the evangelicals' "taste for money" as a sure sign of the Primitives' poverty and, therefore, evidence of the economic origins of an apparently religious movement. In these tellings, anti-missionary sentiment—and the predestinarian Calvinism that, in the Primitives' case, undergirded it—becomes a makeshift refuge thrown together by poor Baptists shaken by the rumblings of the market's boom-and-bust cycle and embittered by the success of their social betters. In some instances, these impoverished, intransigent, and yet honorable Primitives become, as we have seen in chapter 1, emblems of an antique South, of "the persistent Southern struggle to preserve old values in an alien, changing, and often self-righteous world." All that is missing, really, from such accounts are the colorful details: pitchforks and muskets, or, in later eras, a sawed-off shotgun, overalls, and a steely gaze into the black-and-white camera's lens.[5]

This has all been too tidy. The Primitive Baptists' position in the antebellum class structure and the relationship between their Calvinism and the capitalist marketplace were far more complex than the Primitives, their opponents, or their scholarly chroniclers have supposed. The Primitives' relationship to money and the class system was a patched-together affair in which the language of the market and the Christian rhetoric of poverty coexisted and clashed. Primitives quarried the Scriptures for symbols that would help explain the fluctuations of the nation's nascent market economy. In turn, Primitives found the marketplace to be a useful metaphor for describing their place in a fractious religious world. Here, then, was how class and its assorted sociological and historical squires—money, the market revolution, economic development, financial panics, and so on—found themselves connected to the Primitives' revolt: they inevitably entered the lists, but they had not initiated the combat.

For the Primitives, the market is perhaps best understood as a cultural resource, though one they were not always conscious of mining. Consider Cushing Biggs Hassell, the Williamston merchant and Primitive Baptist elder who noted on that fall day in 1834 that true Christianity was "scarce in market and in little demand." Hassell spent a life raging against the modern age's infatuation with money while insisting that the ample profits from his mercantile operation proved God's beneficent foresight. Or consider Joshua Lawrence, the foremost Primitive Baptist polemicist whose patriarchal attacks on money-hungry missionaries carried deep within them, like contraband, problematic affinities with motherhood and dependence. Neither Hassell nor Lawrence were typical Primitive Baptists. But neither were they anomalous figures within an Old School Baptist world filled with fellow believers who heard their preaching and read their published words. Studying them closely suggests some ways that uncertain Primitive Baptist selves, like those examined in the previous chapter, mediated theological and economic concerns—predestinarianism and anti-missionism, on the one hand, and market fluctuations and missionaries' money-raising, on the other—and thereby created meaning and shaped action. In tense moments of emotional labor, Hassell and Lawrence drew on old religious habits, appropriated them as they saw fit, and improvised responses to suit their particular circumstances. In their money-inflected crises, their religion came into being.

Christian Scarcity, or Calvinism in Tough Times:
Primitive Rhetoric and the Language of the Market

It is true that some Primitive thought consciously exhibited Manichaean tendencies that would have been congenial to people who found themselves on the losing end of the market revolution. Drawing on the Scottish Free Church theologian W. G. Blaikie, C. B. Hassell, for example, divided the world into "Sethite" and "Cainite" lineages. The Sethites were "the sons of God": foolish and sinful like all men, but preachers of righteousness and God-fearing. The Cainite lineage, on the other hand, had been responsible for most of the practical and aesthetic advances in human history. They had invented musical instruments and blacksmithing, for example. But the Cainites were the bearers of evil; like their ancestor, they were cursed. To Hassell and other Primitives, the meaning of this exercise in theological genealogy was clear: all manner of human improvements and progress unaided by faith in the one true God were nothing. This sort of bifurcation looked, at times, like a zero-sum game. "While, therefore, the stars of human art and pharisaical enchantments are in the ascendant, the light of heavenly truth appears to be seen nearing the horizon," Hassell wrote. "The more dazzling the former, the more obscure the latter."[6]

This was a deeply pessimistic worldview. It confirmed for the Primitives that their anti-missionary convictions placed them in an inevitable conflict with the religious changes in their churches and with the economic and technological innovations transforming American society. Here market and church fused into a new kind of dangerous wage-labor technology. In the language of an 1834 circular letter from a Primitive Baptist association, missionaries were "hired men," "religion became a trade," and churches decided "who should work the machine." And the machine was mesmerizing. As if transported by railcars or shipped aboard a river-bound vessel, evangelicals were "imagining themselves going to heaven as it were by steam." Indeed, the revolutions in transportation and communication that marked the Jacksonian era and rapidly expanded the nation's commerce often appeared as fiendish co-conspirators with the Primitives' evangelical opponents. Like toll collectors on one of the early Republic's new plank roads, missionary agents wished "death for all who dare to go to heaven by any other turnpike road and not pay toll at their gate." Antebellum America's banking and currency debates also filtered into Primitive discourse. Benevolent enterprises and national missionary societies could easily be compared with the "monster" Bank of the United States, making the differences between evangelicals and Primitives as stark, Joshua Lawrence wrote, as those between "bank notes and love."[7]

But the market's language, categories, and assumptions also nested comfortably in the Primitives' Calvinist theology. Indebtedness became the ruling metaphor. A church clerk, for instance, reminded his fellows of their helplessness in the face of divine judgment: "the debt hang[s] over us," he wrote, "ready to crush us to everlasting ruin, ourselves being unable to cancel the most minute particle of our indebtedness." Meanwhile, "justice" cried "in tones of thunder, pay me what thou owest." In the traditional version of this scenario, Jesus became the atonement. But in the church clerk's hands, Christ also became "our surety," as if Jesus were bailing his believers out of the poorhouse. In the religious verse that graced the back pages of the Primitives' many periodicals, this relationship was succinctly put: "He paid out for a bankrupt crew / The debt that to himself was due."[8]

The Primitives' problem, then, was not that people in the antebellum marketplace trafficked in Christianity, but that so little of the true stuff could be found in the stalls. "Primitive theology is a very scarce commodity in our market," lamented one Old Baptist. Another described God's mercy as a "divine commodity" with "an intrinsic worth . . . which far excels the transitory toys, and all the vain gaieties of this unhallowed world." Meanwhile, missionary societies traded in "quackery, artifice, and deception." Their decision to sell memberships looked to Joshua Lawrence like a crass bit of religious business. "What are they selling at $2? I see nothing," he wrote. And "what are these men buying? Good heaven, said I, what a cunning and intriguing scheme to make money for priests!" As these remarks indicate, distinguishing between divine commodities and religious artifice, between truth and falsity, was a necessary skill for the vigilant believer. But as any antebellum Protestant knew, Satan worked tirelessly to ensnare the gullible in his demonic traps. And as good Calvinists, the Primitives also knew that mankind—fallen, stained by sin, yet proud—was especially susceptible to self-deception. In this loamy theological soil, the language of the market blossomed. In the Primitive Baptists' religious marketplace, the sinner's "promises and promissory notes are nothing worth," wrote the preacher William Garrard to his friend Hassell. "God puts no trust in them." The market was flooded with these false notes. They circulated among the deluded and were accepted by benighted churches ("free-will . . . banking companies," as Garrard acidly described them). There was, however, one bank that issued paper notes guaranteed never to lose their value. The "high bank of heaven," Garrard explained, run by "the great bankers, the Father, Son, and Holy Ghost," made sure that anyone who held their notes would "receive payment in full."[9]

But this heavenly bank chose its customers. Indeed, the constant theme of this kind of Primitive rhetoric was that free will—the ability, if you will, to choose to conduct transactions at the "high bank of heaven"—was, at best, a historical anachronism. What, after all, was God's covenant with Israel but a contract properly understood? And what was the Christian covenant of grace but a new contract to replace the old Mosaic one? In the bargain struck in Sinai's shadows, God promised the Israelites temporal rewards and punishments based upon the Israelites' ability to follow the legal compact delivered to Moses. "Man was a party" to this "contract," as the *Primitive Baptist* biweekly explained. But man—inherently depraved and, therefore, unable to fulfill all the obligations of the Mosaic law—was consigned to damnation under the very covenant to which he had agreed. This awful Mosaic law, however, had been dispatched in blood and thorns at Calvary. Jesus's sacrifice initiated a new covenant. Here the Primitives made a crucial distinction. Whereas "man was a party"—"a contractor"— at Sinai, he was merely a bystander to the transaction at Golgotha. "Christ was the purchaser, and God's people the thing purchased," as the *Primitive Baptist* put it. Man was the subject of this deal between various parts of the Godhead. But precisely because fallen man's redemption was at stake, he could not be allowed to actively participate in the transaction. Of course, these were the terms of the Primitives' Calvinism: God was exalted; man was scorned. By removing man from an active role in the deal, theological exercises like this one seem to attack the ideological underpinnings of the capitalist marketplace. They also suggest how liberating a predestinarian faith could be. That was, at first, how it worked for C. B. Hassell.[10]

Calvinism in Practice: The Labors of C. B. Hassell

For Hassell, the absolute predestination of all things quelled life's chaos. "Were things otherwise," he confided in his unpublished autobiography, "all would be uncertainty and confusion." His father's untimely death, struggles with his mercantile trade, personal slights: these troubles stemmed not from happenstance (he did "not believe in the existence of such a thing as 'luck' or 'chance' anyway"), not from the mundane uncertainties that loosen even the most securely tethered lives, and not, ultimately, from market forces or political developments. Rather, God's hand—"Divine Providence," as Hassell capitalized it—moved all; it leveled the ridges and furrows of Hassell's life. Writing in his characteristic third-person-limited narrative style, Hassell announced: "The omnipotence of this doctrine reconciles to his mind the result of all matters whether apparently adverse or prosperous." One detects here how a seemingly fearsome predestinarian theology could liberate the very people it appeared to shackle. "He is such a strong believer in predestination that he views all his own actions ever to have been for the best," Hassell wrote. How could they not be? God, who was good, predestined them. In prosperous circumstances, such conclusions were irresistible. "And how could he doubt it," Hassell continued, "when he reflected that the Lord had taken him while a pennyless orphan boy, & from that moment to manhood & maturer age had never let him go, but had unceasingly given him & his through him a sufficiency of the necessaries of this life?"[11]

Hassell called himself "an exception to the general rule"—the "general rule" being the inability of Primitive Baptist preachers to combine religious and secular labors. Many elders were too devoted to their churches to engage in other work. Most, however, tried their hands at "domestic employments" but were, as Hassell pointedly noted, "generally . . . unsuccessful" and, therefore, forced to rely upon their flocks' donations for sustenance.[12] Hassell worked hard, and he eventually met with success. He espoused a business ethic of steadiness and caution ("Slow & sure should be the rule through life in all pecuniary matters," he believed). He also believed that such caution "will prove in the end to be the most profitable plan." (Hassell, unsurprisingly, admired Benjamin Franklin, the great American champion of order and moderation.)[13] He weathered the Panic of 1837, a bad mercantile partnership at about the same time, and the economic downturn of 1840. By the mid-1840s, flush times had arrived. His dry goods business was netting him about $15,000 per year, and he continued to collect a salary as the clerk and master in equity of the Martin County court. His increased wealth went hand in hand with his growing civic presence. As the county court's master in equity, he administered the estates of locals who died without descendants who had reached the age of majority. He was not only a member of the board of trustees for the Williamston male and female academies but styled himself "the principal management of both" and "chiefly instrumental in keeping the school[s] going." He was the treasurer of the Williamston Library Association (in private, he described himself as "the first mover in the business"), bought all of the library's books, and housed them in a glass case in his counting room. In the spring of 1847, he made a note in his diary that his family consisted of about forty people. Included in his tally were a new fleet of slaves he had bought a few months before to build his new dwelling house. A year later, the North Carolina state legislature appointed him a trustee of the University of North Carolina. He was just thirty-eight years old. C. B. Hassell was a big man in a small town. He was an exception, and he was proud of it.[14]

God, too, smiled upon Hassell's diligence, and as Hassell told it, the Almighty seemed particularly pleased with his man's business acumen. "The Lord," Hassell concluded, "had blessed him with the means of comfortable living as a reward for his labour in business of various kinds of a secular nature & chiefly that of merchandising." When Hassell wrote those words about himself in the mid-1840s he had been preaching for more than fifteen years and had been an ordained minister for the last four. Yet it was Hassell's work behind the counter that so pleased God. God blessed him with wealth not because he was a faithful preacher but because he was a diligent salesman. Hassell's God was no mercenary; he was simply pragmatic, like his storekeeping servant. For it was Hassell's industriousness in business that made it possible for him to preach without monetary compensation. Hassell's secular labor preserved the altruism of his spiritual labor since not one of Hassell's congregants needed to reach into his or her own pocket to feed the pastor.[15]

When he pondered his successes, Hassell realized that an ethic of service proved similarly valuable in business and religion. The Lord had called him to be a preacher *and* a merchant. As Hassell saw it, "the chief object of his life was to be serviceable to others; and that he could take a wider range of usefulness, by combining secular with spiritual labours than by confining himself to spiritual labours alone." Thinking along these lines had deep roots in Protestant experience, both in Europe and America. But these were Hassell's official pronouncements. They have the booming ring of dogma.[16]

Time and again, though, Hassell's mercantile trade made being "serviceable" in business and in the church a difficult proposition. During national economic panics and local commercial slowdowns, during tussles with county commissioners and embarrassing feuds with business partners, Hassell's business trials strained the bonds he had forged between faith and work. Eventually, Hassell's worsening economic circumstances helped persuade him to modify some of his earlier beliefs about the role of money in the church. He made these changes fitfully and not without a certain amount of shame. Because his worldly success enabled his ministerial career, economic downturns could have a doubly painful effect. A bad business cycle meant financial discomfort, debt, and embarrassment. But it was always more than that for Hassell. It was a cosmic sign but one whose genesis he was nevertheless loath to connect to God. Instead, the frustrated Hassell, beset by debts and afraid of financial ruin, turned his wrath outward toward his neighbors.

In the mid-1830s, Hassell had faced his first financial crisis. Burdened with $4,000 in debt, the young merchant entered a hasty partnership that became the "most unfortunate step" he had ever made. The deal immediately erased his debt, but over the next three years the bad partnership, helped along by the Panic of 1837, led to further losses and much "mortification and misery." Traumatized by his failed venture, Hassell finally dissolved his partnership and moved to a cash-only business. This episode's economic details are interesting, but its religious repercussions are more compelling, for the episode seems to have bolstered Hassell's predestinarian faith rather than undermined it. As he weathered another economic downturn in 1840, Hassell recounted his failed partnership in the first draft of his unpublished autobiography. He brought both stories—his botched partnership, on the one hand, and his as-yet-unfinished life story, on the other—to a close with a declaration of his Calvinist principles described earlier. It was not an unusual ending for a Calvinist narrative where God's sovereignty was to be celebrated, even—or especially—during tough times.[17]

But when a second, larger crisis struck a decade later, Hassell's Calvinistic didacticism struggled to contain his distress. He once again read his ledger books with religious principles in mind, but the stakes were higher. His much-expanded family—nine children now—needed care and sustenance. He also needed to safeguard his increased role in Williamston's civic life. Finally, he had been formally ordained and now tended to several nearby churches. A failed business might lead to bankruptcy, but it would also inevitably lead to humiliation, both of himself and of the Primitive Baptist order he represented.

This second crisis began, as one might expect, in Hassell's counting room, where, in the fall of 1849, he calculated his mounting debts. They rose higher than ever before. Hassell felt himself "wearing away" under their weight. I am "more oppressed & borne down with business than at any other time of [my] life," he wrote. The pressure had been building for months. Earlier that spring he scratched out a diary entry: "Mind very barren in religious things—having a desire to wean away from the world & no ability to do so."[18] By the fall, Hassell's frustrations pointed in the opposite direction. He became exasperated as his pastoral duties insistently called him away from what he described as "urgent & important" business.[19]

As he sank deeper into a financial morass, Hassell's emotional labors intensified. He promised to turn his mind away from its habitual concern with secular matters. He vowed to write less—both in his diary and in his correspondence—about business concerns. He would, instead, meditate upon God's charity. Those efforts proved less than wholly successful. Soon he began telling himself comforting white lies in the way that anxious people often do. He assured himself that, in fact, he had rarely wasted space in his diary contemplating business, and, in any case, he would write even less about such trivia in the future. The diary's pages, inked with an assortment of tallies, told a different story. His public efforts, too, became a kind of masquerade. He would carry on as usual, he decided. He worked—and it must have been hard work, indeed—to take "all things cheerfully & calmly as though nothing had happened & as though nothing whatever troubled him, so that others around him supposed he saw no trouble, but lived at ease. And poor foolish things actually envied his condition in life."[20]

Sometime between 1850 and 1852, Hassell began accepting money for his preaching. He had made the decision in the fall of 1849, but "much mortified" over his financial condition and devoted to keeping up appearances, Hassell delayed the implementation of his plan for at least six months. The mortification, of course, stemmed only partly from pecuniary matters. Or, more accurately, Hassell's pecuniary matters were themselves rooted in religious, if not quite theological, concerns. For Hassell, like all Primitive preachers, inveighed against a salaried ministry, in particular, and against the influence of money in the church, more generally. Now, Hassell had *not* decided to take a salary, but he would be accepting—even soliciting—donations. And while, in Primitive precincts, unprompted donations made by individual believers were, officially speaking, not suspect, the solicitor of those donations certainly would be. That was the anguish of Hassell's situation: the money he accepted for preaching became both the glue that held his life together and the solvent that tore it apart.[21]

The unfolding anguish became particularly dramatic as Hassell's business continued its decline while Methodists increased their presence in Hassell's hometown. The two trends, Hassell realized, must be linked. There were, at first, the empty pews in one of the several churches he pastored. Much of his flock had decided to attend a nearby Methodist revival during the fall of 1850. Earlier that summer, Hassell had become the subject of public denunciation in Williamston when he spoke out against the presence in town of a Methodist preacher sponsored by the Sons of Temperance. And later that winter, Hassell wrote in his diary that more and more townsfolk were angry at him because he opposed the fund-raising being carried out by local Methodists to support a bell raising. By the spring, the situation had deteriorated further. Methodists held a two-week revival in Williamston, Hassell's cousin Asa and his wife had apparently fallen under their spell, and it had become "fashionable" in town to denounce Hassell, who, when he did his books that June, came to the unfortunate conclusion that his economic situation was worse than ever. Three years earlier he had worried that he would soon die, leaving his family debt-ridden and destitute. One year earlier he watched his debts rise from $9,000 to $12,000 as spring became summer. Now he calculated his debts at $15,000. He begged God to deliver him from this "embarrassing condition."[22]

By the fall of 1851, God had yet to take action, so Hassell acted in his stead. One year after attendance at weekly church meetings began declining, Hassell fired one of his longtime clerks whom he accused of wasting thousands of dollars before embezzling thousands more. The clerk's perfidy, Hassell concluded, accounted for last year's losses. He told his hollowed-out church that he would be spending less time with them because he needed to devote his energies to resuscitating his ailing mercantile outfit. Only one month later, however, Hassell stood before his flock bearing a different message. Describing himself as a member of "the other poor," he pleaded like a lowly missionary for the church to establish a fund to pay him regularly. Church members said they would go home and think about it. Finally, desperate and overworked, Hassell enlisted his wife and one of his daughters to take on his paperwork as clerk and master in equity of the Martin County court.[23]

It was an awful turnabout. God had called him to be serviceable, but circumstances, or perhaps God himself, had intervened. The humiliation followed Hassell to the grave. In 1886, Hassell's son Sylvester tried to posthumously absolve his father of the Primitive Baptist sin of acting like a missionary beggar. "Certainly it was not for filthy lucre that he labored in the cause of his Master," the younger Hassell wrote. The facts spoke in a less forgiving key. Proprietor of an ailing business, shepherd of a withered flock, C. B. Hassell had come to depend upon his former dependents—the church, his wife, his daughter—for support.[24]

By then Hassell had pinpointed the cause of his downfall. A cabal of traitorous clerks, local Methodists, and rival businessmen had organized a "very great opposition" to him, his Old School Baptist church, and his business. They were ruining him. And though this struggle appeared to be taking place in Hassell's riverside hometown, it actually unfolded on a much larger stage. It was a cosmic conflict, Hassell concluded: "Man was against him," he wrote in his diary, "but . . . God was for him."[25]

Hassell did finally right his business. As early as June 1852, he noted an increase in his sales and a decrease in his debts, and by that winter he determined that a minor uptick in his yearly sales totals meant that he had staved off the "clique" that had tried to reduce him to bankruptcy. There would be more ups and downs. The Civil War proved especially disruptive as Hassell retreated inland, leaving behind both business and family when Union forces landed in Williamston. As a munitions supplier to the Confederacy, he feared that remaining in town would lead to his capture, imprisonment, or worse.[26]

If there is an end to Hassell's story, it came not at his death in 1880 at the age of seventy-one but six years later with the eventual publication of his and his son Sylvester's mammoth *History of the Church of God*. That book wrought the scraps of Hassell's life into a polished historical narrative. In the *History*, Primitive Baptists find themselves, like Hassell, beset by religious rivals—missionary Baptists, Methodists, revivalists, temperance activists—who seek to destroy them while growing rich on new religious schemes and entertainments. The Primitives, of course, persevere.

But even that ending was a false one, or at least a partial one, for it never accounted for the discrepancy between Hassell's sunny creed and his turbulent life, between his call to be serviceable and his actual dependence. There, in that gap between ideology and practice, between public emotional standards and private emotional experience, life unfolded. In that breach, Hassell scrambled to make sense of his world. The market, as always, functioned not only as a network of commercial exchange but as a venue imbued with religious significance. The imperium of class, market, and economy that has so often ruled explanations of the Primitives' rise cannot adequately account for Hassell's story. That life was shaped by everyday structures of power—marketplace rules, theological strictures, entrenched denominational expectations, gender conventions—but those structures of power lived always in dynamic tension with Hassell's religious practice and imagination.

How might this have worked? Hassell believed God had rewarded him for his secular work, for his "merchandising," as he put it. The wealth Hassell gained from being serviceable behind the counter allowed him to be serviceable to his flock. He had been called to both pursuits. This kind of practical Calvinism worked fine during flush times. Indeed, prosperity appeared to ratify Hassell's religious creed. Hardship, however, put these principles under significant strain. Hassell's own religious logic dictated that God lay behind his financial difficulties, but holding God accountable proved either unthinkable or too painful. Instead, Hassell found others to blame. He railed against the Methodist preachers' "charlatanism" and sneered at the "poor deluded souls" captivated by revivalistic trickery.[27]

But Hassell himself was guilty of a similar sort of masquerade. Recall that he confided to his diary that he pitied the "poor foolish things" in his congregation who were misled by his serene public demeanor while internally he crumbled and sank deeper into sin. Recall, too, Hassell's anger with the means of Methodists' fund-raising. As his own debts climbed, he accused his Methodist rivals of holding not revivals but fairs where they charged admission, hired well-paid entertainers, and made sure that their preachers were handed a healthy balance for their treasury. But Hassell, too, asked for preaching fees, began taking donations, and suggested to his home church that they pay him regularly. Unable or unwilling to hold God accountable, he displaced anger onto more convenient targets. Incapable of blaming himself for his infirm mercantile outfit and fearful of reckoning completely with his decision to accept payment for his preaching, he projected his guilt onto duplicitous clerks, scheming townspeople, and Methodist fraudsters.

At his nadir in early 1852, Hassell attended Sunday services at Williamston's Episcopal chapel. "It was all a dry breast," he wrote. Later that night he attended a prayer meeting at a Primitive Baptist brother's home. He stood to preach and the text that came to mind was from Revelation: "Come out of her, my people, that ye be not partakers of her sins and that ye receive not of her plagues." The text was a Primitive Baptist staple, and after that morning's dryness and the months of growing despair, it may have looked to his besieged mind like an escape route. He could find other Old School Baptists treading the same path out from what they perceived to be the confines of a feminized evangelicalism. But that path forked and then doubled back on itself, a fact that tells us much about the gendered dimensions of the Primitives' predicament and, more generally, suggests some new ways to think about patriarchy and religion in the Old South.[28]

"Come Out of Her, My People": Joshua Lawrence's Compromised Patriarchy

In a farmhouse in eastern North Carolina, in or around the year 1808, Jesus Christ visited Joshua Lawrence. The Son of God stood "face to face" with the awestruck farmer-preacher, gazed "wishfully" at him, and spoke: "Feed my wife," he implored. "Feed my children." Jesus vanished. Joshua Lawrence crumbled. The sublime visitation left him bathed in tears, struggling for breath, laboring under what he described as "the groans of death." Yet the sight of his Savior's face also had buoyed Lawrence. Humbled, but filled with "infinite joy," he quickly set about the task of interpretation. Who was Jesus's wife? And where to find his children?[29]

The answers to these questions arrived quickly. By his "wife," Lawrence supposed, Jesus had referred to the converted and the baptized. Jesus's "children" also could be found within the church's embrace, but many more of them, Lawrence realized, remained estranged from the church's beloved family. Both groups needed Lawrence's paternal care. As both a faithful preacher and a sturdy patriarch, Lawrence vowed to nourish his churchly family with gospel truth while working tirelessly to bring more "children" into the fold. Such were the happy prospects for Lawrence's "family religion."[30]

Soon, though, Joshua Lawrence's religious family was torn asunder. Jesus had called Lawrence to protect and guide his spiritual family, but enemies lurked in the very pews and pulpits Lawrence sought to shelter. These enemies were evangelical missionaries, newly organized emissaries dispatched by the boards and societies that controlled the new Benevolent Empire. To Lawrence and his fellows, the missionaries' zealous search for new funds and new converts corrupted their old-time Baptist faith. The rot was visible. They watched as missionaries' money-raising transformed country churches into ecclesiastical banks. Meanwhile, these missionary intruders' insistence on evangelism and their penchant for the drama of mass conversions marked them as arrogant upstarts eager to seize the power of saving grace from God himself.

For Joshua Lawrence, the battles against the missionary advance became a family quarrel. To be sure, the Primitives' decades-long campaign against the evangelical juggernaut featured disputes about doctrine, the influence of money in the church, ministerial authority, the efficacy of God's sovereign grace, and the role of Christianity in an expanding nation. But in Lawrence's religious imagination, evangelical missionaries seduced daughters, stole wives, and undermined patriarchal authority. Missionaries had broken his church family, and Lawrence—the steady patriarch and devoted preacher—vowed to repair the damage.

That Lawrence envisioned his church as a family, Jesus as a patriarch, and himself as Jesus's fatherly proxy should not surprise us. Hierarchy saturated southern life: white over black, man over woman. Plantation owners and well-to-do farmers could preside over a family (that, in fact, was the word they used) that included not only a wife and children but also assorted other dependents whom the patriarch held in chains. Even lowly subsistence farmers wielded patriarchal authority, ruling over family members who doubled as laborers on the family land. Baptists such as Lawrence saw themselves as part of a beloved community, a spiritual family set apart from the vanity of the secular world. But patriarchy intruded there, too. Within the church, men and women might address each other as "brother" and "sister," and preachers might refuse the honorific "reverend" in favor of the more homely and familial title "elder." But in the Baptists' Calvinist theology, God often appeared as a stern, if loving, father. Men held all church offices. Only men voted on matters of church business, and only men led the congregation in prayer. As for women, Joshua Lawrence advised them to "be content to wear the petticoat, and never, no never, jirk the breeches out of your husband's hands."[31]

At first, missionaries posed little threat to these gender conventions, and indeed, Lawrence's earliest anti-missionary broadside skewered missionaries as money-hunting hirelings, not home wreckers. Dispatched by massive ecclesiastical bureaucracies, paid in wages, and bereft of true gospel feeling, missionaries wandered the countryside searching for funds. That search, Lawrence argued, took the missionaries not to the South's poor and destitute but to the wealthy and the comfortable. "Believe me," he wrote, "these hirelings like to be fed on better fare than the poor can give them—they like the houses of colonels, [and] squires, and to have very rich and fat tables." As the missionaries ignored the needy and feted the wealthy, Lawrence concluded that their claim to be seeking converts for Christ was nothing but a ruse. The missionaries, he reckoned, pocketed the money they raised. How else to explain their cloaks of "the finest black and blue broad cloth," their "fur hats," "silk jackets," and "silver tipped bridles"? The entire missionary enterprise,

Lawrence and his fellow Primitive Baptists concluded, amounted to nothing more than a series of "religious schemes to pick men's pockets."[32]

But the pockets of a man were never as enticing as the purse strings of a lady, or so Joshua Lawrence thought. Time and time again, Lawrence argued that missionaries specifically sought women's donations, encouraged women's fiscal irresponsibility, and tempted women's lax morals. Women, Lawrence reasoned, were especially susceptible to missionary trickery. The Bible said as much. Satan deceived women first. Satan fooled Eve, convinced the wives and concubines of King Solomon to lead him astray, and persuaded Delilah to shear Samson's locks. Lawrence found more examples. He repeated the apostle Paul's warning that one sign of the last days would be the presence of those "creeping into houses, and leading captive silly women." The book of Exodus, too, furnished suggestions, for like the Hebrew women at the foot of Mt. Sinai, southern women were willing accomplices in the fashioning of an idol. "There is as great begging by the priests of the ladies for money and bracelets, as there was by priest Aaron," Lawrence wrote while pondering what seemed to him the golden calf that was the modern missionary system.[33]

The mischief started with the young single male missionary whose grounding in the gospel only disguised his expertise in the "gallanting" of women. Using his "smooth pathetic tongue and enticing words," the missionary convinced women to part with their husband's or father's money. But the real prize, according to Lawrence, was the woman herself. "If it was not for getting a rich wife . . . preachers would be scarce," he observed. "Hunting a rich wife, [and] begging money" went hand in hand. Even married women remained vulnerable. Missionaries "often take the advantage to beg the woman when the husband is from home," he noted. Though women remained, for Lawrence, the weaker sex, he feared their influence over their husbands and fathers. Missionaries, he knew, "have got hold of the right handle," that is, the wives and daughters in each southern household. "They have got hold of the women and led them captive, and be sure the men will follow," he noted bitterly, "for this is a thing of course."[34]

Lawrence was not alone in worrying about women's importance to the missionary cause. Across the South, changes in religious practice and organization threatened to modify, if not overturn, conventional gender hierarchies. The most important of these changes were demographic. By the early nineteenth century, women outnumbered men in Protestant southern churches, perhaps by as many as two to one.[35] Numbers, though, tell only part of the story. Evangelicals and their missionary allies were transforming women's place in church and society. Responding to women's increased presence in the church, evangelicals and missionaries increasingly idealized feminine spirituality and lauded women as the guardians of family morality. In a society where most women remained confined to the domestic sphere, evangelical churches thus became "the chief means of establishing a public life for women" in the antebellum South.[36]

Joshua Lawrence and the Primitive Baptists resisted these changes. This resistance is palpable in Lawrence's anti-missionary invective where evangelical missionaries metamorphosed into seducers and the women who listened to them were castigated as dupes. It would not be inaccurate to describe the Primitives as a patriarchal reaction to the feminizing influence of evangelical Protestantism. The Primitives, after all, understood themselves as "waging war with the mother Arminianism, and her entire brood of institutions." That was how the first issue of the *Signs of the Times*, a Primitive paper out of New Vernon, New York, described its mission.[37]

But this interpretation is too easy and would stop our story short. Recall the vision with which we began. Jesus had called Joshua Lawrence to feed his wife and children—had called him to be a patriarch—and Lawrence had heeded Christ's call. But soon, as missionaries fanned out across the South and more and more women filled the church pews, Lawrence described himself in different terms. Joshua Lawrence became a mother.

This wrinkle in Lawrence's thinking emerged as he contemplated those features that firmly distinguished the false-speaking missionaries from his truth-preaching Primitives. Elders, he pleaded, should "preach as freely as a mother suckles her child." Here the converted and the unchurched remained children, but instead of paternal guidance they needed maternal care. Only by nursing the congregation on what Lawrence described as "the milk of the word"—only by offering up what he called the "warm paps of a preached gospel"—could the faithful preacher answer his call. He imagined the ideal preacher "like a full breasted mother," swollen with the milk of the word and ready to give of it freely. Only then, after parting with the milk, would the "pain in the breast [be] relieved and the hunger of the child ... satisfied."[38]

By contrast, missionaries and evangelical preachers starved their spiritual children and denied them their breast. Surveying his missionary opponents, Lawrence detected not real preacher-mothers but, once again, hirelings. They "are hired nurses," he seethed. "They have no milk in their breast for God's children, they serve for pay and so feed God's children on the pot-liquor of morality and self doings, on which all God's children will starve." Hired nurses—impostor mothers, if you will—were not the only problem. A salaried preacher or a paid missionary essentially charged his own children for milk from his breast. "Would you not think that woman a brute, who would charge the son of her womb for sucking her breast, that the God of nature has freely bestowed and filled for the nourishment of her children? Yes, sir, such a woman is worse than the brutes—so is such a minister of God."[39]

Joshua Lawrence and his fellow Primitive Baptist preachers no doubt refused to consider themselves brutes, but why and how would these preacher-patriarchs envision themselves as breast-feeding mothers? First, consider the Primitive preachers' precarious economic position. They refused to take a salary. God's call—and God's call alone—beckoned them toward the pulpit. A salary, a speaking fee: these could only mean that a preacher had been called not by God but by greed, by the devil. Hence the Primitives' anger at evangelicals, who had introduced a professional, salaried ministry and paid itinerancy. Without a salary, however, Primitive preachers were thrown onto the mercy of their congregations for monetary support. A lucky few balanced small farming or a trade with their ministerial duties. But for the vast majority, only voluntary donations from the laity prevented them from a stay in the poorhouse. In theory, this system guaranteed the purity of the Primitives' gospel message and fostered a mutuality between preacher and congregation that could, in fact, be likened to that between a mother and her child. Called by God to preach, filled by God with the milk of the word, the preacher was, as Joshua Lawrence put it, "like a woman who has a young child and full breast, she is under the necessity of suckling it for her own ease and not for pay." Meanwhile, "the churches are as freely to support him, as obedient children."[40] And, indeed, many Primitives did imagine their elders as breast-feeding mothers. When, for example, Esther Barlow was a new church member, she learned much from the elder at her church, and "when the time came," she wrote, "that I should be weaned from the milk and drawn from the breast," she moved on to other lessons.[41]

In practice, though, this fantasy of mutuality—this wish for an organic relationship between the preacher-mother and the congregation-child—faltered. How could it not? When C. B. Hassell finally started asking for donations for his preaching, gusts of revulsion blew through his life. He was ashamed. He was enraged. He felt besieged. He masked that shame and lashed out at his enemies. At its worst, the system simply broke down. Some Primitive preachers, for instance, complained that their flocks had decided that giving any money at all to their minister violated Jesus's gospel of poverty.[42]

That most situations never became that grave should not distract us from the bind in which Primitive preachers found themselves. Even while pastoring a generous congregation—perhaps, especially while pastoring a generous congregation—the Primitive Baptist preacher realized that he depended on others for his sustenance. In the antebellum South, in Joshua Lawrence's world, to be a dependent was to be a child, a woman, or a slave. White men, on the other hand, claimed independence. White men were patriarchs. No self-respecting white man—and, needless to say, every ordained preacher was a white man—could be deemed a worthy member of society if he were a dependent. But this was precisely the position in which the unsalaried Primitive Baptist preacher found himself: a patriarch by presumption, a dependent in fact. This was a peculiar position, and its emotional implications were vast and complex.

The preachers' split status—part caretaker, part cared for—had deep affinities with women's roles as mothers in male-dominated households. Even financially secure preachers, such as Lawrence, seem to have felt something of this bind.[43] Lawrence's slaves saved him from outright dependence, and he often laced his prose with patriarchal invective. Still, Lawrence felt that as a preacher he was a caretaker, a nurse, and, like a breast-feeding mother, a provider of sustenance. But in a patriarchal society, such as the antebellum South, these affinities with motherhood had to be blunted or controlled. It comes as no surprise, then, that Primitive Baptists wielded the language of patriarchy far more often than they summoned the images of maternity. The Primitives' maternal images, nevertheless, offer us a clue as to the causes and consequences of their fight with evangelical missionaries. Consider, once again, Joshua Lawrence. Lawrence's rhetoric split his fantasy of the preacher-mother in two. In classic fashion, Lawrence's split image allowed him to control his worrisome identification with motherhood. On the one hand, Lawrence offered his followers an idealized picture of the Primitive Baptist preacher as nourishing mother. Against this romanticized portrait, Lawrence propped up the diametrically opposed image of the withholding or impostor mother. Lawrence and his fellow Primitive Baptists attributed this latter image to their missionary opponents. But we know, both from historical data and logical inference, that the Primitive preachers glimpsed something of themselves in this awful portrait. Were they, too, frauds and impostors? Lawrence often wondered about his own motives for preaching: "I did it [that is, preaching] only to get applause and a great name," he admitted. "I could see a principle in me coveting applause . . . I find it in me at times to this day."[44] While some doubts, such as these, crept through to consciousness, others found different outlets.

Many of the Primitives' accusations against the missionaries—that they were seducers and wife hunters, for instance—had their genesis in the Primitive preachers' own seldom-acknowledged sense of dependence, a sense of dependence that was distinctly uncomfortable for supposed preacher-patriarchs in the Old South. But because Primitive Baptist practice mandated an unsalaried ministry—because, in a sense, God himself had decreed such austerity—the Primitive Baptist preacher had few conscious avenues along which to channel his anxieties. Rather than abandon their posts or condemn God's law, Primitive preachers projected their own anxieties onto the young missionaries seeping into their churches and communities. In Primitive Baptist rhetoric, we see a stunningly accurate transposition of the Primitives' worries about their own peculiar, compromised form of patriarchy. According to Lawrence, young male missionaries sought out rich women, both for their fortunes and for their beds. With a well-to-do wife—one with property and slaves—a missionary could settle down, earn a healthy income from his wife's assets, and assume the pastorship of a church just as he assumed his patriarchal prerogatives. In the Primitives' eyes, such a plan exposed not only the deceit undergirding the missionary's cause but also the fraudulence of his claim to be a southern patriarch. After all, the missionary depended on his new wife's fortune to secure his manly status. This made him a dependent, an impostor patriarch. These same worries, of course, rattled Primitive Baptist preachers. As unsalaried ministers, they depended on the church for sustenance just as the missionary depended on his stolen wife for riches. Jesus had called on Joshua Lawrence to feed his wife and children, but the task proved complicated. The fact remained, though seldom acknowledged, that for many Primitive preachers it was the church itself who fed them. And Lawrence's ambivalent descriptions of his role as preacher remind us that in the task of feeding his wife and children—that most fundamental expression of what it meant to be a man in the Old South—he found himself transformed, momentarily and imaginatively, into a mother. For Lawrence and his fellow Primitives, theirs was a complicated patriarchy, indeed.

Borrowing the language of John's Revelation, Lawrence urged believers in the primitive way to "come out of her," to leave the precincts of a feminized evangelicalism whose innovations in doctrine and practice promised only chaos. But Lawrence and the Primitives never did completely escape "her." Haunted by their own compromised patriarchy, worried by their affinities with mothers and other dependents, Lawrence and his fellow Primitives fortified their old faith by fighting some very familiar enemies.[45]

IF THE ERA of the Baptist schism was also the era of the market revolution, it was, too, the age of confidence and confidence men, the age of deceptions both artful and criminal. Indeed, the antebellum marketplace often seemed to its participants to be a realm of confusion where one weathered unpredictable panics, negotiated deals with strangers, and tangled oneself in lines of credit.[46] Americans braced themselves against the market's gales by lashing themselves to a variety of steadying institutions and ideologies. Primitive Baptists watched in anger as their Protestant contemporaries bolstered themselves with an increasingly Arminianized faith that celebrated men and women's ability to, if not quite save themselves, choose to receive God's grace. Arminianized Protestantism (dismissed by Primitives as mere "will-worship") ratified an emergent culture of control where rationality, self-reliance, and discipline promised to subdue chance and tame the marketplace's caprice.[47]

The culture of control was not entirely foreign to the Calvinistic Primitives, but they defended themselves against the market's volatility by rehearsing their faith in predestination and an inscrutable God even as they identified enemies who, they claimed, were the real cause of their troubles. For as uncertain as the antebellum marketplace was, as labyrinthine were its credit networks, as slippery were its commercial relations, the market—for Primitives, at least—objectified the unidentifiable. The market's uncertainty paralleled the Primitive's Calvinist uncertainty. But even the unpredictable market provided a kind of solidity that Calvinism and Primitive Baptist traditions could not. It presented them with their cash-bearing enemies. C. B. Hassell spied them wandering Williamston's streets, soliciting funds for temperance campaigns and foreign missions and driving away his customers and his congregation. From his perch in the burgeoning commercial center of Tarboro, Joshua Lawrence found similar enemies. The young itinerant missionaries threatened to replace a sovereign God with a pliable one and the Old South's patriarchal rule with gender disorder. That each man cast his enemies from his deepest fears and that each did so with only partial awareness tells us much, of course, about them and, I think, about Primitive Baptists more generally. Hassell's and Lawrence's predicaments suggest, at the very least, how Primitives mediated the various social forces that surrounded them. In a broader sense, these portraits suggest how a history that hovers close to believers' emotional experiences can deepen the categories we use to make sense of antebellum life—that the market could be both a social force and a personal resource and that patriarchy's edifice might still stand but its walls, we should note, were deeply compromised by doubt and ambivalence.

4 Rocking Daniel

From a distance it looked like a gathering of decrepits. Men and women, bent at the waist like invalids, shuffling in circles, moaning something strange and inchoate. Thirty or forty of them shambling single file, counterclockwise, feet scraping out crooked rhythms on the wood floor. But then the trumpet blast shout: *Rock Daniel, Rock Daniel*. With hands now clapping like the patter of rain on the church roof and the pace quickening so that from the now-churning circle a hot tempo darted through the slower tempo, finally a "regular step or motion" materialized as if it had been incubated in the maelstrom: *Rock Daniel, Rock Daniel*. Still they moved, faster now. And then a refrain growing louder like a fanfare: *Rock Daniel till I die!*[1]

Afterward, after they had "worked up to a high state of excitement," after their leader had given the signal to stop, after the tight circle had dispersed like so many exhausted acolytes, after the clamoring praise had given way to a church house hush, no one could explain to the curious white woman who had been watching them—had been visiting with them for weeks now, had come south to central Florida, to, of all places, DeLand, a speck of a town resting on a ridge amid drained lakes of pine and citrus, to study "the negro," to observe, in particular, his religious life—no one could explain to her the origins of their sacred dance. Legatees to an ancient rite, they had, even by 1902, just a generation removed from slavery, collectively forgotten the origins and history of their own particular church. No matter. They harbored a deeper truth. That is what they told the woman, a University of Chicago–trained sociologist, Annie Marion MacLean was her name, who was so clearly fascinated by them, even sympathetic to them, but ultimately so baffled by them that she could only remark that theirs was "a noisy religion" and that their whirling shout reminded her of nothing so much as "an Indian war dance"—except that it was, she added, "on a somewhat tamer plan." But the saints made sure MacLean took down their truth. "With much vigor," she noted, the church members asserted that they composed "the original Baptist Church; that the so-called 'Missionary Baptist' . . . is a false body, which withdrew from the mother church in 1832." They pointed with pride to great men of the past who were, like them, Primitive Baptists. We believe, they told

MacLean, "in the scriptures of the Old and New Testaments, in predestination, in the fall of man, in the covenant of redemption, in justification, [in] regeneration, in the resurrection and general judgment, baptism, the Lord's supper, and foot-washing."

It was this last rite, foot washing, that had immediately preceded the shout and was itself immediately preceded by the taking of communion. There, in the crumbling church, its windows unadorned, its cracking shell bare since it had been raised who knew how many years ago, the saints had dragged their benches into two large squares, one for men and one for women, on either side of the pulpit. Following their preacher's lead, they washed each other's feet. MacLean, a remarkable scholar who later reported that her time in DeLand had convinced her that its three black churches lay at the heart of the town's black social life, that these churches—to borrow the words of her colleague, another young sociologist, W. E. B. Du Bois, the man who had asked MacLean to contribute to his mammoth study of the black church—were "the real units of race life," then asked the members of the St. Annis Primitive Baptist Church what it all meant. And the saints answered her, gave her an answer as plain as the meetinghouse they called home: "This, they say, is merely carrying out the example of Christ."[2]

To carry out the example of Christ in the Jim Crow South was difficult work even in holy company, even when the Spirit moved and beckoned. For black Baptists of all stripes, the Jim Crow era was, as the historian Paul Harvey explained, "not one of triumph but of struggle, of small victories hard won and even harder kept." Yet the black Primitive Baptist story has escaped notice, even though its burdens and aspirations tell us something new about both African Americans and Calvinism's complex fate. For black Primitives, the last decades of the nineteenth century were ones where their pasts stalked their futures, where freedom's vistas were shadowed by racism's and sexism's looming presence, and where dreams of spiritual autonomy were draped with the moth-eaten garment of interracial fellowship.[3]

Yet for a particular group of black Primitives—the people most closely examined here, the ones who eventually, improbably, organized the National Primitive Baptist Convention of America—these also were years of dynamism and change. In Huntsville, Alabama, they founded schools of all kinds—Sunday schools, graded schools, a "select" school, even an industrial college—forged interdenominational ties, and lodged themselves in the heart of the city's social and political life. In Florida's northern pinelands, they dispatched evangelists and slowly opened church offices to women, and along its Atlantic coast, they raised money with an unclouded joy that marked them as heralds of something new. The movement spread: to Texas, North Carolina, Virginia. In 1907, when these black Primitives gathered for their first national convention meeting, they culminated several decades of work building a movement that allied a renovated Calvinism to the advancement of the race and denomination alike. Of course, to many Primitives, white as well as black, the rise of a national convention of Primitive Baptists seemed equal parts farce and tragedy. In a pocket of central Georgia, far from the hurtling energies in Huntsville and Daytona Beach, a group of orthodox "old-line" black Primitives scoffed at "these modern human vanities and follies." They declared themselves surrounded, enemies pressing in. "Seeing more and more of the evils of the religious institutions of men," they wrote, "we have less and less confidence in them, and less and less fellowship for them." All they could do was pledge to do that most Primitive of things—"to continue to walk in the good old paths." Those old-liners in Georgia were right that the national Primitives represented something modern and different: they, just as much as the emergent Holiness churches or the more established black denominations, were reinventing African American religious life. Yet the national Primitives also trod the old paths. Their primitiveness was not conjectural. They celebrated their hard-shell distinctiveness, steadied themselves against the stanchions of Calvinist doctrine, and replenished themselves from the deep well of Afro-Baptist ritual. Like all Primitives, they looked backward to go forward. But the old paths, they said, led them a new way.[4]

Duskland

Even after the war, they worshipped together: black and white Primitives in the same church as it had been in the days, not long past, when one party owned the other. They sang together, were baptized together, took communion together. This happened for years, for decades even, long after the thrill of emancipation had been supplanted by the misery of Jim Crow. But the mind remembers and expects, and so African American Primitive Baptists, like black believers across the post–Civil War South, eventually left the churches of their former masters to build their own. In Primitive circles, at least, this leave-taking was a slow, meandering affair that trundled across the half century separating the Civil War from the Great War. In the heady days after the Civil War's end, many black Primitives struck out on their own. Sometimes whites sanctioned and even aided these departures, and sometimes they seethed like ineffectual autocrats as black believers marched toward freedom and independence. But there were other journeys, ones more circuitous and complex, ones where fledgling bonds of interracial fellowship came lashed to Jim Crow's sad freight, ones that heralded a promising future even as they curled back into a darker past.

There were so many beginnings: in 1865, south of Nashville, Tennessee, when "the Lord through His Spirit" revealed to a group of emancipated black Primitives "the answer to their prayers," and so, cast out of the church by whites, they turned to each other, "knelt and laid their hands on each other's heads," and then "arose and started out to preach, to baptize, and to establish churches"; in 1869, just outside Macon, at the edge of Georgia's Black Belt—"that strange land of shadows," as Du Bois put it—when a presbytery of white Primitive Baptist elders ordained several of their black brothers, some of whom were perhaps their slaves little more than four years earlier, so that these new black pastors could in orderly fashion found the Colored Primitive Baptist Association of Georgia, which itself soon birthed more associations of black Primitives so that by 1900 there were in Georgia more than 4,500 black believers in more than 170 Primitive Baptist meetinghouses; in 1870, in the portion of the Tennessee River Valley that winds through northwest Alabama, when black Primitives who had been "regularly dismissed by letter" from a white-dominated association founded their own association that, two decades later, boasted more than four thousand members in twenty-seven churches across three states; in 1868 in tropical Key West, Florida, when enterprising black Primitives, while still members of the "white" Primitive church, organized themselves into what they called a "Baptist Friendly Society," bought a tract of land at the heart of the island, and, when "given their marching orders, they had their property paid for and walked out and began business for themselves, and gave the licensed preacher $300.00 and sent him to Virginia to get his ordination." Beginnings like these were collaborations. To be "regularly dismissed," as the Alabama Primitives had put it, was vital. It meant that their new churches and associations were in gospel order, were right in the sight of God and man alike. And for their white counterparts, the regular dismissal preserved some sense of their authority; it allowed them to console themselves that though the black exodus rolled on, God had not hardened their hearts like Pharaoh's of old.[5]

In many other places, however, whites refused to let go, solacing themselves instead with the old myths of black contentment and black loyalty. "I do not believe the colored members wish to separate from the whites," tut-tutted a white elder in eastern North Carolina in 1877 when his black brothers and sisters begged leave to organize their own churches. In any case, he continued, the white "brethren in general did not yet feel that the colored brethren were prepared to maintain gospel order and hence they could not dismiss them in gospel fellowship."[6] Instead, black believers were to remain tenanted in white-run churches where they might be baptized into the beloved community and approach the communion table as brothers and sisters in Christ, but where, as was the case in associations across eastern North Carolina in the 1860s and 1870s, fretful whites maintained control of church discipline and governance. Even in the late 1880s, it was obvious to these white Primitives "that the colored people should remain as they are" so that "many thousands of them continue to have the benefit of regular preaching by white as well as by colored ministers."[7] And with the proper white supervision, those black ministers could be beneficial indeed. In a "remarkable narrative" that white Primitives never tired of circulating from the end of the Civil War through the early twentieth century, an elderly black Primitive preacher attested to the benevolence of his former masters, the mercifulness of God, and the consolations of the plantation. When he recounted the Union occupation of Williamston, North Carolina, the black man said, "The Yankees asked me if I did not want to go with them and have freedom. I told them I did not want to go from my old home, where I knew my people, off with them, where I knew nobody; and besides, that I was already free—that I had a freedom that no man could take from me, even the saving knowledge of our Lord Jesus Christ."[8] This was, for white Primitives, an enchanting story, a fantasy of black fidelity to the primitive faith and its white patriarchs, a purportedly true narrative they could retell even as so many of the African Americans in their churches sought spiritual equality and independence.

While most white Primitives in the decades following the Civil War soothed themselves with the thin milk of paternalism, many others simply recoiled at the continued presence of blacks in their midst. Often white-run associations flatly refused black churches that asked to associate with them. Here the other old myths—about black degeneracy and black cursedness—returned. In 1876, when Isaac Berry, a black man who had received a hope in Christ, asked the all-white membership of a Florida Primitive Baptist church if he might join them in fellowship, two elders refused him on racist grounds. As an early chronicler of this episode put it: They "preached to their church that if they received negroes into the church they would have to treat them the same as white Brethren, put them up to the table to eat with white brethren and in the bed just the same." Some of these same white brethren attempted to placate the incensed preachers and their followers by reminding them that while the church "had no right to reject any nationality of people regardless to color," the aggrieved party could nonetheless discard its fears about the dinner table and the bedroom: "Treat him as a brother in spirit but not in sociality as a man, which is contrary to the laws of our country," they advised. But even this bit of genteel racism seemed a provocation. Within two years, the elders had cut their churches loose from any Primitive association that would baptize African Americans. Meanwhile, a similar incident unfolded in eastern North Carolina where a group of white Primitive Baptists declared that they "did not believe the negroes had a soul." Rather than commune with their black brothers and sisters, these white Primitives followed their leader, a bitter elder named Taylor, who, on a hill bearing his name, erected a cavernous lean-to out of pine boughs and weatherboard so that he and his minions might find God without the damnable presence of black Christians.[9]

Between peaceable separation and acrimonious division lay other possibilities, such as those that played out in northern Virginia's Bethlehem Primitive Baptist Church. When the church reassembled itself five years after Appomattox, one of its first items of business was to listen as "a colored brother . . . and a colored sister" related their experiences of grace. The church accepted Edward Francis and Nelly Roberson on a Saturday, baptized them in the river on a Sunday morning, and added their names to the rolls, where they joined the Bethlehem church's black majority. Their pastor, however, was a white man, though the entire church—white and black—declared itself "favorably impressed" with the gifts of a black preacher, Charles Mason, who delivered the word to them regularly. When another black brother sought ordination, "all the members present both white and colored voted against his having such privilege as they did not consider his preaching edifying." By 1874 a kind of parallel black church operated inside Bethlehem Primitive. When disputes arose between black members, Elder Mason, the black preacher, tended to them. When black converts sought church membership, whites turned to their black brethren for advice. But when white and black members quarreled, the church appointed investigative committees with a majority of white men. And in 1879, when "the case of the colored members having full liberty to act in all church business was then taken up," a white elder rose from his seat to speak to the church's black members about "the disorder of such a course." He "besought them to be satisfied with such church privileges as was customary in all the primitive baptist churches in this section of country."

He averred that such forbearance on their part "would be for their good as well as for the peace and prosperity of the church." He called for a vote, and the vote came in: "the colored members of this church are entitled to such church privileges, *and no more* than is customary with churches in this section of country of our faith and order."[10]

But what were the customary privileges in a church that eagerly listened to black preaching, that baptized white and black folk side by side, that met in fellowship with independent black Primitive Baptist churches in northern Virginia and Washington, D.C., and that for a decade after this vote continued to gather in black members, many of whom had left black-run churches—both missionary and Primitive—to join the fraught fellowship at Bethlehem? And what, precisely, were the customary privileges prevailing "in this section of country" when it came to African American Primitive Baptists? Consider that not far from Bethlehem lay another Primitive church that had also taken up the question of the extent and limits of the rights of its black members. At the Quantico church, there had long been a rule barring blacks from voting on matters of church business. But in 1882, just three years after the confrontation at Bethlehem, the Quantico church revisited the issue. Something had changed. The old custom would not do any longer. The whites at Quantico revoked it, and now, when church business was at hand, white and black Primitives voted together.[11]

What a bewildering landscape! And yet like expert witnesses, we confidently trace the broad contours of the scene without having been there. For in the closing decades of the nineteenth century, we know that African Americans left biracial churches to form their own; that they escaped the oppressive oversight of white churchgoers and celebrated their own spiritual autonomy; and that they relied on their own institutions to help them through an era of lynching, disfranchisement, and segregation. The "black church" embodied resistance and liberation; the "white church" answered with unrelenting bigotry and violence. This is our map, and we know it well,[12] just as we know that death ate away at the Bethlehem church ("We feel we may soon become *extinct*," they—all twenty of them, and just one of them black—wondered aloud in 1910, forty years after Edward Francis and Nelly Roberson had joined a band more than 100 strong) and that the Quantico church, abandoned by its members when its pastor died in 1939, is now nothing but a clump of foundation stones and a lone support beam.[13] But in the deeper past, the black Primitive Baptists at Bethlehem and Quantico and so many other places across the South lived in a duskland where custom might be conjured up, hardened, and dissolved in the time it took to ride from one meetinghouse to the next and where a less-than-perfect interracial fellowship could recede into the gloaming before growing luminous for reasons that reticent church records leave inexplicable. Just as there were so many beginnings to the black Primitive Baptist story, there were so many roads. While some led to orthodoxy, to what we now call "old-line" Primitive congregations, others led elsewhere. To Huntsville, then.

Big Spring

In the beginning, they worshipped at night in the slaves' burying ground with their ancestors' mounded graves keeping them silent company. They had no meetinghouse, but no matter. They dubbed themselves the African Baptist Church of Huntsville, Alabama, recruited in 1820 a "free coloured man" named William Harris to be their pastor, and soon dispatched delegates to the Flint River Association, which was otherwise composed of white-run churches. When the missionary schism rippled through Alabama in the 1830s, African Huntsville walked what white and black Primitives alike called "the old paths": against organized missions and benevolent efforts and the like. African Huntsville held to those Calvinistic old paths, and soon members found more and more souls eager to join their journey. The church grew rapidly: from 76 members at its founding in 1820 to 241 worshippers just fifteen years later when it was by far the largest Baptist church—white or black, missionary or anti-missionary—in the entire state. Missionary Baptists fumed. William Harris and his flock of "unsuspecting coloured brethren" had been held in thrall to some baleful white elder, they said. There had been "vast consequences," they said. "False views and false practices"—the so-called election of grace—had spread like a malady all over black Huntsville. All of it "came from one man's decisions . . . and now thousands of people walk in his track as anti-Missionaries."[14]

The frustrated missionary Baptists were right: in Huntsville—black Huntsville—the Primitive Baptist church was *the* Baptist church. By 1874, not long after its members had renamed it "St. Bartley's" after their long-serving pastor, Bartley Harris (William Harris's grandson), the church had amassed a membership of more than two thousand souls, absorbing black Primitives from town and country like some great ingathering at the end of days. When summer arrived, St. Bartley's anchored an annual associational meeting thronged by eight thousand to nine thousand saints and curious onlookers agog at the massive crowds. Sure, Huntsville's black missionary Baptists finally managed to cobble something together by the 1890s, but even they conceded it was a slight affair, a church "bound hand and foot," they said, by its small numbers and meager resources. By contrast, St. Bartley's was big and old and born of ambition. No one in Huntsville could ignore it. Each spring, the saints of St. Bartley's made sure of that.[15]

The *New York Times* correspondent who passed through town in 1874 found the whole thing remarkable, had gawked at it all. "So many excitable negroes," he marveled: thousands of them, "a throng . . . from all parts of the surrounding county" crowding Huntsville's streets. They had arrived on foot or atop doddering mules or piled in "wagons, carts, old carriages, [and] rickety coaches drawn by oxen." They loitered outside shops, lounged on creek banks, perched on rooftops, rode through town both jaunty and circumspect—and all of them waiting on a Sunday afternoon for the Primitives' grand procession that would begin at St. Bartley's and wend its way through town for more than an hour before ending finally at the city's heart, at what locals called the Big Spring, an inexhaustible source of water that poured out from a craggy rock face like some biblical tableau.[16]

Each year in late May it happened like this. After Sunday services, one hundred young men in dark suits, their heads swathed in white cotton kerchiefs, stationed themselves in the streets and began to sing the old surging Watts hymns that soared and canted and crashed in great, irrepressible sheets of sound. Then came the cavalcade: first the elderly pastor, enfolded in gray flannel robes and flanked by two deacons; then the baptismal candidates—women first and then men; and after them the entire congregation. They marched—all of them—through the streets "singing and shouting at the top of their voices": "Am I a soldier of the cross, a follower of the Lamb?" they thundered. "And shall I fear to own his cause or blush to speak his name?" When they arrived at the Big Spring, a teeming crowd under a canopy of umbrellas greeted them with shouts of praise. The pastor knelt on the banks in prayer while the candidates waded knee-deep into the spring. When the pastor met them in the center of the water, he called their names out one by one, took their hands, blessed them in the name of the Father and the Son and the Holy Spirit, and threw them under the water so that when they rose up—"borned again!" as they cried out—they felt a kinship with their risen Savior. "Never die no more," the congregation would shout out. "No, never die no more!"[17]

Methodists scoffed at the pageantry—"Niggers is sinful fond of show, and the Baptists gives it to 'em sure," said one—but what else could they do? The crowds kept coming. Whites groused about "negroes . . . loafing

The St. Bartley's baptisms at the Big Spring, ca. 1895. Courtesy of the Huntsville–Madison County Public Library Special Collections, Huntsville, Ala.

around the Big Spring" and demanded that the authorities halt this "lounging nuisance at the only place in our city that would be a pleasant, cool resting place . . . for white ladies and children." When, just a few weeks before one of the Primitives' annual baptisms, Huntsville's Republican mayor, a man indebted to the city's black residents for his election, "advanced a suggestion that, in view of numerous strangers visiting in the city soon," the city "should beautify the Spring park somewhat by introducing flower beds, etc.," white aldermen balked. Visitors seemed not to mind the lack of flowers. So popular was the baptism ceremony that unscrupulous city boosters would regularly paper the countryside with bogus handbills, hoping to lure sightseers to Huntsville on various weekend excursions throughout the spring. If the Big Spring's waters were vacant of black Primitives, well, the sightseers had already paid their railroad fare, and certainly there was a chance they might visit one of the town's many saloons. (City worthies boasted that their fair burg hosted two churches for every saloon, a bit of boosterism that had the benefit of appealing to the saintly and the sloshed alike.) By 1895, visitors could even purchase a postcard of the "Negro Baptising." Huntsville's black Primitives had become a tourist attraction.[18]

Postcard of "Negro Baptizing, Huntsville, Alabama." Courtesy of Alan C. Wright.

For a church whose early years were spent in a slave graveyard beyond the city limits, the metamorphosis was startling and inescapable: from death to life, from slavery to freedom, from periphery to center. In the first exhilarating days after Appomattox, when their pastor waded into the spring to baptize 140 souls and then, just a week later, 200 more before "a vast concourse of spectators," the converts leaped from their watery graves like "the contortionist trying to jump through himself." "Freed from slavery—freed from sin," a woman, one of the newly saved, shouted. "Bress

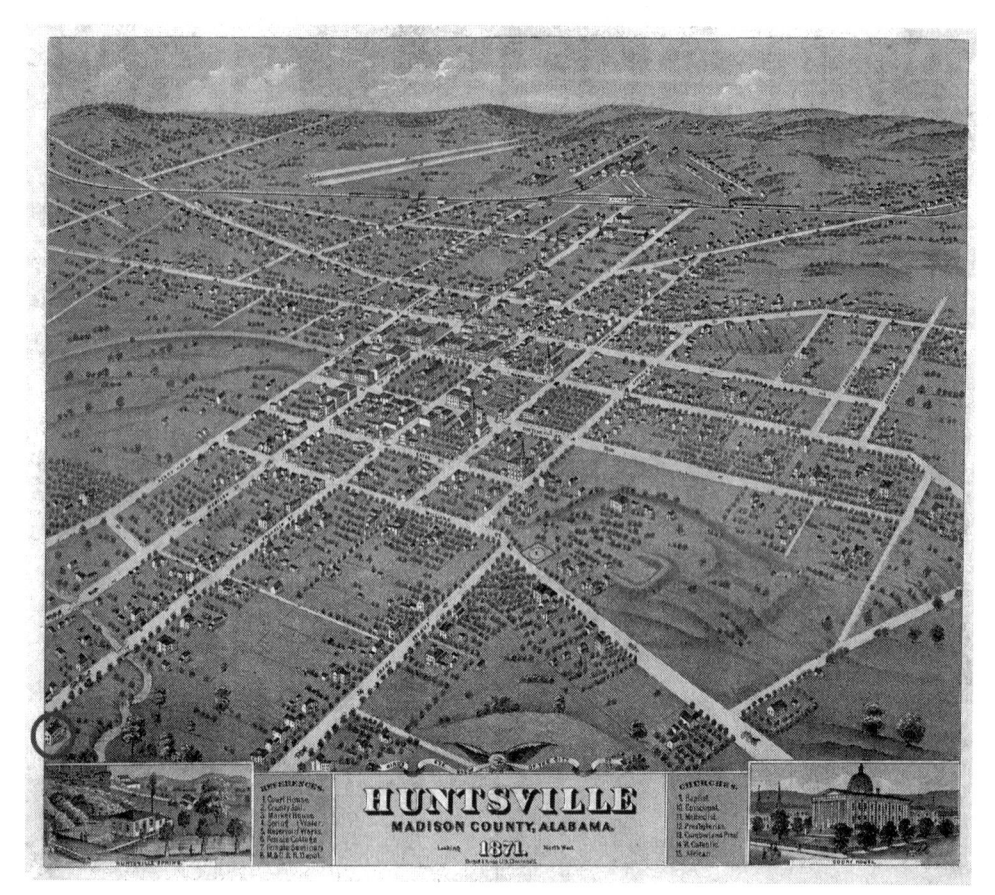

A bird's-eye view of the city of Huntsville in 1871 with the Primitives' African Baptist Church in the lower-left corner. Courtesy of the Library of Congress, G3974h PM000070.

God and Gen. Grant!" The contemptuous newspaperman who took down the scene found the woman's bodily gyrations "ludicrous in the extreme," but even he understood the significance of her loud celebration of the new birth of freedom both she and her nation had experienced. St. Bartley's new souls had been "brought into 'active service,'" he wrote. They were "new recruits to the side of RIGHT." In the difficult years that followed those days of jubilee, the Primitives built their church into a kind of landmark that no Huntsvillian could ignore. When, for example, lithographers crafted a bird's-eye view of Huntsville in 1871, St. Bartley's—still at that point called the "African" church—was the only black church to appear. A year later the Primitives decamped from that meetinghouse—a wooden structure they had fashioned beside the old slave burial ground—for a new brick edifice, gothic windows and all, close to the town center.[19]

They always remembered their journey. In the 1880s, long after they, like Huntsville's other African Americans, began burying their dead in the new "colored cemetery" with its manicured walks and generous shade trees, and when, regrettably, hogs and cattle began grazing through the old slave burial ground where their church had been born, the Primitives successfully lobbied the city government to repair the graveyard's fences so that their ancestors' resting places would no longer be "subject to depredations and neglect." A half decade after this incident, at a time when many Huntsvillians continued to register their disgust with the city for acquiescing to the Primitives' earlier request (an 1885 mayoral candidate used his campaign to stoke this grievance), a farmer simply decided to take matters into his own hands, decided, that is, to move the burying ground's fences in some thirty feet so that he might have more land to plow. But by then a black alderman—one of two, in fact, who belonged to St. Bartley's—intervened. Once again, the board of mayor and aldermen decided to "give immediate attention to this desecration of graves."[20]

When the men and women of St. Bartley's formed their own church association in 1870, they named it Indian Creek after the stream that flowed out from the Big Spring. Indian Creek cradled their baptismal waters; it was where they experienced the new birth. But those waters had also enslaved them. In the early nineteenth century, Indian Creek meandered south and west of the Big Spring for five miles before it became navigable by boats of any size, boats that could carry cotton and foodstuffs and slaves back and forth to the Tennessee River and then to the world beyond. By 1818 Madison County's merchants began dreaming of a waterway that would more firmly anchor Huntsville to the region's booming cotton economy and allow them to escape the clattering expense of overland travel. When, in 1831, their money finally allowed them to gouge a canal out of the slender creek, they heaped keelboats with cotton and celebrated their good fortune. The merchants' triumph was the slaves' catastrophe: a cheaper and quicker transportation network only made their masters more wealthy and their fates more bleak. Emancipation itself could not completely ameliorate their condition. The creek, after all, still ran to the river, and so many of the St. Bartley's faithful cropped the land or served the white people who owned it.

But each year on a spring day, the order of things changed. Loudly and freely they marched through city streets where they and their ancestors had once been shackled silently. Proudly they paraded past the courthouse, under whose majestic portico so many of them had once been bought and sold. And then they approached those glorious and troubled waters. But on this day, God's spirit rippled through Indian Creek, and the men and women who had once been slaves "took charge of the waters"—yes, that is what they called it when their young men, their heads wrapped in white, waded into the spring to ritually prepare it to receive the new converts. During the Big Spring procession and baptism, they conjured the past and rewrote it. These rites were their sturdy almanac, a yearly reminder to themselves and to all of Huntsville about who they were now and who they had been before.[21]

That Huntsville's Primitives would remember their dead and baptize their living is unremarkable; what is noteworthy is that they insisted all along that their fellow citizens acknowledge, if not respect, their decision to do so. The fights over the burial ground, the skirmishes about the "loafing negroes" at the Big Spring: these were battles over belonging and identity, over whether and how a group of black Primitive Baptists in the Deep South—in a town that had, not many years before, let the Klan bloody its streets—could lodge a claim for recognition and respect in what we now habitually and antiseptically refer to as "the public sphere." For those who crowded the pews at St. Bartley's, marched through the city's streets, lined the Big Spring's banks, and took charge of its waters, the answers were urgent and obvious: they were fierce soldiers of the cross and meek followers of the Lamb, they would be heard and seen, they would harness their political power to protect their own, they were dead to sin but alive to God, they had once been slaves but were now free, and they would not forget.

Hard-Shell Schooling

When Georgia Ann Ware knew the end was near, she put on her wedding dress and lay down to die. "Death would be a welcome messenger," she said. When they buried her, her friends showered her grave with calla lilies and white hyacinths. They remembered her practicality and industry, her frugality and selflessness. They said all who knew her "knew her life was centered in her husband." It was true; she had devoted herself to Charlie Ware. Twenty-two years earlier, in 1875, they had been married: she a young woman, just nineteen, who had swept into Huntsville, Alabama, from Kentucky not long after the war, and he, three years her senior, a brickmason who fell in and out of work with the seasons. Georgia Ann kept house while Charlie scuffled for work, and she was by his side when, a decade later, he made his improbable rise to city hall to become a four-term alderman and a pillar of Huntsville's black community. But Georgia Ann Ware had causes other than Charlie. When she died in the spring of 1897, her work had for more than a decade buttressed a massive Primitive Baptist educational movement that resulted in a fleet of church-built schoolhouses, the founding of the Huntsville Primitive Baptist Graded and Industrial School (what the Primitives, in the parlance of the day, referred to as their "college"), and, eventually, the construction of a national black Primitive Baptist movement that would, ten years after her death, bring itself into being in the church she had called home.[22]

In Huntsville as elsewhere, teachers, like sutlers, rode in the wake of the Union army's serpentine advance. Not long after Federal forces swept into northern Alabama in the spring of 1862, Treasury Department officials in Huntsville organized a school for freedpeople, one of three or four such schools established in Alabama before Appomattox. Within just a few years, about six hundred black children in Huntsville were annually attending schools of various sorts.[23]

When Huntsville's newly freed Primitives started their own school, the local Freedmen's Bureau agent—a white man—sighed. In an 1867 report, he grumbled that the Primitives' little academy was run by a black man "not in any way qualified for this work," a man audacious enough to charge each of his fifty-six pupils one dollar per month, a man, he admitted, who worked in earnest but whose "zeal is not according to wisdom." That man was William H. Gaston, a thirty-seven-year-old former slave, illiterate in the summer of 1863 when he traded his shackles for Union blues, and a wounded sergeant major, the record keeper for his regiment, and quite literate indeed when he mustered out three years later and declared himself a teacher to anyone who asked. For much of the next three decades, Gaston continued to run what he called his "select school" out of St. Bartley's. The subjects ranged from "practical" arithmetic and hygiene to natural philosophy and U.S. history. By the early 1880s, he had added night classes, organized ten-month-long school terms, and still charged one dollar a month for tuition. "If we wish good material," he explained, "we should be willing to pay for it."[24]

But Gaston's interests were never narrowly pecuniary or sectarian; instead, like his fellow black Primitives in Huntsville, he devoted himself to broader civic, educational, and religious efforts designed, as he explained, "to lay hold and push forward every facility for elevating our people." In 1872 he traveled to the Republican National Convention in Philadelphia and helped nominate President Grant for a second term. Back home, he helped organize the Indian Creek Primitive Baptist Association. By the early 1880s the congregation at St. Bartley's had chosen him as their church clerk and ordained him as an elder. Then, just as attendance at his select school began booming in 1882, Gaston chaired a new effort to establish a nonsectarian industrial college in Huntsville "for the benefit of our rising youth." He and his committee of prominent black men—some of them Primitives but most of them not—called on "leading colored men" from across the South and "leading ministers of every denomination" to join their campaign. They imagined a school "entirely untrammeled from sectarianism" where "no eligible gentleman or lady shall be prohibited from becoming a teacher or pupil on account of color or religious opinion." "A Hardshell Baptist myself," Gaston declared, "I am free to confess that my children have gotten the most they know from teachers of other denominations." The efforts to build an industrial college soon fizzled out, but when a similar plan surfaced in the early 1890s, Gaston found himself elected as one of seven trustees tasked with purchasing a lot on which to build a new black primary school. And there were still other endeavors: he served as secretary of the Madison County teachers' institute and regularly traveled to Selma for meetings of the black State Teachers' Association; he prosecuted pension claims on behalf of African American Civil War veterans and their widows; and from 1883 to 1889, he served three terms as an alderman from Huntsville's Fourth Ward, a position he used to champion efforts to improve the city's black schools and build new ones.[25]

Gaston's constant bustle had a consistent aim: the advancement of his race. "If my people rise, I rise with them," he wrote. "If they go down, I shall go down with them, from New Brunswick to [the] California Peninsula." But though they might journey together, Gaston knew that it would be men like him who would need to lead the way: "The more educated of our people . . . must know that it is to you that the illiterate are looking to be led in the way to peace, elevation and prosperity." Gaston had become the most visible and vocal Primitive Baptist in Huntsville, but he was hardly alone in his enthusiasm for black civic and educational causes. Other Primitive Baptists—elders and lay members, men and women—taught school, sat on school boards, coordinated school fund-raisers, organized Republican Party meetings, won public office, and graced the dais at what had become, by the early 1880s, a constant stream of education-related meetings in Huntsville's black community.[26]

It was these men and women who decided in the summer of 1885 that black Primitives in Huntsville and its hinterlands needed their own college—something more extensive and ambitious than Gaston's comparatively tiny select school—and that they would, therefore, soon "purchase ground and erect an Institute for educational purposes, owned and controlled by Primitive or Old School Baptists, but entirely free from sectarianism as to imparting knowledge and selecting teachers." The proposed academy—it was to be called the National Industrial College—would charge tuition for those who could afford it, educate and clothe free of charge those who could not, and "embrace all necessary and classical branches of education." The plan proved popular. Primitives of course endorsed it, and it also found enthusiastic backers in Madison County's white superintendent of education and the principal and teachers at Rust Normal Institute, a black school in Huntsville attached to the Methodist Episcopal Church (North).[27]

Indeed, the National Industrial College seemed designed to meet the needs of both Huntsville's black Primitive Baptists and the city's larger black community. For years, calls for African Americans to invest more time and money in educational pursuits had filled the pages of the city's black-owned newspaper, the *Huntsville Gazette*. Correspondents pleaded with the *Gazette* to urge its black readers to renounce their frivolous pastimes, abandon their Odd Fellows halls and Masonic lodges, and pour their energies instead into building new schools. "Mr. Editor, can't you use your pen against these follies?" wrote the pseudonymous Jack Daw. "Tell our people the true course to pursue—show them that if this money had been spent for schools and teachers, that we would have had school houses on a thousand hills, where now we have none." The *Gazette*, meanwhile, blamed "the people" who were "depending too little on their own efforts to educate their children, and too much on the State and the benevolences of the North." Perhaps the Primitive Baptists, who, after all, disdained fraternal orders and had, in Gaston, a leader who had long demonstrated an ability to run a school without aid from government agencies or northern philanthropists, were positioned perfectly to allay the kinds of paternalistic worries dotting the *Gazette*'s pages. Perhaps, too, Huntsville's Primitives, who had proven their organizational strength since slave times, could succeed where the earlier effort to build a nonsectarian school—the one Gaston backed in 1882—had failed. Certainly, the city itself seemed unable or unwilling to act. When it finally came time in the early 1880s for Huntsville to build "a colored city school," the government, as southern municipalities were wont to do, resorted first to the kind of dilatory proceduralism that would become a hallmark of the Jim Crow state and then built a white school instead.[28]

Despite these setbacks, African Americans in Huntsville remained publicly optimistic about education's ability to uplift the race. In 1884, just a year before the Primitives' remarkable announcement, Gaston, for example, had addressed a standing-room-only education rally at the Methodist Episcopal church. "The color barrier every day is giving way," he declared, "and merit, shift and industry will bring their just rewards alike to black and white. . . . Today the world looks to see the fate of 4 million people come up out of darkness and oppression. We have vindicated, are vindicating and will continue to vindicate to it our manhood and ability. Not by blood, not by sword, not by cannon and musketry, will we walk into a proud position of respectability and power, but by the pen." On a platform packed with Huntsville's black elite, Gaston was clearly the star. To the *Gazette* reporter, he seemed a manly hero, "an old warrior" who "took possession of his audience, was bold, aggressive." Gaston's prominence revealed his denomination's significance. Huntsville's black Primitive Baptists stood at the center of their city's political and religious life. They shared platforms and pulpits with ministers from the city's other black churches. They held public office. They planned the future of their church and imagined a brilliant future for their race.[29]

But a sense of grievance rumbled beneath the surface optimism and ecumenism pushing these plans. The Primitives' National Industrial College would become a refuge and a bulwark against what they felt were the depredations of the leading African American educator in the state, William Hooper Councill—a man whose presence overshadowed even Booker T. Washington. Councill had been born a slave, sold on the Huntsville courthouse steps, and, through sheer doggedness, guile, and craven self-interest, transformed himself within years of the war's end into a teacher, lawyer, AME church minister, and political operator. In 1874, he traded his support of the successful Democratic gubernatorial candidate for an appointment as the head of Huntsville's new normal school. Even the ever-obliging Washington found Councill's eager horse-trading with Democrats and "oily flattery" of white powerbrokers repellant. The man, Washington wrote, was "in every way an undesirable individual." Yet Councill, ever resourceful, found plenty of admirers among Huntsville's white and black elite—"gentlemen of distinction," as they called themselves—who, just months before Councill shot a Primitive Baptist man named Blount McCravy, lionized him as the man whose introduction of industrial training had made the State Normal School "second to none in Alabama." William Gaston himself wrote the commendation.[30]

Blount McCravy earned no such accolades. He loaded coal on the Memphis & Charleston line, was a member of St. Bartley's, and was the uncle to a twelve-year-old girl, Martha Mary Ellen Clay, who said that Councill, on an early spring morning in 1885, took her to an upstairs room at his schoolhouse and raped her. When McCravy learned of his niece's allegations, he confronted Councill at the schoolhouse where the alleged rape occurred. Councill brandished a gun, chased McCravy out of the school, and shot him through the hand. While Councill awaited trial for rape and assault with intent to kill, his fellow black citizens held mass meetings to call for his ouster from both the State Normal School and the AME Church and to defend themselves against charges circulated by Councill's white allies that "the colored people . . . have attempted to incite a mob against Mr. Councill." In early July the grand jury refused to indict Councill, and by the end of the month the normal school's commissioners had reelected him as principal. In between those verdicts, the Primitives had called a meeting at St. Bartley's where they decided that if the State Normal School could not be trusted, they would simply build their own. And so the idea for the National Industrial College was born.[31]

Still, the Primitives' grievances festered. In 1887, they charged Councill and the State Normal School with subverting their faith and refusing to hire Primitive Baptist teachers. "Our children have been educated against us," they declared. "Our teachers, male and female, have been debarred." For many years, they had labored to change the regrettable situation at the normal school, but the wound, they concluded, had been "for too long and too openly developed for us to want a change any longer." They recommended instead that Primitive Baptist parents across the Tennessee Valley remove their children from the State Normal School at once: "We have no better time to begin than now." Two years passed. Councill and the State Normal School continued to refuse the Primitives' entreaties. Councill's obstinacy rankled. This time the Primitives petitioned Alabama's state superintendent of education; begged him to intervene on their behalf; insisted that "we have been, without any just cause, *discriminated against, as a sect*, in the selection of teachers for said school"; reminded him that "our children are a great factor of nearly all the colored schools of Madison county"; and finally, with respect, requested "that a lady or gentleman of our sect be given a position in the school in Huntsville to teach." They sent their petition south to Montgomery where the Honorable Solomon Palmer or, perhaps, his secretary looked it over momentarily before forwarding it to Councill, who once again denied the Primitives' accusations and said that he would, in any case, "be unfit to manage such a great and growing school" if he bent to the Primitives' demands.[32]

The church's male elders carried on the public tussle with Councill and his white allies, but, in the nine years that lay between the Primitives' decision in 1885 to build their academy and its opening in 1894, it was the women of St. Bartley's who sustained the church. When fire swept through the church, women spearheaded pledge drives to pay for the repairs. When those pledges were collected, women contributed 70 percent of the donations. When the repairs were completed, women kicked off rousing educational meetings, shared the stage with church elders and Huntsville's mayor, delivered addresses to cheering crowds, and sang hymns to stir the faithful. And when, in 1889, St. Bartley's announced that it had just finished construction on "a very neat school building," one that would receive students for primary instruction and would, therefore, supplement their forthcoming academy, William Gaston made a point of announcing that Georgia Ann Ware, who, on a spring day some eight years later would put on her wedding dress to wait for death's appearing, had "largely contributed to the erection of said school, and has been the prime mover of it."[33]

When Huntsville's black Primitive Baptists seized control of their education, they only did what so many African Americans across the postwar South also were doing. When their Graded and Industrial School (the institution that they had earlier called the National Industrial College) supplemented a classical liberal education with industrial training, they embraced an educational philosophy that, despite Booker T. Washington's efforts to make carpentry and blacksmithing the mainspring of the race's ascent, was popular with black academies across the South. And when they made their church "a deliberative arena"—a place "where individual souls communed intimately with God" and where they "discussed, debated, and devised an agenda for their common good"—they only did what black Baptists across the nation had learned to do as well.[34]

Yet these Primitives knew they were different. They described themselves as a "sect," a leaden one-word counterweight to all their decades of ecumenical work. When missionary Baptists and other evangelicals derided Primitives as "hard-shells," people stubbornly resisting the march of Christian progress, the African American Primitives examined here celebrated their hard-shell distinctiveness, even going so far as to stamp up bronze lapel pins—price: ten cents—emblazoned cheekily with an image of a hard shell. The money raised from pin sales would, of course, go to support black Primitive Baptist academies.[35]

And here, too, there was a difference. Decades earlier, at the apogee of the Baptist schism, white Primitives also had seen themselves as a people set apart, a people who needed, as they put it, to "come out" of churches blighted by greed and impudence. These white Primitives, afflicted by uncertainty, lashed out at their enemies—missionaries, itinerants, revivalists, seminary-trained preachers—who seemed to grow more numerous and more insidious each day. In the State Normal School, William Councill, and Councill's white allies, Huntsville's black Primitives found their own enemy. But they harnessed their anger, organized themselves, and founded schools that both embraced their denominational identity and, when it came to the classrooms themselves, held it at bay. In doing all this, the black Primitive Baptists in Huntsville floated a new kind of Primitive-ness, a new kind of American Calvinism—born in slavery, reborn in freedom, and then reconceived in the twilight between Reconstruction and Jim Crow as an educational movement that moved nimbly between black Calvinist sectarianism and optimistic ecumenicism.

By the turn of the century, 162 students were attending the Huntsville Graded and Industrial School. Two teachers—one woman and one man—guided their work at the elementary and secondary levels. It was a modest enterprise. (Washington's Tuskegee Institute, by contrast, featured 85 instructors who taught more than 1,000 students.) But it would serve as a model for the denomination's fledgling academies and its more ambitious efforts: a combined industrial school and theological seminary in Winston-Salem, North Carolina; a similar institute in Tallahassee, Florida; a Primitive Baptist college in Texas; three denominational academies in rural Alabama; and, by 1907, a new institution—a national convention of black Primitive Baptists—that would not be modest at all.[36]

Union, Peace, and Progress

It might as well have been an old-time revival. Two thousand bodies cramming the pews, everyone "wild with enthusiasm," preachers starting low, rising high, striking fire, then sitting down inside a storm of "amens"—though if one entered through a different door or appeared at a different time of day, implacable sobriety reigned. Calls to order were read. Delegates were counted. Roll was called. Motions were made. Votes were taken. Eleven different committees filed reports.

Above all, however, the six-day-long gathering in Huntsville in July 1907 was an exercise in exegetical polemic and, in that sense, a most traditional Primitive Baptist affair. A zealous young preacher hauled out Luke 1:1 and, as if he were the apostle himself drafting a new gospel, "laid the claim that the Primitive Baptist was the only true church of Christ." More men took the floor. A saint from Florida related his experience. He called his address "Why I Am a Primitive Baptist." An elder from Huntsville denounced the evil effects of secret societies. Another called for the development of a distinctly Primitive Baptist literature. A professor from North Carolina measured his audience. "Turn the sword to the enemy," he said. "Get together." And then in the summer Alabama heat, they saluted the London Confession of Faith like the gray English Calvinists of 1689. It was as if the old ghosts of Joshua Lawrence and C. B. Hassell had returned, strictures in tow.[37]

But these were black men and women, and they had come to Huntsville in July 1907 for the first meeting of what they called the National Primitive Baptist Convention of America (NPBC). The convention's very name advertised its ambitions, and its motto—"Union, Peace, and Progress"—glistened with optimism. According to its organizers, the convention would "uplift the Primitive Baptists of America." To do this, NPBC delegates fastened their faith to their race: "A careful consideration of the conditions and needs of the Primitive Baptists in America, and likewise the conditions and needs of the race," they asserted, "show that much has been done and much more remains to be done." They resolved to "declare education a necessity," to mandate various annual collection days to support the denomination's academies, and to build still more schools: a new industrial and theological seminary in Tallahassee, Florida, that would match the one already operating in Winston-Salem, North Carolina; a Primitive Baptist college in Mexia, Texas; and yet another denominational academy in Alabama's Black Belt. They organized a Woman's Auxiliary, a Young People's Congress, and the delightfully named Predestination Aid Society. By the time the Primitives gathered a year later for a second national meeting, this time in Nashville, Tennessee, both the AME Church and the distinctly non-Primitive National Baptist Convention sent emissaries. They each waited, though, as Nashville's mayor finished his welcoming address.[38]

C. F. Sams, a thirty-seven-year-old minister from Key West, Florida, was identified as "the originator of the movement" in the program of the first annual meeting. For seven years, he had, as one of the conventioneers put it, "labored zealously," pouring his own time and money into a monumental effort to unite black Primitive Baptists across America. In the year before the delegates descended upon Huntsville, Sams spent more than $450 of his own money (about $12,000 in 2015 dollars) on printing, postage, and travel related to organizing the convention. If the minutes from that first national meeting are to be believed, Sams's introductory sermon, "The Divine Plan of Organized Government," embraced modern science, ancient history, and the marvels of statecraft. "As a defender of the Faith, he has no equal," the minutes read. "It can be truthfully said that through this powerful sermon was the organization effected." That must have been an impressive sermon. Of course, Sams himself recorded and compiled the minutes. Into those minutes he also shoehorned photographs of his wife and four-year-old daughter. The man was not shy.[39]

Sams had emerged from a black Primitive Baptist culture in Florida that prized organizational ingenuity and peripatetic efficiency. By 1880, an association near Tallahassee ran its own Sunday schools and boasted a "chief evangelist." Associations across the state soon followed suit, and by 1901 they had banded together to form an overarching Primitive Baptist General State Convention that endorsed these same aims of education and the spread of the gospel. In the east-central part of the state, where Sams bounded between churches, black Primitives celebrated what one newspaper called their "glorious results, both spiritual and financial." Preachers raised money with an impresario's agility: gospel quartet concerts, Saturday-night entertainments arranged with community social clubs, even Easter egg hunts. A denominational newspaper launched in 1901. The editor? "The genial Rev. C. F. Sams," reported the *Daytona Gazette-News*.[40]

A similar enterprising spirit galloped through the NPBC, and if it ever flagged, Sams was there to prod it along. The first meeting in Huntsville? "That was the getting together meeting," Sams announced when they all had gathered once again, this time in Nashville. "This will be the money raising meeting." Sure enough, the convention asked for various annual membership fees that would be assessed at the individual, church, associational, and state convention levels. And delegates were offered the privilege of buying for ten cents the official convention button—the one inscribed proudly and waggishly with that image of a hard shell. "Talk is cheap," Sams wrote. "Our expenses are heavy." But this was a convention, and so talk became both currency and reward. In Huntsville, "the meeting went wild" when a keynote speaker laid out "the great future that lies before us." The theme proved irresistible. A teacher from Chattanooga—the man, in fact, who had been the first principal of the Huntsville Graded and Industrial School—made "a pledge of future triumphs." A professor from Texas showed how "to carry the Primitive Baptists to the maximum mark of intelligence."[41]

But couched among the noisy solicitations and triumphant stem-winders was Calvinism's low hum. Responsive readings leaned on the first chapter of Ephesians, rehearsing the passages on predestination that had long been Primitive Baptist favorites. A "National Hymn" composed by the effervescent Sams nonetheless voiced the trembling uncertainties of the old Primitive Baptist self. "We're weak, but Thou art strong," read the song's plea to the Almighty. "Lead these old Baptists right / Through the dark shades of strife." But if Sams's dark hymn surprises, it need not be so. Six years before the first national convention, Sams had "labored day and night" on what he and his fellows called the *Primitive Baptist Manual*, a handbook that would soon be solemnized as the National Convention's *Discipline of the Primitive Baptist Church*. The manual presented a lacquered faith—pages of polished rules and hard decrees—and what it reflected back was Calvinist orthodoxy. Original sin, total human depravity, an "eternal and particular election of a definite number of the human race, chosen in Christ before the foundation of the world," the irresistibility of God's grace, and the perseverance of the saints: it was all there under the heading "What We Believe." Preachers were told to sink into a determined course of study about predestination, justification, and the will; to turn again to the London Confession of Faith and general accounts of church history and Christian theology; to read an array of histories of the Primitive Baptists' early nineteenth-century split with missionary Baptists; and to follow the peregrinations of the Primitive Baptist soul, which meant reading, among other harrowing conversion narratives, the autobiography of Rebecca Phillips, who had wondered two generations earlier whether anyone could "fathom or control the human mind," for she knew she could not.[42]

Yet the white Rebecca Phillips was, at best, a peripheral female figure in NPBC churches where black women struggled for their own kind of control over spiritual matters. In each church, a woman—usually a longtime member—held the office of "church mother," an elected position whose responsibilities reflected the ambiguities of women's status in meetinghouses with predominantly female lay memberships and exclusively male clerical leaderships. In white-run Primitive churches, the office of church mother did not exist. Throughout the nineteenth century, white Primitive Baptist women had largely been content to rely on the church for sisterly affection while their men fortified themselves on Pauline staples, such as the dark warnings about "silly women." The national black Primitives also read their Paul, though they thumbed other passages. They pointed out that Paul praised Phebe, the "deaconess" of the church at Cenchrea. And did she not succor many, they asked, including Paul himself? And should we spurn the Philippian women who labored side by side with Paul? Certainly, they concluded, the church mothers in Huntsville and Daytona Beach had forebears in the earliest churches, and like their predecessors in the ancient world, these church mothers took "the watchcare of [all] the members." Still, their motherly roles meant that these women fell into conventionally female occupations: visiting the sick, tending to the churches' sisterhood, and, alas, keeping the meetinghouse in order. "They shall see that the church is kept clean and that pulpit is kept in order," read the *Primitive Baptist Manual* that Sams and his male colleagues had authored. It is difficult to read the manual's decorous, stodgy prose and not hear in it a tragic call to domestic service, precisely the same kind of menial work African American women were largely confined to *outside* of church. But it would be a mistake to conclude that the unrelenting social order of the Jim Crow South had imprisoned national black Primitive churches. For in the legalese of the manual, these black Primitives revealed themselves. Phebe, the model church mother, was in their language a "deaconess." But the language of their Bible—and for these black Primitives, like their white counterparts, it was the King James Version only—described Phebe not as a deaconess but as a "servant," a word that the men who compiled this handbook clearly would not abide. Instead, they turned to the New Testament's original Greek, where they found Phebe described as a *diakonos*, the same word used to describe male deacons.[43]

It may be foolish to make too much of lexical vetoes such as this one, yet the Primitives' linguistic choices always seem handpicked. For example, in the minutes to their first national convention meeting, they sometimes referred to their organization as the National *Colored* Primitive Baptist Convention of America, but by the next year, they had banished "Colored" from their name. And then, when language alone would not do, they sang themselves into the nation's history with their "National Rally Song," a paean to Primitive perseverance sung to the tune of the "The Battle Hymn of the Republic," as if these black Old School Baptist saints had donned Union blues and the nation's destiny lay at their feet:

> They unfurl the Primitive Banner and behold the thousand rise.
> They are looking in prayer to Him enthroned beyond the skies.
> They are lifting up their brother from ruin where he lies.
> Our cause is marching on.[44]

Rock Daniel Till I Die

What Annie Marion MacLean had witnessed, though she did not know it—what she had heard and seen at the St. Annis Primitive Baptist Church in DeLand, Florida, in 1902 when the saints were "Rocking Daniel"—was a ring shout, the circle dance ceremony that African slaves had brought with them through the Middle Passage. The pastor at the St. Annis church was none other than C. F. Sams, the exuberant innovator who helped launch the National Primitive movement. But clearly, when Sams and his people walked into the future they had fashioned for themselves, they moved to the ancient rhythms of the Afro-Baptist past. The hitching and shuffling, the quickening pace, the counterclockwise movement, the call-and-response singing, the multiple rhythms and meters born of hand clapping and sliding-gliding-stomping footwork: all the features of the St. Annis Primitives' "Rocking Daniel" of 1902 could have been found centuries earlier coursing through the various forms of the circle ritual performed by the Igbo, the Akan, the Mende, and so many other ethnic groups in West and Central Africa. In its African contexts, the circle ritual cemented the connections between the dancers and their ancestors, between the singers and their gods. On American soil, the ritual—eventually dubbed the "ring shout"—continued to shoulder those responsibilities while taking on others. Students of the shout have variously described it as "the principal context in which black creativity occurred," "the foremost means by which a sense of community was forged among the [enslaved] African-based population," "a principal mechanism by which Africans of varying ethnicities were able to span their differences," "the foundation of Afro-American music," and "a two-way bridge connecting the core of West African religions—possession by the gods—to the core of evangelical Protestantism—experience of conversion." The ring shout, it seems, was a cultural dynamo. It transformed Africans into African Americans and sutured the cultural wound that had lain bleeding since the Middle Passage had sundered slaves from their ancestral lands.[45]

"Rock Daniel," too, has been a meaning-making powerhouse. As a song, it has led a fugitive existence, bellowed in a Delta church house in 1941 while the folklorist's disc-cutting machine whirred in the background and burnished to a metallic shine in a Harlem jazz club just a few years later before disappearing for three decades, only to resurface first as a sun-dappled Bahamian ditty and then, at the turn of the twenty-first century, as a jazzed-up melody used to sell Uncle Ben's rice. In the 1930s, a black gospel singer recalled how her once-enslaved grandmother used "Rock Daniel" as a generic name for the slaves' "holy dance." The late folklorist Alan Lomax described "Rock Daniel" as a particular instance of a ring-shout song. His colleagues John Work, Samuel Adams, and Lewis Jones endorsed that view, though they also noted that "Rock Daniel" occasionally slipped the circle ceremony to appear at "church entertainments, at quiltings, and at house parties" as a partner dance. In these instances, men and women would put their hands on each other's shoulders and "have a rock." (That certainly sounds chaste, though it is worth pointing out that one song collector moving through low country South Carolina in the 1920s noted "the sensual rocking motion of the hips at the command 'rock, Daniel, rock.'") Meanwhile, the black Baptists whom all of these folklorists spoke with in the early 1940s told them the song was an "old-time slavery song," an "old jubilee song," an "old spiritual" that conjured up visions of slavery's dark times and of Daniel in the lions' den because those old struggles were, as a Mississippi preacher told Lomax, "the same trouble that we are going through now" in the Jim Crow South. Closer to our own time, the McIntosh County Shouters, who bill themselves as "perhaps the last, active practitioners" of the ring shout, have performed a version of the song—theirs is called "Move, Daniel"—whose meaning, they say, lies in the mundane realities of slave life and not, as one might suppose, in the apocalyptic visions of a biblical prophet. "See, Daniel was a slave, and the slaves all were havin' a little party across the field one day," recalled the group's leader. "The smokehouse was up there . . . and they send Daniel in to get a piece of meat so they could put the party on sure enough! And old boss was coming down through there so the slaves going to sing a song to let Daniel know to get out the way." Here, the ancient ring, the rattling plantation praise house, the clandestine brush arbor meeting—all of these have vanished, and the sung command to "Rock, Daniel, rock," or to "Move, Daniel, move Daniel," is simply a coded instruction to hide from the slave driver.[46]

Despite—or, perhaps, because of—this legion of possibilities, the meaning of the St. Annis Primitives' dance remains opaque. When Professor MacLean asked the church members about the origins of what they called "Rocking Daniel," they and their usually voluble pastor remained mute.[47] Maybe when they rocked Daniel, they, like the Mississippi Baptists who spoke to Alan Lomax in 1941 about their own "Rock Daniel," summoned their ancestors' travails, poured out their souls' complaints, and pictured some future moment, beyond calendared time, when they would "slip and slide" down heaven's streets like a band of Lindy-Hopping angels. Three times for each refrain, they sang:

I'm gonna tell my Lord.	(Daniel)
How you do me here.	(Daniel)
This ain't none of my home.	(Daniel)
Put on your moving shoes.	(Daniel)
Slip and slide the street.	(Daniel)

Or was it that the St. Annis shout was, as the McIntosh County Shouters have suggested, simply a sliver of musical code—a song about the necessities and pleasures of "puttin' on ole massa"—engrafted onto the hoary trunk of the traditional communion service? Perhaps, though, between these two interpretive poles—one about prophetic deliverance from this world, the other about day-to-day existence in it—lies a third possibility.

All the versions of "Daniel," whether they unfolded outside the smokehouse or inside the meetinghouse, whether they addressed a divine interlocutor or a fellow slave, whether they spoke about heavenly deliverance or earthly trials, whether performed on the Cotton Club's stage or in front of a church pulpit, were fundamentally about movement. In Mississippi, the saints sang quite literally about leaving the world below for a better home above. The McIntosh County Shouters' version operates as a kind of pantomime with the leader issuing commands that the shouters follow. "Go the other way, Daniel," the leader sings, and the shouters reverse direction. A command to "do the eagle wing, Daniel" unspools the shouters' arms. Other "Daniel" variations also lyrically evoke the hitching shuffle of the ring shout. In Sister Rosetta Tharpe's version, recorded with Lucky Millinder's rhythm and blues big band in the 1940s, the singer called the saints to order at "a meeting tonight" so they could "straighten out the business at hand." What business? We do not know; it was left unnamed. But something was crooked, and here was how Tharpe proposed to make it right:

> We are going to learn a new thing *(repeated three times)*
> A rhythm and a rock, and a rock got rhythm
>
> We come out tonight (Rock Daniel) *(repeated three times)*
> Oh, oh, oh (Rock Daniel)
>
> No, it ain't no harm (Rock Daniel) *(repeated three times)*
> Oh, oh, oh (Rock Daniel)

The real business at hand, then, *was* "Rock Daniel." That was why the saints had gathered—to learn a new rhythm, to learn to rock, to move. "Come and rock (Rock Daniel)," Tharpe and her chorus sang. "Rock, rock, rock, rock, rock Daniel." Like an earlier era's "Jump Jim Crow" or a later generation's "The Twist," Tharpe's "Rock Daniel" was an invitation to perform the "dance" it named. Her lyrics laid bare the churning logic behind all the versions of the "Rock Daniel" shout.[48]

So though the St. Annis Primitives remained tight-lipped about the precise meaning of "Rocking Daniel," their shout spoke for them. It bespoke a religion of movement and perseverance, a religion like the one that could march gallantly through Huntsville's streets each spring and sedulously reinvent itself at a national convention each summer. The song itself was a kind of self-activating prayer, a call to action, a set of instructions that referred back to itself like some recursive incantation: keep moving, keep shouting, keep rocking, keep the circle together and never stop, not until you die, not until your people are delivered, not until they reach the promised land.

5   The Lonesome Sound

Several years ago, W. J. Cash lodged himself in my mind. He was like an uninvited houseguest; I could not get rid of the old man. Or perhaps I should say, I could not rid myself of the old man's ideas, especially his strange and beguiling contention in his 1941 book, *The Mind of the South*, that a Calvinist "feeling" had come to dominate the southern mind. Cash described how besieged southerners took refuge beneath a makeshift Calvinism and its omnipotent God. "The South would have a Baptist Church, a Presbyterian Church, a Methodist Church of its own," he wrote. "But this Southern Methodist Church would be one which was not strictly Methodist any more. For as the pressure of the Yankee increased, the whole South, including the Methodists, would move toward a position of thoroughgoing Calvinism in feeling if not in formal theology . . . everybody did come increasingly, and without regard for his traditional creed, to think and speak of Him as being primarily the imperious master of a puppet-show. Every man was in his place because He had set him there. Everything was as it was because He had ordained it so."[1] Like much of Cash, this passage managed to be at once immoderate and insufficient. This was Calvinism disguised as fatalism, and Cash's "everybody" referred only to white southerners since it was only they, presumably, who, forced by "the pressure of the Yankee," sought justification for the South's racial caste system in the inscrutable doings of their "imperious master."

Despite such flaws, Cash proves useful to think "with" and not just think against. And Cash, I should note, has not been alone in suspecting that a Calvinist mood, rooted in the folkways of the Primitive Baptists, exerted an inordinate cultural influence. In his 1972 classic, *A Religious History of the American People*, Sydney Ahlstrom noted that though Primitives numbered more than 120,000 by 1890, "Hard-Shell tendencies were far more pervasive than these figures suggest." The Primitives, Ahlstrom wrote, "won acceptance for Hard-Shell doctrines among countless persons and churches who never became affiliated with Primitive Baptist associations." And so I, too, began to wonder if something like a Calvinist feeling had, in fact, seeped into the South's cultural life and, if so, where I could find

Music discussed in this chapter can be heard at the author's website: strangersbelow.net.

it. Would it be possible to write that history if it existed? How would I describe religious changes that were not necessarily reflected in creedal statements and denominational demographics? What happened when a theology, already bent and abraded by centuries of adaptation, slumped into decline? Would it molder, or would some part of it linger like a fantastic rocky outcropping on an eroded plain? Or might its energies release and reconstitute themselves in new and surprising ways?[2]

As so often happens with fanciful questions, the answers arrived in just about the most mundane way possible. I found them in my Volkswagen. On the radio, to be precise. They arrived while I was listening to "O Death," a chilling a cappella deathbed plea chanted out by the elderly bluegrass musician Ralph Stanley. Hearing that song on country music radio will make the mind turn. I was not the only one arrested by Stanley's performance. Soon it would win Stanley a 2002 Grammy Award for best male country vocal, and at last count it had sold a stupefying total of more than 9 million copies. Fans and critics alike rhapsodized about Stanley's voice. (They still do.) It was haunting and ghostly and otherworldly, they said over and over again. And, above all, it was real. But the enthusiasm for Stanley's prowess substituted for elucidation of it. I knew that something similar, though on a much smaller scale, had happened a generation earlier when an until-then unknown singer from eastern Kentucky, Roscoe Holcomb, made a splash among folk revival audiences. Holcomb's music had stunned me when I first heard it in the late 1990s while ringing people up at the register of a Los Angeles record store, but I cannot say that Holcomb had been much on my mind until that evening, several years later, when something in Stanley's quavering rendition of "O Death" sent me scrambling back to him—to his elastic and unaccompanied "I Am a Man of Constant Sorrow," a song that shared its anguish and slender hope both with "O Death" and with the experiences of the old Primitive Baptists about whom I was just beginning to learn. The connection I sensed that evening is this chapter's conceit: Holcomb's and Stanley's popularity marked the eruption into American popular culture—on LPs, in movies, and through a car stereo's speakers—of a Calvinist feeling, a lonesome sound, that had, by all rights, been buried at least a century before.

Now Calvinism had not exactly vanished by the mid-twentieth century, but even as early as the eve of the Civil War, increasing numbers of Americans had concluded that they could not abide notions such as original sin or human depravity. Or, as Catharine Beecher succinctly put it, "*there must be a dreadful mistake somewhere*" when it came to consigning obviously good people to hell simply because they had died—accidentally, no less—in an unregenerate state. In these years, Calvinist orthodoxy came for Beecher and so many other Americans to sound like the "senseless jargon of election and reprobation." Calvinists themselves slipped into endless squabbling to, in the historian Mark Noll's terse summation, "self-immolation."[3]

In the lonesome sounds of Stanley and Holcomb we hear Calvinism's strange return and inevitable transformation. The texture of Stanley's and Holcomb's singing recalls the older voices from the Primitive past, of men and women who thought the mistake lay not with religious doctrine but inside themselves. Remember Thomas Hill, who felt himself to be "a stranger in a strange place," a man "standing on a narrow point of time"; Mary Bristow, chased for years by "gloomy phantoms" even in gayest company; Lee Hanks, who was "alone in every sense of the word"; Sarah Ann Hollister, who trembled with uncertainty about the authenticity of her vision of Jesus; Joshua Lawrence, who scoured his soul "until I doubt almost every thing, and can believe nothing concerning myself, but what is bad"; and J. H. Purifoy, who, assailed by withering doubts and unable to trust his own senses, spent thirty years begging a silent God for moments of respite. Stanley and Holcomb brought these voices back to life, and their audiences sensed that an exhumation was taking place even if they remained blind to the details. No longer hardened doctrine or the subject of contention in a fight over evangelicalism's future, Calvinism was free to become a feeling, a mood—a lonesome sound whose echoes connected audiences to the past even while signaling their distance from it.[4]

How to Sing a Really Lonesome Song

It was as if they had met a ghost. Or a prophet. For sure, though, the man was a "visionary" and his appearance before them something "miraculous." He spoke softly, his speech unfurling like lines of poetry. He spoke about the meaning of life, of raw "experience," of violence and poverty and loneliness, too. And then he walked away, leaving them to ponder his greatness. He had come to them, they knew, from a better place, "from a time and place before the race of Americans had fallen." There would be other visitations: in basements and college hallways, outside East Village cafés, and backstage in Bremen, Germany. A notable one—a "spiritual experience" was how the young folksinger later described it—took place in a New York City loft. That was when Bob Dylan met Roscoe Holcomb.[5]

That these awesome encounters were with a fifty-something-year-old unemployed construction worker from the mountains of eastern Kentucky may at first seem strange, but something in Holcomb—a bony, retiring man who, when he was away from his Kentucky home, as he invariably was during these meetings, wore horn-rimmed glasses, a beige fedora atop his thinning hair, and a neat suit with a thin tie and had about him the appearance, if not quite the temperament, of an old encyclopedia salesman—provoked raptures. To 1960s folk festival audiences and to the handful of musicians, producers, and fans who met him, Holcomb seemed to be everything: ancient yet not bound by time, a specimen of Appalachian poverty and a universal symbol of struggle, the embodiment of yellowing tradition and an avatar of the future.

And Holcomb's sound? It, too, was a kind of miracle, a collection of opposites without contradictions. "So archaic, and so abstractly avant garde" was how the folk music enthusiast John Pankake put it after hearing Holcomb perform at the 1961 University of Chicago Folk Festival. Bob Dylan heard in Holcomb's voice "a certain untamed sense of control." The fiddler Howard Armstrong also heard categorical and temporal distinctions crumble under the pressure of Holcomb's sound. "Roscoe only plays the music itself," Armstrong said. "The rest of us—Beethoven, Bach, Louis Armstrong—put in our decorations and ornaments. Roscoe just plays the music straight without any of that other stuff." Praise like this fell upon Holcomb like a vitalizing rain, showering him with encomiums that singled out his music's naked power and heralded its unique status as an art of both wisdom and guilessness.[6]

In the late 1990s and early 2000s, as Holcomb's music migrated belatedly onto compact disc, listeners heard and felt much as they had more than a generation earlier. Fans and critics alike described the music as "intense, raw." It "pushe[d] the envelope—not to the next step, but back to the foundations, way back in time." It "was radical, and avant-garde, as well as being hard core and rock bottom." It was "Shakespeare without the comic relief . . . an opportunity to experience the very depths of another person's being, undisguised by artifice but nevertheless great art." The man himself was "a living archetype" of a nearly vanished Appalachian past. He was practically the undead.[7]

But in all the critical and popular commentary surrounding Holcomb, it has been the word "lonesome," above all others, that has come to signify his sound. It was there already in those first dispatches in *Sing Out!* about an unnamed Kentucky folksinger and the "wild and lonesome sound he gets." John Cohen, the young folk revivalist who wrote that early report in 1960 after he "discovered" Holcomb deep in a Kentucky holler, soon coined the phrase "the high lonesome sound" to encapsulate Holcomb's style. Within a few years, the coinage gave its name to a Cohen documentary, a Holcomb album, and eventually an entire genre of music, bluegrass, that Holcomb never played.[8]

The high lonesome sound. That once-ripe phrase spoiled long ago, reduced to a cliché summoned to describe nearly any kind of string band music played by white people. But that expression—the high lonesome sound—still has much to tell us, as do the billows of repetitive but ardent reactions to Holcomb's music cited above. They signal listeners' fascination with Holcomb's person and sound—a fascination that could at times seem like the aural equivalent of gawking but more often signified either a deep longing for, or a fleeting yet sincere identification with, the yearning and struggle in Holcomb's voice. Listeners have heard something of themselves in Holcomb, or at least something worthy of aspiration. In their fascination with Holcomb's drawn visage and, especially, his piercing voice—those attributes of his that made him seem a relic and sound so raw—listeners have somehow, even as they remained largely unaware of the historical and cultural particulars, imaginatively connected with sources of Holcomb's sound, which lay in the dispositions and beliefs of dissenting Protestants reaching back to the seventeenth century. In this admittedly enigmatic way, Holcomb's singing smuggled into postwar America's college campuses, cafés, and folk festivals a Calvinistic sense of longing, struggle, and defiance that had largely vanished from the American landscape. But listeners, ignorant for the most part of the abstruse particulars of Calvinist history and the development of what late eighteenth-century critics were already describing as the "Old Way" of singing, were free to hear instead a more abstract or existential loneliness, a lonesomeness that fit their era even if it was summoned from another.

By the time anyone outside of eastern Kentucky encountered Roscoe Holcomb and his music, they also had met, whether they knew it or not, John Cohen. In 1959 Cohen became Holcomb's discoverer and, after a fashion, his manager. He arranged Holcomb's recording sessions, booked his stage appearances, and produced his albums. He shot the documentary-style photographs of Holcomb that adorned his records' covers, and he wrote the studious liner notes tucked inside. Cohen was a musician, too. He played guitar in the New Lost City Ramblers, organized hootenannies during his undergraduate years at Yale, and gathered with the other young "folkniks" at the Sunday sings in New York City's Washington Square Park. John Cohen was a folk revivalist. He also was, to use the historian Benjamin Filene's apt term, a "cultural middleman," whose tastes and choices of whom to document, record, and publicize inevitably shaped the folk traditions he sought to preserve. It is in this sense, then, that Holcomb became Cohen's discovery and creation. Their meeting happened by chance outside the lumber camp of Daisy, Kentucky, during the summer of 1959. Cohen was scavenging eastern Kentucky's mountains for Depression-era songs that he and his bandmates could include on an upcoming album. Having exhausted his list of local musicians, Cohen, on a whim, pointed his car down a dirt road, ran into a man he had recorded the night before, and decided to listen to him play again. After awhile, "a little guy," Cohen said, wandered in. It was Holcomb, and he offered up a song. The Roscoe Holcomb of the folk revival—the iconic Holcomb, the one with the etched face and gnarled hands, the man holding his banjo in front of a wooden shed and staring into the camera, the one whose image became emblematic of Appalachia—did not appear until a year later. Cohen was right by his side.[9]

It was then that Cohen's Kentucky field recordings, including a half dozen made on Holcomb's front porch, found their way onto *Mountain Music of Kentucky*, a Folkways Records release that set the terms for Holcomb's public reception. Cohen conceived of the LP as what we would now call a multimedia experience, in which a collection of music, text, and images would immerse listeners in the culture and history of eastern Kentucky. The record came packaged with a suitably grave booklet that upon first glance looked like something from the photographic arm of Franklin D. Roosevelt's Farm Security Administration. After Cohen's introductory notes and transcriptions of the song texts, there were fifteen pages of black-and-white prints with spare titles (usually just the place name where the photograph was taken) and no commentary. Cohen's photographs amplified his liner notes (overshadowed them, really) and, seen together, portrayed Perry County, Kentucky, as a place of empty spaces and grueling labor. Meanwhile, Cohen's notes grounded the music in eastern Kentucky's cultural traditions and longstanding poverty. The music, he noted, was homemade and raw, recorded on front porches and in kitchens and living rooms. There were no second takes. The musicians were tradition bearers. Cohen described them holding the old styles close, nurturing them, even modifying them occasionally while jukeboxes and rock 'n' roll radio stations cawed in the background. "I did not sense that this old musical tradition in Kentucky is a dying one," he wrote. "Rather it is changing and continuing while maintaining much of its earlier character." The musicians were skilled, but not too skilled. The most supple of them had left to seek riches elsewhere. "As soon as they get good," Cohen wrote, "they move out to the big cities to try to earn a living with their music if possible."[10]

Roscoe Holcomb as talisman. Photo by John Cohen. Courtesy of the Ralph Rinzler Folklife Archives and Collections, Washington, D.C.

As for Holcomb in particular, Cohen created what he later described as a "talisman image." Included in the photograph collection and also emblazoned on the album's cover was the now-iconic picture of Holcomb: the rutted face with black-framed glasses, the sleeves of his work shirt rolled up above his elbows, his muscular arms reaching toward the five-string banjo slung over his shoulder, the stiff pose in front of the clapboard shack, and, most powerfully, the steady, interrogatory gaze that seemed to make Holcomb a cousin to the Alabama sharecropping family Walker Evans had famously photographed more than twenty years earlier. In his notes, Cohen described Holcomb in ways that would soon become familiar: Holcomb "makes his living with his hands" and, though little appreciated by his neighbors, his "music has become a deeper means towards a lonely and passionate artistic expression." Here, then, were the basic terms upon which Holcomb would be understood by revival audiences. He was an outcast, a symbol of Appalachian poverty and defiance, and an ancient craftsman. "Like it or not," Cohen explained, "my task was to shape Roscoe's image."[11]

Cohen's image-making continued when Holcomb took the stage to perform for audiences in the urban North. Along with Ralph Rinzler and Israel Young, Cohen founded the Friends of Old Time Music (FOTM), an

Bud Fields and his family at home. Photo by Walker Evans. Courtesy of the Library of Congress, Prints and Photographs Division, FSA/OWI Collection, LC-DIG-ppmsc-00234.

organization dedicated to introducing traditional southern musicians to New York City's folk music enthusiasts. Holcomb, they decided, would top the bill at their first concert in February 1961. That concert, like the thirteen others that followed over the next four years, was something more than a musical exhibition. It was both refuge and celebration, a place that would, as Rinzler observed, "satisfy both the capacity of the performer and the appetite of the audience" by honoring the "real article"—the authentic artist—rather than commercial imitators. But Cohen and his fellow organizers conceived the FOTM concerts not only as a bulwark against the lacquered tones of commercial folk musicians such as Harry Belafonte and the Kingston Trio but also as a means to differentiate themselves from two older factions in the folk song movement: the politically motivated bloc most closely identified with Pete Seeger and tied ideologically to the Popular Front of the 1930s, and the collectors of folk-song-as-art-song who, like John Jacob Niles, might sing "John Henry" with an opera-house vibrato. The modern folk song movement, Cohen wrote in 1959, dwelled "no longer on social reform" but was instead "focused more on a search for real and human values." "We are looking within ourselves," he continued, and not "for someone to lead us."[12]

Holcomb was ideally suited to meet the goals of the FOTM and, by extension, the urban folk audience who bought his records and attended his concerts. His very life qualified him. He hailed from Appalachia, was poor, and looked even older than his fifty-some-odd years, and his body was compromised from years spent in the mines and a lumber mill where he had broken his back. He sang about murdered lovers, moonshining, orphans, and graveyards. He was someone revival audiences could believe in. He was the "real article," as Rinzler put it, which is another way of saying that Holcomb was transparently sincere (not an ideologue or a commercial showman) and therefore the ideal vehicle for legitimizing Cohen's modern folk song movement. "'Sincerity,'" wrote Pierre Bourdieu in his discussion of how artistic value is created, "is only possible—and only achieved—where there is a perfect and immediate harmony between the expectations inscribed in the position occupied (in a less consecrated universe, one would say 'the job description') and the dispositions of the occupant."[13] Holcomb, as Cohen quickly realized, fit the job description perfectly: "1959 was a time when the 'vision' of the urban Folk Revival was in need of 'revision,' and Roscoe's music presented me with the weapon to achieve a change in that perception."[14]

It is difficult to know for certain, but it seems that Holcomb consented to, if not collaborated in, Cohen's image making. One thing we do know: Holcomb's wife, Ethel, and many of his neighbors loathed Cohen's now-ubiquitous photo of Holcomb standing in front of his shed. As far they were concerned, it was a naked piece of exploitation. Holcomb himself was unfazed: "You see, we live in these old mountains here and we've been raised up pretty rough and a lot of them does the best they can and they take it as if you take the worst you can find to make a picture to take back to New York to show the people. That's the way a lot them feel about it. *Course it don't matter with me.*"[15]

None of this was sinister. Cohen wanted to close the gap between traditional southern musicians and their urban audiences. He offered himself up—naively, idealistically—as the bridge. In doing so, he of course participated in the longstanding Western cultural dialectic between country and city of which the postwar folk revival was but one instance. The stink of exploitation often rose from this cultural traffic between city and country, between, in this case, rural Appalachia and urban America. But the back and forth also could be imaginatively productive, if not always well mannered. In this instance, the key point is that the context of Holcomb's presentation enhanced, rather than swamped, his sound. Listeners were prepared to hear in Holcomb something deeply unfamiliar and yet powerfully magnetic, something that came from without yet reflected their deepest selves. The question was, "Would he deliver?"[16]

Roscoe Holcomb played the blues, frailed his banjo at square dances, picked his guitar to a lyric about Cincinnati's Coney Isle amusement park, bent notes on his mouth harp, set British broadside ballads to musical accompaniment, learned tunes first cut on 78 rpm records by Ida Cox and Bessie Smith, worshipped at a Holiness church, and sang the old lined-out hymns he first heard as a child in Old Regular Baptist meetinghouses. He even on occasion scraped a fiddle. Leafing through such a diverse repertoire, one is tempted to describe Holcomb as a songster, a jack-of-all-musical-trades. But the label does not quite fit. Holcomb demonstrated neither the showmanship of an old-time songster such as Uncle Dave Macon or the studied professionalism of his contemporary Doc Watson on the folk festival circuit. Without these presentational tools at his disposal, Holcomb might have had only a short-lived stint on revival stages. Instead, he performed for nearly twenty years, and his music found its way onto a handful of solo albums and several compilations.

Holcomb's voice carried him and drew listeners toward him. That voice was a singular instrument: reedy and compressed, its tones pooling deep in his chest but ringing out as if they had been ejected directly from the back of his throat or deflected, laser-like, off his hard palate. And as observers never failed to point out, Holcomb pitched his voice high. This piercing combination of timbre and pitch defined Holcomb's singing.

In his early conversations with Cohen, Holcomb regularly described his sound as lonesome. Cohen, then, took the musician's cue when he hit upon the phrase "the high lonesome sound" to describe Holcomb's music. According to the bluegrass historian Neil Rosenberg, Cohen used the word "high" as a synonym for "very" or "extremely" and not—or, at least, not only—as a descriptor of pitch: "Cohen had heard the title of a song, 'High Lonesome,' an obscure early recording by the Country Gentlemen. Though there was no mountain or aural image in the song—composer John Duffey had used the word *high* as a synonym for a more common intensifier, *really*—the unusual combination of words appealed to Cohen."[17]

It is, of course, Bill Monroe's music, not Holcomb's, that is most often defined as "the high lonesome sound." Indeed, for many fans and critics, the phrase signifies bluegrass music itself and calls up in an instant all of the music's totemic images—the little cabin on the hill, the old mountain church, blue moons, rocky tops, and happy valleys. And why not? Those keening vocal harmonies are as important to bluegrass music as are its breakneck banjo rolls and rapid-fire mandolin lines.

But Monroe's lonesomeness was not Holcomb's. They were different by kind and degree. Consider, first, that listeners heard them differently. Monroe's voice has been analogized to an oboe, a pearl, an air horn, and fresh cream, while Holcomb's whine most often elicited comparisons to dark moods, not things: eerie, taut, deathly, chilling. Monroe's voice was polished (like that pearl), finely tuned (like that oboe), powerful, and necessarily capable of the fierce precision demanded of the bluegrass singer. Bluegrass music, said Monroe, was like "putting a motor together."[18]

Monroe's weeping wail in a Blue Grass Boys song was fundamentally sentimental, rooted in the traditions of the hillbilly "heart song," which was itself tied to the tenderhearted Victorian parlor song. Here parted lovers pine for each other in waltz time:

> No answer to my love letter
> To soothe my aching heart
> Why did God ever permit
> True love like ours to part

Or the singer, exiled from domestic bliss, can only sit home alone and wonder:

> What is a home without a baby
> To love and to tease and adore?
> What is a home without a sweet wife
> To kiss you each night at the door?
> What is a home without sunshine
> To spread its bright rays from above?
> You can have wealth and its pleasures
> But what is a home without love?

Or the widower struggles to take comfort in the memories of his lost love:

> It seems I'll never more see you
> Till we meet in Heaven it seems
> But I hold you close to my heart love
> In my beautiful memories and dreams

Often when the singer's situation grows more grave, such as in "Roane County Prison," where the townspeople shun him before the jury declares him guilty, he still finds comfort in family:

> When the train pulled out poor mother stood weepin'
> And sister she sat all alone with a sigh
> And the last words I heard was "Willy God bless you"
> Was "Willy God bless you, God bless you, goodbye"[19]

These lyrical themes echoed in the rising and falling action of Monroe's singing. In his discussion of Monroe's vocal technique, Robert Cantwell has explained that the texture of Monroe's voice evoked "a sweet bereavement, a kind of homesickness," as it scaled sonic heights and then, like a receding siren, sailed away: "What Monroe is doing is cleaving his voice to certain *terrestrial* laws, at once overcoming and being overcome by them . . . and thereby provoking an inestimable sensation of loss of the summit to which we have become emotionally and musically, deeply committed." This was Monroe's high lonesome sound: a sonic drama of achievement and loss that mimicked the sentimental dramas played out in the lyrics of his songs.[20]

Then again, how lonely, really, is the bluegrass singer? Even when the meter speeds up and the singer seems only to exist as an isolated traveler in a decaying landscape—

> I'm on my way back to the old home
> The road winds on up the hill
> But there's no light in the window
> That shined long ago where I live[21]

—his loneliness is tethered, for bluegrass music is an ensemble sound and the singer performs his lonesomeness within the embrace of his band. Alan Lomax deemed bluegrass an orchestral music, and those who saw the Blue Grass Boys perform would agree, I think, that Monroe's presence—standing at center stage costumed like a southern planter and driving his band with his mandolin—bespoke authority much like a tuxedoed conductor poised, baton in hand, before his armada of woodwinds, strings, and brass.

Holcomb, by contrast, seemed the embodiment of solitary struggle. It was not just his gaunt appearance or the fact that he, a man of average height, reported his weight in 1964 as 116 pounds. Those who perused Cohen's liner notes knew that Holcomb's biography read like an inventory of hardships. He had loaded coal in the mines, broken his back working in a lumber mill, picked up highway construction jobs when he could find them, and was, by the time they saw him perform, unable to work because his body would not allow it: "I thought I was getting better but it was just a thought. I wasn't. That's what got me worried. If I's to get a job I couldn't hold it—be more worries. Man just as soon have his brains shot out as to be in that condition, the way I feel." Religious crisis also gripped him. He had at one point spent ten years away from his banjo and guitar because the Old Regular Baptist church in which he was raised despised musical instruments for their associations with frivolity and iniquity. Finally, after a decade away from his instruments, Holcomb began attending the nearby Holiness church, where he could play guitar. It proved difficult, however, to shed his guilt. In the early 1960s, he told Cohen that he continued to "get disgusted and think sometimes I'll quit [playing music] anyway."[22]

Holcomb's singing voice amplified his biography so that even those listeners unfamiliar with the details of life would nevertheless hear an aural representation of it. Holcomb chose, as Cohen has pointed out, to pitch his songs at the very top of his vocal register, ensuring that he needed to strain to hit his notes. Even the unbearably shrill notes of "In the Pines" were not reached by using a falsetto. There was, then, in his songs a built-in yearning—sonically encoded—no matter the topic. Many bluegrass musicians achieve a similar effect. Some of Monroe's former sidemen tell stories of their erstwhile boss practicing songs before a performance by pitching them a half tone higher than he had sung them just the night before. But successful bluegrass singers always hit their notes even as they preserve a dramatic tension between the notes sung and their ability to reach them. In bluegrass singing, to hit the wrong notes or to hit the right notes too easily constitutes failure. A Holcomb performance was far more elastic. In the first place, Holcomb's vocal phrasing, as on "Little Maggie," was malleable, with vowels smeared across the staff while his fingers traced an insistent rhythm on banjo. Here, as with many of his performances, the meter was tied more to Holcomb's breath than to a consistent beat. So pinched were his tones and so stretched were his phrasings that some critics complained they could not understand a word of what he was singing. Holcomb replied that the sound mattered more than the individual lyric: "The music is saying just the same as I am saying, otherwise what good is it?" It is, perhaps, an obvious point but one still worth emphasizing: Holcomb's approach foregrounded the voice, even creating the illusion of untethering it—for a few beats here and few phrases there—from the instrumental accompaniment. The combined effect is one of momentary aural dislocation, or, rather, a series of such moments: a man singing impossibly high, lyrics that seem disconnected from standard phrasing, a sense of vocal and instrumental lines moving not only to different pulses but on entirely different plains. One hears this most dramatically on Holcomb's "Across the Rocky Mountain," in which with each breath he stretched vowels over several bars atop buzzing guitar: "Aaaaaaaaaaaaaaaaacross the rocky mountain, I walked for miles and miiiiiiiiiiiles / Across the rocky mountaiiiiiiiiiiin, I walked for miles and miles." Here Holcomb used an unusual open G tuning in which he tuned his lowest string up to G so that the same note rang out from both his fifth and sixth strings. As his thumb rained down on the top string a drone swelled up from the persistent thump-thump, and Holcomb's voice rose even above that before breaking off, like a balloon floating in the air and then bursting.[23]

That taut soaring voice possessed a history. It was always Holcomb's own but it was, too, an inheritance collected during childhood while attending Old Regular Baptist church services. The Old Regular Baptists sang hymns in high voice like other Old-Time Baptist sects. In the 1920s, for example, an early song collector in the Appalachians noted the "weird effect" achieved by Primitive Baptist singers, especially women, who "pitch[ed] the air an octave too high." One can still find a similar style of high-pitched hymn singing among the Calvinistic, Gaelic-speaking residents of the Hebrides. Both the southern Highlanders and the Scotch islanders were the inheritors of a style of unaccompanied psalm singing rooted in the reformed Protestant sects of the seventeenth century and stubbornly preserved through the years, often along Calvinist principles. High pitch, however, was only one of several key features in a style that early eighteenth-century psalm books already referred to as the "Old Way." Slow tempos, nearly imperceptible rhythms, nasality, the addition of extra pitches or so-called ornaments, a precentor whose job it was to "line out" the hymn to his illiterate congregation before they sang it back to him—these were all Old Way singing traits found in, say, a seventeenth-century Scottish parish church and an Old Regular Baptist meetinghouse in eastern Kentucky just after the First World War. Conventional harmony was rare as congregations sang as one but with individual voices falling in and out of phase depending on each singer's breath or taste. The folk singer Jean Ritchie, who grew up attending an Old Regular Baptist church not far from where Holcomb lived, recalled hymn singing "that rose and crashed with the majesty and immensity of great mountainous waves on the ocean," a description that, when you think about it, sums up Holcomb's high lonesome sound quite well.[24]

In the nineteenth century, the Old Regulars and their Primitive cousins preserved the Old Way of singing as a stream of trained singing masters (think of them as musical missionaries) traveled the nation preaching a gospel of part harmony, note reading (including shape notes), "purity and fullness" of tone, and ear-catching melodies. A century earlier, Anglican and Congregational reformers had introduced organs and trained choirs to codify "regular" psalm singing, which used the conventions of art music to "improve" worship and, it was thought, create a more pleasing sound for God's ear. The musicologist Nicholas Temperley has found that musical reforms such as these were linked, in both England and America, with a retreat from Calvinistic theology. The Old Baptists resisted these changes just as they refused to support missions, Sunday schools, and Bible tract societies. Their musical intransigence ought to be seen as one aspect of their overall hostility to the sweeping changes affecting nineteenth-century American Protestantism, especially those that they believed threatened the autonomy of the individual church at the expense of larger ecclesiastical or benevolent networks.[25]

A Holcomb performance recapitulated this history and became, in its own way, a kind of public worship—"in its own way" because a Holcomb performance decontextualized Old Baptist history, stripping it of denominational politics and doctrinal wranglings, even as it preserved, in condensed form, its ethos. Holcomb began each show much like a sinner relating his conversion experience to the church. He told audience members of his limitations. He assured them he would do the best he could. Or, as he wrote to Cohen in 1963: "It takes a long time to make a musician . . . me especially. I ain't never made it yet." Then, too, reports abound of Holcomb visibly suffering during performances. Singing so loudly at such a high pitch would often leave him exhausted after only two or three songs. Ritchie remembered performances that ended midshow because Holcomb's voice had reached its breaking point. If a song is a compressed drama, then a Holcomb performance—with its yearning and regular failings, its split-but-simultaneously-executed meters—seemed a musical enactment of the nineteenth-century Old School Baptist self with its uncertainty, its hunger for God's grace, its struggle for emotional control and its persistent failures at finding it, and even its occasional dogged duality.[26]

Holcomb's banjo and guitar work thrilled audiences, but it was his a cappella singing that most dramatically represented an Old Baptist feeling. He often sang hymns directly from the Old Regular Baptist hymnbook he carried with him, but some of his most effective performances were those in which he adapted traditional material to fit his a cappella Old Baptist style. In "I Am a Man of Constant Sorrow," for example, he took the Stanley Brothers' loping bluegrass melody, brought it inside the meetinghouse, stripped it of everything except its lyric, and turned it into a quavering first-person testimonial. The song, Holcomb said, was "too true," and it took him several tries in the studio before he could get through an entire take without breaking down.[27]

Many of Holcomb's songs, like Monroe's, were moistened by the teary themes of the sentimental tradition, but the pressure of his Old Way singing style scrapes away any mawkishness. One of Holcomb's favorite tunes, "Wandering Boy," veered between the perspective of the misty-eyed "boy"—now clearly a man—and his seemingly dead mother, who nonetheless prayed that her boy not succumb to dissipation:

> As I travel this wide world over
> Friends I find wherever I roam,
> But to me there's none like Mother
> None like Mother dear at home.
> . . . .
> Oh God wilt thou have mercy
> On my darling precious boy,
> Save, protect him Lord I pray thee
> Let not sin destroy his soul.

Like so many Appalachian songs, the lyrics flirted dangerously with bathos. But sung a cappella in the Old Way style, the song, like "Man of Constant Sorrow," became a powerful lament, a prayer of sorts that regularly drove Holcomb to tears. Stunned audiences simply applauded. John Cohen's 1963 documentary, *The High Lonesome Sound*, closes with Holcomb singing "Wandering Boy" unaccompanied, lining it out in the Old Regular Baptist hymn style. The tune can be found in the Old Baptist songbook that Holcomb often carried with him. As Holcomb chants the tune's opening lines, Cohen's camera creeps inside the singer's empty house, catching a picture of Jesus tacked to the wall in a room illuminated by a bare lightbulb. The camera ensconces Holcomb in shadows and dwells on his thick-veined hands. He is alone in the house, singing the hymn as if he were a member of a church of one.[28]

Holcomb understood his unaccompanied singing as something beyond musical performance. Even as he drew closer to the Holiness Church, Holcomb retained the Old Regulars' lexicon by which music making was

Roscoe Holcomb and the Stanley Brothers (Ralph at left) singing the old hymns. Photo by Mike Seeger. Courtesy of the Southern Folklife Collection, Louis Round Wilson Special Collections Library, University of North Carolina at Chapel Hill.

confined to sounds produced using instruments. Unaccompanied singing, as Holcomb and other Old Regulars pointed out, was not in this sense music. It was, instead, the medium used to approach the Almighty. Old Regular believers talk about "being *tuned up* with the grace of God and His Holy Spirit." Old Regulars believe that singing "illuminates the soul of the singer" and "glorifies God." All of this has led an ethnographer of Old Regular Baptists to conclude that their hymn singing "carries the full weight of both the mundane and ineffable meanings of Old Regular beliefs."[29]

By 1966, Holcomb was, according to the *New York Times*, "something of a rural star." That was about as famous as Holcomb ever became. That year his album, *The High Lonesome Sound*, earned a Grammy nomination in the category of "Best Folk Recording." A few years later, a song of his wedged its way between Pink Floyd and the Grateful Dead on the soundtrack to Michelangelo Antonioni's *Zabriskie Point*. He died in 1981 at the age of seventy. His presence has continued to hover on the edges of popular culture—Charles Frazier, for instance, claims Holcomb's music as an influence on his best-selling novel *Cold Mountain*—but it would be Holcomb's younger contemporary, the bluegrass singer and banjo player Ralph Stanley, who popularized the lonesome sound.[30]

In Ralph Stanley's Meetinghouse

Listening to Ralph Stanley's music is like crawling into a crypt. Dark, dank, and moss-covered, this musical sepulcher summons the past's ghosts, conjures up visions of the afterlife, and leaves us—its intruders— with memories haunted by our encounter. In truth, this is only one way of hearing Ralph Stanley. But it has been a popular way to listen. "Haunting," "ghostly," "sepulchral," "otherworldly"—these words bounce around the written discussions of Stanley's music as if in some kind of literary echo chamber. And like reverberations in such a chamber, these depictions of Stanley's grim strangeness float on the air, the sources that generated them long since obscured by the fog of repetition and decay.[31]

The apotheosis (or, depending upon one's point of view, the nadir) of this way of listening occurred in the months and years after the release in late 2000 of the movie *O Brother, Where Art Thou?* and its accompanying soundtrack. In movie theaters, Stanley's voice echoed from behind a Ku Klux Klan mask as the white-sheeted hordes gathered for a lynching. But it was on the movie's soundtrack, away from the film's visual hyperbole, that most listeners first encountered Stanley. There they heard him sing the old ballad "O Death," impersonating both a dying man and the Grim Reaper collecting his quarry:

O, Death
O, Death
Won't you spare me over till another year
Well, what is this that I can't see
With ice cold hands taking hold of me
Well I am Death, none can excel
I'll open the door to heaven or hell
O, Death someone would pray
Could you wait to call me another day
The children prayed, the preacher preached
Time and mercy is out of your reach
I'll fix your feet till you can't walk
I'll lock your jaw till you can't talk
I'll close your eyes so you can't see

> This very hour, come and go with me
> Death—I come to take the soul
> Leave the body and leave it cold
> To draw the flesh off of the frame
> Dirt and worm both have a claim

Stanley's turn as Death himself caught the popular imagination. The film managed modest box office returns, but the soundtrack, with Stanley's harrowing performance at its heart, quickly lodged itself in a host of Billboard charts, sold more than five million copies by the end of 2002, earned Stanley a Grammy award, and spawned a series of concert tours featuring the collection's musicians. By 2011, a decade after its initial release, more than nine million copies of the album had been sold, placing it securely, if strangely, on a list of the all-time top-ten best-selling movie soundtracks alongside *Grease, Saturday Night Fever, The Lion King, Titanic,* and *The Bodyguard.* To celebrate Stanley and company's success, Lost Highway Records issued an expanded tenth anniversary version of the *O Brother* soundtrack. From the moment the soundtrack's sales took off, critics have wondered what lay behind the public's enthusiasm for a collection largely ignored by modern country radio and filled with obscure field recordings, classic bluegrass tunes, and some more current renditions of old blues songs performed in traditional styles.[32]

The question here—What is the source of Stanley's musical power?—is a subset of that larger question, and its answer lies hidden in plain view. We find it in the contours of Stanley's biography and the folkways of his Primitive Baptist faith. What we discover there, if we would only look for it, and what we hear there, if we would simply listen for it, is nothing less than a drama of death and resurrection, a drama of loss and life that undergirds Stanley's music the way Jesus's trial on the cross powers Christianity. Nowhere is this drama more urgently represented than in Stanley's voice. It is, after all, Ralph Stanley's voice that has led to the steady accretion of ominous adjectives I listed above. But those disembodied descriptions drift above the historical, cultural, and theological roots of Stanley's sound. As of this writing, Ralph Stanley is eighty-eight years old, but his voice is nearly three centuries older than that. It is the voice of dissenting Protestantism, a Calvinist voice whose quavers and slides dramatize a lonely soul's search for grace in a fallen world.

In early promotional photos, Ralph Stanley looked more like a cheerful television cowboy than a frontier preacher. Record companies presented Stanley and his brother Carter as a conventional brother duo, much like the

Cheerful bluegrass cowboys: Ralph Stanley and the Clinch Mountain Boys, ca. 1967 (from left to right: Curley Ray Cline, Melvin Goins, Larry Sparks, and Ralph Stanley). Courtesy of the Southern Folklife Collection, Louis Round Wilson Special Collections Library, University of North Carolina at Chapel Hill.

Blue Sky Boys or Jim and Jesse McReynolds, and poured these bluegrass musicians into the same cowboy mold used to market country and western singers. Early photographs of Ralph's own band, the Clinch Mountain Boys—formed in the wake of Carter's death in 1966—continued in this vein.

Stanley's metamorphosis from youthful banjo-playing cowboy to mature mountain preacher began in the early 1970s as he switched record labels and began to take his music in a new direction. During these years, Stanley emphasized the religious character of his repertoire, and so his record label posed Stanley and his band like reverent soldiers in front of a mammoth cross and stood them solemnly in front of the plain white siding of a mountain church. These band photos almost invariably presented Stanley as the literal or figurative minister while the Clinch Mountain Boys served, alternately, as his choir, congregation, or band of pilgrims. Stanley's iconography gradually changed over the ensuing decades, but both the solemnity of the 1970s-era images as well as his outward, off-camera gaze became hallmarks of Stanley's presentational style.

The Lonesome Sound

Ralph Stanley as preacher and the Clinch Mountain Boys as his band of pilgrims, from the covers of *Cry from the Cross* and *Clinch Mountain Gospel*. Courtesy of Rebel Records.

The biggest changes in Stanley's photographic representation have occurred in the last fifteen years as he has been recognized as bluegrass music's foremost elder statesman and his music has gained a popular audience with its inclusion on the *O Brother, Where Art Thou?* soundtrack. The more recent images have continued to emphasize the sobriety of the earlier band portraits, but the band itself has vanished. Instead, Stanley appears alone, often set in vast empty spaces that serve to reinforce his isolation. His gaze, too, has shifted. No longer does he look heavenward like a supplicant. Instead, he peers at an unseen point past the viewer or, like Roscoe Holcomb, stares directly at the camera's lens with a look that alternates between impassive and imposing. Death, too, intrudes. In a series of portraits taken for Stanley's eponymous 2002 release, the photographer Mary Ellen Mark posed the elderly singer in front of his own grave. The increasing grimness of Stanley's photographic representation seems a calculated response to the success of his a cappella version of "O Death," but it also embraces his long-term critical portrayal as the creator of "ghostly" and "haunting" bluegrass music.

And, again, what about bluegrass? It is a music that prizes instrumental virtuosity above all else. It is impossible to imagine the music without Earl Scruggs's nimble three-fingered banjo rolls or Bill Monroe's quicksilver mandolin runs. Bluegrass, as Alan Lomax famously put it, is "folk music in overdrive," a frenzied ensemble sound held

Ralph Stanley outside and inside the old mountain church. Photos by Mary Ellen Mark.

Ralph Stanley in front of his own grave. Photo by Mary Ellen Mark.

together—precariously, beautifully, and masterfully—by the instrumentalists' dexterity.[33]

Such dexterity has hardly been absent from Ralph Stanley's art, but he has consistently downplayed it. His bands, he insists, play "old-time mountain music," not bluegrass. And he especially enjoys featuring clawhammer banjo playing, the older, slower, clanging, down-stroking manner of playing that dominated southern folk music until shortly before bluegrass's birth.[34]

Rather than the banjo or the mandolin or the fiddle, the bellwether of Stanley's music has been the voice, especially his own. "Singing," Stanley explains, "is the weak spot in bluegrass. Now, I feature singing more than I do instruments. I've always liked it better. If I sing a song I think people want to hear the song. Course, it's good to have some music to take a break, but the song is what they're interested in. *The instruments are there to bolster up the singing.*"[35]

This voice-based approach to bluegrass stems not just from Stanley's personal preference but also from a deep cultural and religious wellspring in the Primitive Baptist church. Stanley is a Primitive Baptist; he has been since a child. Primitive Baptist worship revolves around the voice—not only in the lengthy sermons that elders spin out in a kind of speak-chant but, even more important, in the unaccompanied congregational singing that is the hallmark of any Primitive service. In those services, there are no responsive readings, no recitations of creeds. It is only in song that congregation members, as a whole, lift up their voices to God. Like Old Regular Baptists, Primitives long sang in the Old Way. They did not allow instruments in their churches. They sang loudly and slowly. Hymns were lined out. Harmonies were rare. Everyone sang lead. Vocal ornaments— quavers, slides, passing notes—marked each performance. The oldest hymns unfurled in minor keys and skillfully combined the volume of open-throated singing with the pinched tones of sounds pushed either through a clenched throat or into the nasal cavity. These features used to be ubiquitous in Primitive churches, and the church of Stanley's youth certainly sang this way. Over the course of the twentieth century, however, as many Primitive congregations adopted hymnals with musical notation (for decades Primitive hymn books were text only), Primitive singing slowly changed. The pace quickened, harmony became more predictable and uniform as congregations adopted the part-singing style of shape-note singing, and those distinctive vocal improvisations receded into the background. But one can still visit Primitive Baptist churches where members line out the hymns and sing them in the Old Way. And even in many of the churches that use shape-note part-singing, one finds singers embroidering their notated parts with the shakings of the Old Way. To hear well-known texts and tunes, such as "Amazing Grace," sung by Primitive Baptist believers is to have something familiar made radically new and centuries-old all at the same time.[36]

Even the early editions of the Stanley Brothers' bands featured a density of vocal material that set them apart from their contemporaries. A comparison with Bill Monroe's Blue Grass Boys proves useful. Monroe's bands paired a lead vocal with a tenor harmony part. The Stanley Brothers, by contrast, introduced a third part—what observers have dubbed a "high baritone"—to the vocal mix. To be sure, this was not Primitive Baptist singing per se but rather the leading edge of a cultural disposition toward vocal display that would continue to make its presence felt as Stanley's career unfolded.

That presence hovers especially around the music Stanley made shortly after his brother and bandleader, Carter, passed away in 1966. Ralph's voice, already a powerful instrument, dominated his recordings like never before. To his ears, his banjo became but an extension of his voice as he did his "best to make them strings sound just exactly like I'm a-saying it. Like I'm singing it."[37] More revealing, perhaps, is the way that even Stanley's harmony vocals—what bluegrass musicians refer to as the tenor part—took on the character of the ensemble's lead voice. "I just about lead the lead singer with my tenor," he explained to one interviewer. "There's not many tenor singers that does that. . . . I don't listen to the lead; I just sing it and they're usually in with me." Recall that one of the defining features of Primitive Baptist singing in the Old Way was the lack of harmony parts. In the meetinghouse, everyone sang in unison. Everyone sang lead. In Stanley's comments, we hear precisely these sentiments. And in Stanley's music from this period, we hear how his Primitive Baptist singing style uncannily undid bluegrass harmony parts even as he sang them. On tunes such as "You're Drifting On" from 1971's *Cry from the Cross*, one hears Stanley's quavering harmony part periodically bubble up and over the lead and baritone vocals.[38]

The most significant change in Ralph Stanley's music at this time came from what both he and his fans identified as his return to an archaic aesthetic. The hallmark of this turn toward the antique became the unaccompanied, lined-out hymns that punctuated each Stanley performance. Stanley has described the a cappella singing he introduced on his early 1970s Rebel Records albums as "the same singing we learned to do in church." He drew these hymns from the Primitive and Old Regular Baptist repertoires, but, as on the 1972 performance of "Village Church Yard," a song that appeared in an Old Baptist songbook, he arranged them for four-part harmony even as he preserved the Old Baptists' trademark vocal quavers and grace notes. Reviewers quickly seized on the unaccompanied quartet pieces as innovations in bluegrass performance style that drew their strength precisely from their ability to resurrect older, authentic mountain traditions. One critic advised listeners to put "Village Church Yard" "on the turntable and wander back through your childhood and through the ages." Another thought the music was timeless: "To hear this is to hear music as it has always been sung, way back up the creek." The Clinch Mountain Boys' rendition of "Village Church Yard" sounds only distantly like the kinds of Old Way Primitive hymns one might hear in church on a Sunday. When Primitives turn to Old Way singing, harmony appears only occasionally, and when it does, it is not nearly as elaborate as what the Clinch Mountain Boys create. Of course, their version of "Village Church Yard" is not a replica but a representation. It is a fantasy, an imagining, of an Old-Time Baptist meetinghouse. Here Stanley is the song leader, chanting out lines that his congregation, the Clinch Mountain

Boys, sing back in that loud and slow, ornamented style. Reverb saturates the recording, fabricating not only the meetinghouse space but also a congregation of electronic echoes.

Stanley's music, in fact, does more than just imaginatively reconstitute the old mountain church. It recalls an entire history of Calvinist-inspired Protestant dissent. Stanley has often described his style as the "lonesomer sound." "Me, I like it just as lonesome as you can get it," he has said. "Something that'll bring tears, sweat, this that and another." He has repeatedly used the same term—lonesome—to describe his ancestors' voices ("Our grandpas and great-uncles and so forth were of the old Baptist faith, and they all had lonesome voices to sing out those sad old hymns") and his father's voice ("My father had just an old-time lonesome voice, down to earth like he dug it right out of one of these mountains") and to mark what differentiated his style from his late brother's ("Carter didn't like them as lonesome as I did, I guess. He always wanted to experiment"). That lonesome sound, Stanley has explained, was a gift from God. "That's the way it was with my voice," he wrote in his autobiography. "It was lonesome and mournful and it wasn't like nobody else's. . . . I think God gives everybody a gift, and He wants them to use it. I've always done my best to honor what God gave me. I've never tried to put any airs on it. I sing it the way I feel it, just the way it comes out." In the two ethnographies of Primitive Baptist hymnody, we find believers using precisely the same term—lonesome—to describe the distinctive sound of their slow, quavering, ornamented congregational singing. And of course, we know already about Roscoe Holcomb's self-described lonesome sound rooted in Old Regular Baptist folkways that very closely align with those of the Primitives.[39]

Why so lonesome? Primitive Baptists are, theologically speaking, men and women of constant sorrow, lonely pilgrims whose hopes of a heavenly reward are tempered by the most severe doubts about their own worthiness. Consider again Primitive Baptists' lived religion: their predestinarianism, their sense of an inscrutable and obdurate God whose clemency they crave, their knowledge of their own fallenness. Without claiming that contemporary Primitive Baptists live in a world apart, it is still possible to recognize that they remain an order removed from the sort of sunnily pragmatic Christianity that, in H. Richard Niebuhr's words, turned the faith "into a utilitarian device for the attainment of personal prosperity or public peace" wherein "some imagined idol called by his name takes the place of Jesus Christ the Lord."[40]

When Ralph Stanley describes his work as the "lonesomer sound," he indexes something more than musical style. He invokes a cultural disposition that is itself reflected in musical practice. This disposition is that of the lonely Calvinist pilgrim longing for God's grace but always unsure of receiving it. Realizing that his unknowable fate turns on the whims of an all-powerful God, the Calvinist scours the landscape in search of a sign—any sign—that might indicate his salvation. Stanley's ancestors, for example, prized the nasality of their singing. For these dissenting Baptists in England, the summoning of the nasal sound marked the presence of the Holy Spirit, and they referred to it as the "nose of the saint." That nasality—that hint of the Holy Spirit—resounds in Stanley's voice as well, though it is not its most characteristic trait. That remains his vocal ornaments, his quavers, the way he affords each syllable of a lyric two or three notes of melody, the way that tones shiver in Stanley's throat. "Primitive Baptists are different," say Stanley. "They're strictly business when it comes to their hymns. It's more sad and it's more mournful and it fits my voice like nothing else." The quavering uncertainty of this style mimics the Calvinist pilgrim's uncertainty in the face of his unknowable fate. That Stanley always hits his notes should not bother us. Like ritual crying, Stanley's quavering is an elaborate cultural performance—scripted, in a sense, but nevertheless indicative of deep emotion.[41]

The lonesome sound embodies two centuries or more of Old Baptist uncertainty. When Primitives, such as Stanley, call forth lonesome sound—the sound revealed in the old minor tunes whose melodies are marked by pentatonic structures—they express, according to the folklorist Beverly Patterson, "their acceptance of a certain lack of control, and they reveal their sense of the world as a realm in which uncertainty plays a fundamental role." That sense of uncertainty is encoded in the music. In her study of Primitive singing, Patterson explains that the old lonesome tunes "do not lend themselves to predictable harmonic progressions of major and minor chords. Instead they are more apt to promote a sense of ambiguity." In Stanley's "lonesomer sound," we hear the wayfaring stranger, the man of constant sorrow, the stranger below.[42]

There is just one problem, or, at least, one final twist. After all, how can we call Stanley a Calvinist pilgrim beset by doubt when his song catalog brims with tunes proclaiming the certainty of a heavenly reward? "Death is only a dream," he sings. "Bear me away . . . to my immortal home." "I'll meet you on God's golden shore." "I'll not be a stranger when I get to that city / I'm acquainted with folks over there." "I hold a clear title to a mansion / That Jesus has gone to prepare." Similar lyrics abound. How, then, can we square Stanley's lyrical certainty with his dramatic vocal performances of uncertainty?[43]

Stanley is, indeed, a Primitive Baptist, but he belongs to a specific subdenomination of the faith. His church describes itself as a Primitive Baptist Universalist congregation. Outsiders call them the "no-hellers." The Primitive Baptist Universalists do, in fact, believe in hell, but they locate it here on earth, in this world. Heaven, on the other hand, remains open to all—not just God's elect—in the next life. This amounts to a stunning reorientation of Calvinist doctrine, though not an erasure of it. The Calvinist drama lingers, but the "no-hellers" confine such tension to earthly existence. Life itself remains a vale of tears. Men of constant sorrow still roam the hills. But death, as Ralph Stanley sings, remains only a dream.[44]

Death, of course, pervades Stanley's music, as it does much of bluegrass. But Ralph Stanley is no grim reaper. In Stanley's music, death—in classic "no-heller" fashion—is figured most often as a happy family reunion, a longed-for gathering in the gracious presence of the Lord. Death ends earthly suffering. Just as Jesus died on the cross so that humanity might receive the gift of a new birth, the Primitive Baptist no-heller sees his or her own death as redemption from the pain of this world. Stanley's voice dramatizes that pain even as his lyrics promise deliverance from it.

"As One That Is Born Out of Due Time"

Calvinism's long eclipse is not in dispute. Historians, in their various bailiwicks, continue to bicker about more finely tailored questions of periodicity and causation, but the idea that orthodox Calvinist doctrines, whatever their import to varieties of American Protestantism from the seventeenth through the nineteenth centuries, had by the twentieth century given way to other sets of formal and informal Protestant theologies is not a controversial one. A few Ralph Stanley tunes and some Roscoe Holcomb records do not change the grand narrative. Maybe the two old mountain musicians are just bit players in Calvinism's final scene. Holcomb after all was an Old Regular Baptist who in the end opted to attend the local Holiness Church. And Stanley counts himself a member of a Baptist subdenomination so small (just under six hundred members at last count) and bearing a theology so unlikely that adherents seem to have taken literally the Pauline injunction to be a "a peculiar people."[45]

But there is another way to think about Calvinism's presence in modern American culture. It is a will-o'-the-wisp presence, flickering here and there, fluttering on the periphery, disappearing sometimes when approached directly. It is difficult to measure, except perhaps by a fan's ardor or the sudden popularity of a deathbed chant in those unsteady months after the terrorist attacks of September 11, 2001. At certain moments—perhaps especially those moments of national crisis like the folk revival's Vietnam-scarred 1960s or our own time's preoccupation with terrorism—popular audiences have inclined toward "the folk." And among those audiences, some have found their worries mirrored and even relieved in the lonesome quavering of Old Baptist singing. In the spring of 2002, *Newsweek* magazine, for instance, pondered what it called "an esthetic national emergency," a companion crisis, one imagines, to the global tumult engaging the United States at the same time. The magazine sulked about the country's dismal pop music, its blandness and naked commercialism. As *Newsweek* saw it, the national emergency could be contained—even rolled back—by the "mountain-pure" Ralph Stanley and the other *O Brother* performers who were "about as far from industry product as you could get" but had garnered the admiration of millions by making music "with nothing going for it but authenticity: no hype, no radio, no MTV."[46]

The ironies abound. A mass-market publication hyping a product by claiming it has no hype. Even better, the idea of a music soaked in Calvinist folkways appearing as a solution to a crisis in popular culture. Disjunctures such as these have caused some critics to dismiss the concurrent Stanley and *O Brother* booms as little more than episodes of postmodern minstrelsy in which white, well-to-do listeners of National Public Radio dress up in "real" country outfits instead of degrade themselves by donning Nashville's rhinestone-studded wares.[47] We do not need to dismiss such perceptive critiques entirely to note that they are overdrawn, that they too easily shrug off the impassioned responses to the singing of Stanley, Holcomb, or other folk artists.

I suspect that Americans' fascination with Stanley's a cappella rendition of "O Death," the song that propelled him to belated national stardom, had more to do with the aesthetic and moral power of his performance than with its putative whiteness. Audiences clamor for that tune. "A cappella, we want the a cappella," they shout. "People ask for it more than anything else," Stanley has remarked. "In fact, they demand it." And in its trembling melody, they hear old and mystic things. "They say that it puts them in mind of the sacred chanting at a Navajo ceremony," Stanley writes, "or the gospel singing from ancient times, way back to the olden days before the written word, when people first sung out their troubles."[48]

In the song, Stanley inhabits two characters, a dying figure and Death itself. "Won't you spare me over till another year?" he begs before answering, "Time and mercy is out of your reach." Stanley oscillates between the two characters, and it is a measure of his prowess that he thoroughly convinces in each role. But even this dramatic metaphor does not quite convey the burden of the performance. What one hears when listening to "O Death" is not, first of all, Stanley jumping between parts but rather these two voices—one withered and fearful, the other violent and unrelenting—speaking through him almost at once. The dialogue is internal and existential. It unfolds in that liminal space between life and death. It is a song of grief and fear, of a fallen man stained by sin, seeking reprieve, and realizing he may not get it—that he may not deserve it. That man, like Thomas Hill two hundred years ago with a rifle's muzzle buried in his chin, stands on a narrow point of time. And this is what makes the performance harrowing and spectral and all those other adjectives used to describe Stanley's sound. It is what makes it lonesome. Even if we consider Death in this song not to be an internal voice but instead a metonym for Satan, the performance loses none of its power. For, again, the effect in performance is not of Stanley playing Satan but of Satan speaking through Stanley. It is a presence felt but not seen: "Well, what is this that I can't see / With ice cold hands taking hold of me?"

Stanley's performance offered, then, a private counterpoint to the kind of Satan being offered up in the nation's political discourse at roughly the same time. That more public Satan was a familiar one: a wholly external evil, one located in foreign lands and foreign ideologies, one that needed to be subdued and then stamped out. In the Calvinist mood of Stanley's "O Death," a far more intimate evil lurks. The song's stark text and the fierce trembling of Stanley's voice evokes an evil that hovers nearby or, like original sin, resides within.[49]

"I am neither company for the living nor the dead, but as one that is born out of due time, without a heart for any thing as I could wish," wrote an anonymous Primitive Baptist in 1834. Stanley's "O Death" is that letter's postscript. It is conjecture, I know, to say that this is what Americans heard in Stanley's singing or that members of an earlier generation were drawn to Roscoe Holcomb's voice for similar reasons. One cannot find an overt and unbroken line of descent from music examined here to the uncertain Primitive Baptists in this book's earlier chapters. But to me, the echoes from the past are unmistakable. In suggesting these connections, I have been guided, of course, by listeners' fascination with these musicians' beguiling sounds. I have also been prompted by the musicologist Nicholas Temperley, who has done so much to excavate the history of the Old Way of singing. Temperley has not exactly found Cash's Calvinist feeling, but he has discovered that the slow keening sounds of the Old Way have a stubborn persistence: "In places where congregations are left to sing hymns without musical direction for long periods, a characteristic style of singing tends to develop. The tempo becomes extremely slow; the sense of rhythm is weakened; extraneous pitches appear, sometimes coinciding with those of the hymn tune, sometimes inserted between them; the total effect may be dissonant." Another scholar argues that the Old Way of singing has flourished among Old Colony Mennonites. Others hear similarities between the Old Way and sounds heard in Indonesia and East Africa. That is, when left alone, people seem to sing in a way not entirely unlike the Old-Time Baptists. Perhaps those strange old sounds are not so unusual after all.[50]

Epilogue
The Subterranean River

I heard them first. The long, sonorous swells, the modal melodies, the hymns sung so slowly as to melt their texts into an amalgam of chant-speech that sounded to me like people calling up spirits. It stopped me dead. I had never heard anything like it. It reminded me of the twisting cantorial lines I heard sung in shul as a boy or of a feverish *qawwali ghazal* reduced to smoldering ash. The sound itself seemed funereal and luminous all at once. It was beautiful.

The label on the cassette said the singers were Primitive Baptists. The name intrigued me. That's what had caught my eye as I scanned the shelves at the Southern Folklife Collection, where I was working during the summer to pay my rent. The singers who so mesmerized me—the ones who lined out the hymn "Guide Me, O Thou Great Jehovah"—hailed from a church in the North Carolina mountains. I made myself a copy and kept listening. And as I listened, the questions arrived. Who were the Primitive Baptists? What made them "primitive"? Why did they sing like this? I read up on them. I tracked them down. I found them in the archives and in the phone book. I learned that they were Calvinists, that they opposed missionaries, and that they had split acrimoniously from their fellow Baptists in the nineteenth century. These bare facts only raised more questions. Evangelicals opposed to missions? Predestinarian Calvinists in the come-to-Jesus South? Doubters planted among the legions of the assured? How might I tell their story, and how might their story affect the stories of southern evangelicals and American Calvinism?

While I have tried my best to answer these and other questions in the pages you have just read, I still find myself puzzling over these believers. It is difficult, I think, even for the trained observer to keep the Primitive Baptists in focus. At one moment they seem so finely carved, their differences impossible to miss even in the busy scenes of southern evangelicalism. At other times, though, they seem flattened out, like a worn bas-relief whose figures have been reclaimed by the surrounding rock. The bleary-eyed ought to be forgiven.

One is always measuring the Primitives against their evangelical adversaries, but in doing so one realizes the extent to which these adversaries were so much alike. Consider an example. The chief accomplishment of American evangelicals in the nineteenth century was, as the historian Beth Barton Schweiger has explained, not temperance or antislavery but instead their ability "to organize the country into a set of denominations that endures to this day." Among many other developments, it was the organization of these vast networks that so troubled the Primitives, for the organizing could not and did not stop at the denominational level (troubling enough, as the Primitives saw it) but instead extended across ecclesiastical lines in the formation of interdenominational benevolent efforts with tiered bureaucracies and worldwide reach. Oversuspicious though they could be, the Primitives realized quickly—more quickly than most—that awakening and organization went hand in hand. To slow this process and, they hoped, to roll it back, the Primitives organized themselves into regional church associations that might remind their fellows to search "for the old paths." Schweiger sees this as ironic, though to me it seems only practical. In any case, the Primitives' associations were, organizationally speaking, slack affairs. More than anything else, they were networks of fellowship, offering believers from across a large swath of territory the opportunity to meet together annually for several days at a time in order to sing their old hymns and hear preached the doctrine of election, total depravity, particular redemption, effectual calling, and the final perseverance of the saints. In their broadsheets, the Primitives extended the bounds of fellowship across the nation as believers writing from, say, Pennsylvania, Alabama, North Carolina, and Maryland could fill any one issue. And, *pace* Schweiger, all this meeting and corresponding can look very much like the various organizational processes put in motion in the more evangelistic evangelical denominations.[1]

The resemblances are important—they mark Primitives as evangelicals—but they also are superficial. From afar, the annual associational meetings could look like protracted revivals or, perhaps, state denominational conventions, but there were no anxious benches or frenzied crowds or budgeting meetings. The pages of the *Primitive Baptist* or *Signs of the Times* showed that the Old School Baptists were just as adept as their New School brethren in using printing press and railroad to communicate over great distances. But the Primitives' periodicals were filled almost entirely with first-person testimonies—with believers relating their hope of grace—and not larded, as many evangelical publications were, with dispatches about the progress of the gospel in Burma or instructions on child rearing. And while one might reasonably contend that nineteenth-century southern evangelicals of all stripes were deeply suspicious of human agency and deeply invested in theories of innate human depravity, such arguments about a putative "collective religious consciousness of antebellum southern evangelicals" run headlong into the actual testimonies of those same believers, many of whom would have been shocked and repulsed to find out that they shared much of anything with the ignorant hard-shell or the Bible-thumping "passion-exciter" down the road.[2]

Another reason one sometimes loses sight of the Primitives has to do with the timing of their birth during the Second Great Awakening. Historians, overwhelmed by the sheer variety of popular religious movements, may have understandably overlooked a small sect such as the Primitives whose historical moment seemed to be slipping away from them almost as soon as it began. Even when viewed within the confines of Baptist history, the Primitives might be seen as just one of many subdenominations in a notoriously schismatic movement. But this observation returns us to the original problem—namely, Primitives' awkward relationship to their fellow Baptists in particular and to their fellow evangelicals in general. In fact, it has been historians' thematic preoccupations rather than any counting problems that explain the Primitives' here-and-there existence in the historiography of American Protestantism. Unlike the modern-day televangelist whom we view through narrowed eyes or the enthusiasts of the First Great Awakening (an era described memorably by one historian as an "interpretive fiction"), "revivalism between the Revolution and the Civil War," writes James Bratt, "has gone untouched as a success story of popular Protestantism defeating all comers to bring evangelical Christianity to its apogee of influence in American history." From these historiographic heights, the Primitives seem small indeed, which has been why, I think, the chief historiographic response to their presence has been to ignore them, to see them as anachronistic, or simply to fold them into a much larger evangelical movement when, in fact, they represent a crisis within that movement.[3]

To study the Primitives is to plunge into that crisis. And so *Strangers Below* crawls inside the Second Great Awakening's organizing processes— sees them from the inside out, as it were—by focusing first on believers' experiences. In this regard, *Strangers Below* complements Schweiger's insight rather than overturns it; it shows, for instance, how we might take account not only of believers' emotional experiences but of the consequences of those experiences both for believers and for the structuring forces they were living with and against. In the case of antebellum Primitive

Baptists, these structuring forces were the processes of denominational consolidation that Schweiger mentions, the tumult of the antebellum market, and the formal theology of Calvinism. To examine these processes from the believer's point of view is not to slip into endless psychologizing or the hoarding of biographical trivia. Nor is it to laud religious believers as autonomous agents, hail them as intuitive resisters of power, or unmask them as nothing more than passive receptacles of cultural meaning. It is, instead, to find the significance of the antebellum Primitive Baptist movement in the endless interaction between experience, religious idiom, and social circumstance, and it is also to suggest that a comparable approach might profitably be taken with other believers. This approach, moreover, shares similarities with the Primitives' struggle against what they saw as modern evangelicalism's reification of faith's mysteries. On this count, the Primitives were right, or at least partially so. Revivals often did become rehearsed, and the various arms of the Benevolent Empire often did want to wrest a measure of control away from the whims of individual churches. And certainly evangelical enthusiasm often became an end in itself.

But because Primitives' fury could itself harden into a granitic monument, I have tried not only to follow George Santayana's advice that "the feeling of reverence should itself be treated with reverence" but also to be properly critical. For the Primitives' rage had a watchman's eye, seeing threatening figures where there were none at all. While the consequences of their anger were felt most often and directly in the fight against the "machine-made Baptists" of the missionary movement, the Primitives were fully capable of turning their rage inward. And so it was that after the missions schism had fractured Baptist churches from Florida to Illinois, many Primitives turned upon each other, arguing that even preaching about the saving power of the gospel amounted to a kind of idolatry. In 1860, during a dramatic but hardly atypical meeting of the Alabama River Association in southeastern Georgia, one man rose, held the Bible aloft, and addressed his fellow Primitives: "You have been told that this is the word of God; do you believe it? I say it is not, it is ink and paper." The man continued: "The gospel had no saving efficacy in it to the awakening of sinners; it was only for the feeding of the flock." God alone saved. His Holy Scriptures? Man-made, a mere instrumentality, no more than words on a page.[4]

The African American Primitives in Huntsville had no time for an annulling faith like that. More important, they had no evidence for it. They knew that Calvinism's sharp decrees could float a movement that awakened sinners, could feed the flock, and could advance the race all at once. Their own lives proved it so. They were anti-missionaries, and they built schools. They hallowed the old Calvinist creeds, and they founded a national convention. They walked the old paths, but they acknowledged that the way was not always as clear as their white and black old-line brethren made it out to be. The Primitives "claim to have descended from the apostles," wrote C. F. Sams, the ebullient young minister from Florida who, more than anyone else, animated the national convention movement. But, Sams continued, "it is true that the line of descent can not always be traced." Better, Sams explained, to think of the Primitives as "like a river, that now and then in its course is lost under the surface of the ground, and then make[s] its appearance again."[5]

The Primitives' subterranean river of faith is like the enigmatic lonesome sound that modern music audiences have craved—a sound drawn from the past but surfacing in the present where, like an accident of grace, it might minister anew to some uncertain soul who knows nothing of its origins. The lonesome sound is the sound of the stranger below, the sound of an American Calvinism thriving for two centuries in Primitive Baptist churches but that has found a second, altered life in its encounter with the folkniks in Washington Square Park in 1961, the sweating crowds at Bonnaroo in 2007, and a worried nation in the wake of the harrowing fall of 2001. Those were unlikely meetings, but they were vital ones, American ones.

Notes

Abbreviations

BHC   Baptist Historical Collection, Wake Forest University, Winston-Salem, N.C.
CBH   Cushing Biggs Hassell Papers, 1809–1880, Southern Historical Collection, Louis Round Wilson Special Collections Library, University of North Carolina at Chapel Hill
CDA   *Christian Doctrinal Advocate and Spiritual Monitor*
DMR   David M. Rubenstein Rare Book and Manuscript Library, Duke University, Durham, N.C.
GM   *Gospel Messenger*
HG   *Huntsville Gazette*
HJ   *Huntsville Journal*
NYT   *New York Times*
PB   *Primitive Baptist*
PBL   Primitive Baptist Library, Elon, N.C.
ST   *Signs of the Times*
UKY   Special Collections Library, University of Kentucky, Lexington

Introduction

1. Abbott's Creek Baptist Church Records, 4 July 1832, BHC; Henry Sheets, *A History of the Liberty Baptist Association. . . .* (Raleigh, N.C.: Edwards and Broughton Printing Co., 1907), 197; 2 Thes 3:6 (all Bible references are to the King James Version); Abbott's Creek Primitive Baptist Church Records, 4 February 1832, BHC; William Dowd to Samuel Wait, 24 April 1832, Samuel and Sarah Wait Papers, Special Collections and Archives, Wake Forest University, Winston-Salem, N.C. For clarity's sake, I have standardized the spelling of "Abbott's" in my narrative, but when quoting directly from either the missionary and primitive records, I have retained the various original spellings, such as "Abbot's" or "Abbots" or "Abbotts."

2. Silas H. Durand and P. G. Lester, *Hymn and Tune Book for Use in Old School or Primitive Baptist Churches* (Greenfield, Ind.: D. H. Goble, 1886), 214.

3. Joshua Lawrence, "Declaration of the Reformed Baptist Churches in the State of North Carolina," *PB*, 14 May 1842, 129–33. Lawrence drafted this declaration in 1826, and the Kehukee Association adopted it in 1827.

4. William T. Stott, *Indiana Baptist History, 1798–1908* (n.p., 1908), 57; Abbott's Creek Primitive Baptist Church Records, 5 May 1832, BHC.

5. "Address to the Particular Baptist Churches of the 'Old School' in the United States," *ST*, 3 July 1833, 241–49; Jeffrey W. Taylor, "'These Worms Will Cut the Root

of Our Independence': Fears of a State Church among the Anti-mission Baptists of the Nineteenth Century," in *Fear Itself: Enemies Real and Imagined in American Culture*, ed. Nancy Lusignan Schultz (West Lafayette, Ind.: Purdue University Press, 1999), 83–92. Both the dating of the schism and its geographic trajectory tend to get obscured by a persistent, though understandable, focus by both believers and scholars on the split's "signature" declarations, such as the 1827 vote in the Kehukee Association and the 1832 Black Rock Address issued by the "Particular Baptists of the Old School" who had gathered that year at the Black Rock Meeting House in Baltimore, Maryland.

6. Richard M. Newport, "Imposition Exposed," *ST*, 2 April 1834, 134; Cushing Biggs Hassell to William Garrard, 25 June 1847, in *Friendly Greetings across the Water, or the Love Letters of Elders Garrard and Hassell* (New York: Chatterton and Crist, 1847), 17; Samuel Trott, "Union of Christ with the Church," in *A Compilation of Elder Samuel Trott's Writings: Copied from the "Signs of the Times" Embracing a Period from 1832–1862*, ed. Marc Jacobsson (Salisbury, Md.: Welsh Tract Publications, 1999), 43. Trott's article was originally published in 1833.

7. Joseph Kelly Turner and John Luther Bridgers, *History of Edgecombe County, North Carolina* (Raleigh, N.C.: Edwards and Broughton, 1920), 417. "Primitive Baptists" became the label these believers most often used to identify themselves, although many also retained a fondness for the "Old School" moniker. In both respects, I follow their usage. For more nomenclatural insight, see Jerry Newsome, "'Primitive Baptists': A Study in Name Formation or What's in a Word," *Viewpoints: Georgia Baptist History* 6 (1978): 63–70.

8. Benjamin Griffin, *History of the Primitive Baptists of Mississippi. . . .* (Jackson, Miss.: Barksdale and Jones, 1853), 65; Joshua Lawrence, *The American Telescope, by a Clodhopper, of North Carolina* (Philadelphia: printed for the author, 1825), 9; Darren Dochuk, *From Bible Belt to Sunbelt: Plain-Folk Religion, Grassroots Politics, and the Rise of Evangelical Conservatism* (New York: W. W. Norton, 2010).

9. William H. Brackney, *The Baptists* (New York: Greenwood Press, 1988), 13; Christine Leigh Heyrman, *Southern Cross: The Beginnings of the Bible Belt* (New York: Knopf, 1997), 5.

10. Heyrman, *Southern Cross*, 27. Heyrman estimates that in the South alone, Baptists' ranks increased from 40,492 in 1790 to 290,141 by the mid-1830s. See *Southern Cross*, 261–66. Between 1792 and 1832, Regular Baptists' numbers across the entire United States increased from 891 churches with 65,345 total members to 5,320 churches with 384,920 members. In 1792, Regular Baptists were 1.6 percent of the U.S. population. By 1832, they were 2.8 percent. See Mark A. Noll, *America's God: From Jonathan Edwards to Abraham Lincoln* (New York: Oxford University Press, 2002). Another way to consider growth is to look at denominations' institution building. American Baptists had six multichurch associations in 1780. By 1820 the number had risen to at least 100, and by 1860 there were more than 500. See Jon Butler, *Awash in a Sea of Faith: Christianizing the American People* (Cambridge, Mass.: Harvard University Press, 1990), 269–70.

11. Albert Henry Newman, *A History of the Baptist Churches in the United States* (New York: Christian Literature Company, 1894), 437–38; Benjamin Franklin Riley, *A History of the Baptists in the Southern States East of the Mississippi* (Philadelphia:

American Baptist Publication Society, 1898), 172; Griffin, *History of the Primitive Baptists*; John G. Crowley, *Primitive Baptists of the Wiregrass South: 1815 to the Present* (Gainesville: University Press of Florida, 1998).

12. Bertram Wyatt-Brown, "The Antimission Movement in the Jacksonian South: A Study in Regional Folk Culture," *Journal of Southern History* 36, no. 4 (1970): 511. I have used the term "Calvinist" and its variants as shorthand descriptions of Primitive Baptist theology, but, like that most famous American Calvinist, Jonathan Edwards, the Primitives did not often cite John Calvin by name. Nonetheless, Primitive theology drew upon, and was refracted through, a series of Calvinist writers and doctrines. Simply examining the articles of faith for nearly any Primitive church will reveal, for instance, Calvinism's famous five points. In this context, using "Reformed" or "Orthodox" or another brief theological denotation would lead to more confusion than the somewhat imprecise designation "Calvinist." For more on Primitives' relationship to the entirety of Calvinist doctrine, see John G. Crowley, "The Primitive or Old School Baptists," in *The Baptist River: Essays on Many Tributaries of a Diverse Tradition*, ed. W. Glenn Jonas Jr. (Macon, Ga.: Mercer University Press, 2008), 158–81.

13. Benjamin Lloyd, *The Primitive Hymns, Spiritual Songs, and Sacred Poems: Regularly Selected, Classified and Set in Order and Adapted to Social Singing and All Occasions of Divine Worship* (Greenville, Ala.: published for the proprietor, 1841), 293.

14. James R. Mathis, *The Making of the Primitive Baptists: A Cultural and Intellectual History of the Anti-mission Movement, 1800–1840* (New York: Routledge, 2004); Jeffrey Wayne Taylor, *The Formation of the Primitive Baptist Movement* (Kitchener, Ont.: Pandora Press, 2004).

15. Ira Durwood Hudgins, "The Anti-missionary Controversy among Baptists," *Chronicle* 14, no. 4 (1951): 147–63; T. Scott Miyakawa, *Protestants and Pioneers: Individualism and Conformity on the American Frontier* (Chicago: University of Chicago Press, 1964); William Warren Sweet, ed., *The Baptists, 1783–1830: A Collection of Source Material* (New York: Cooper Square, 1964); Wyatt-Brown, "Antimission Movement in the Jacksonian South"; Sydney E. Ahlstrom, *A Religious History of the American People* (New Haven, Conn.: Yale University Press, 1972), 721; Keith Robert Burich, "The Primitive Baptist Schism in North Carolina: A Study of the Professionalization of the Baptist Ministry" (M.A. thesis, University of North Carolina at Chapel Hill, 1973); Crowley, *Primitive Baptists of the Wiregrass South*.

16. See, for example, Charles Sellers's landmark synthesis and the separate volume of commentary, especially the essays by Daniel Walker Howe and Richard Carwardine, that were published several years later. Charles Sellers, *The Market Revolution: Jacksonian America, 1815–1846* (New York: Oxford University Press, 1991); and Melvyn Stokes and Stephen Conway, eds., *The Market Revolution in America: Social, Political, and Religious Expressions, 1800–1880* (Charlottesville: University Press of Virginia, 1996). Howe has become Sellers's fiercest critic. See his *What Hath God Wrought: The Transformation of America, 1815–1848* (New York: Oxford University Press, 2007). Jill Lepore's "Vast Designs: How America Came of Age," New Yorker, 29 October 2007, 88–92, reviews the Sellers-Howe debate. The dispute between Sellers and Howe closely tracks the interpretive disagreements over the origins and character of early nineteenth-century evangelical revivalism. That debate has been vast, but see Paul

E. Johnson's *A Shopkeeper's Millennium: Society and Revivals in Rochester, New York, 1815-1837* (New York: Hill and Wang, 1978) and Nathan O. Hatch's *The Democratization of American Christianity* (New Haven, Conn.: Yale University Press, 1989) as representative examples of the conflict's interpretive poles. For overviews of that debate, see Paul E. Johnson, "Democracy, Patriarchy, and American Revivals, 1780-1830," *Journal of Social History* 24, no. 4 (1991): 843-50; Curtis D. Johnson, "Supply-Side and Demand-Side Revivalism? Evaluating the Social Influences on New York State Evangelism in the 1830s," *Social Science History* 19, no. 1 (1995): 1-30; and Jerald C. Brauer, "Revivalism Revisited," *Journal of Religion* 77, no. 2 (1997): 268-77.

17. For instance, both Heyrman's *Southern Cross* and Stephanie McCurry's *Masters of Small Worlds: Yeoman Households, Gender Relations, and the Political Culture of the Antebellum South Carolina Low Country* (New York: Oxford University Press, 1995) place Primitive Baptists under evangelicalism's generous canopy, figuring the Primitives as exemplars of southern evangelicalism's adoption of the South's patriarchal social mores. On the need to, as he puts it, disturb the interpretive peace that has for too long let the story of popular Protestantism during the Second Great Awakening be told as one of unqualified success, see James D. Bratt, "Religious Anti-revivalism in Antebellum America," *Journal of the Early Republic* 24, no. 1 (2004): 65-106. Philip N. Mulder's *A Controversial Spirit: Evangelical Awakenings in the South* (New York: Oxford University Press, 2002) operates in a similar vein.

18. Robert Orsi, "Everyday Miracles: The Study of Lived Religion," in *Lived Religion in America: Toward a History of Practice*, ed. David D. Hall (Princeton, N.J.: Princeton University Press, 1997), 7, 10 (emphasis in the original).

19. Quoted in Ann Taves, *Religious Experience Reconsidered: A Building-Block Approach to the Study of Religion and Other Special Things* (Princeton, N.J.: Princeton University Press, 2009). Orsi's comments appear on the dust jacket of Taves's book. For an overview of the prospects and problems of the turn in religious studies toward the examination of practice, see Courtney Bender, "Practicing Religions," in *The Cambridge Companion to Religious Studies*, ed. Robert A. Orsi (New York: Cambridge University Press, 2012), 273-95.

20. Catherine Lutz, *Unnatural Emotions: Everyday Sentiments on a Micronesian Atoll and Their Challenge to Western Theory* (Chicago: University of Chicago Press, 1988), 5. The other key constructionist ethnographies are Michelle Z. Rosaldo, *Knowledge and Passion: Ilongot Notions of Self and Social Life* (New York: Cambridge University Press, 1980) and Lila Abu-Lughod, *Veiled Sentiments: Honor and Poetry in a Bedouin Society* (Berkeley: University of California Press, 1986). For a psychologist's critique of one key theory of the universality of emotions, see James A. Russell, "Is There Universal Recognition of Emotion from Facial Expressions? A Review of the Cross-Cultural Studies," *Psychological Bulletin* 115, no. 1 (1994): 102-41.

21. In American history, the turn toward historicizing emotional expression has been led by Peter Stearns and Carol Stearns. See, especially, Peter N. Stearns and Carol Z. Stearns, "Emotionology: Clarifying the History of Emotions and Emotional Standards," *American Historical Review* 90, no. 4 (October 1985): 813-36; Peter N. Stearns, *American Cool: Constructing a Twentieth-Century Emotional Style* (New York: New York University Press, 1994); and Peter N. Stearns, "Emotions History in the United

States: Goals, Methods, and Promise," in *Emotions in American History*, ed. Jessica C. E. Gienow-Hecht (New York: Berghahn Books, 2010), 15-27.

22. William M. Reddy, *The Navigation of Feeling: A Framework for the History of Emotions* (New York: Cambridge University Press, 2001), 121; Barbara H. Rosenwein, *Emotional Communities in the Early Middle Ages* (Ithaca, N.Y.: Cornell University Press, 2006); John Corrigan, *Business of the Heart: Religion and Emotion in the Nineteenth Century* (Berkeley: University of California Press, 2002), 231-32 (emphasis in the original); Nicole Eustace, *Passion Is the Gale: Emotion, Power, and the Coming of the American Revolution* (Chapel Hill: University of North Carolina Press, 2008).

23. Corrigan, *Business of the Heart*, 231-32 (emphasis in the original); Richard Rabinowitz, *The Spiritual Self in Everyday Life: The Transformation of Personal Religious Experience in Nineteenth-Century New England* (Boston: Northeastern University Press, 1989), 98. The emotions literature in other fields is vast, but some of the key texts that historians have relied on include Arlie Russell Hochschild, *The Managed Heart: Commercialization of Human Feeling* (Berkeley: University of California Press, 1983); Unni Wikan, "Managing the Heart to Brighten Face and Soul: Emotions in Balinese Morality and Health Care," *American Ethnologist* 16, no. 2 (1989): 294-312; and Lutz, *Unnatural Emotions*. To listen in as historians of emotion discuss the influence of some of this literature, see Jan Plamper, "The History of Emotions: An Interview with William Reddy, Barbara Rosenwein, and Peter Stearns," *History and Theory* 49 (May 2010): 237-65; and Nicole Eustace et al., "AHR Conversation: The Historical Study of Emotions," *American Historical Review* 117, no. 5 (December 2012): 1487-1531.

24. Rosenwein, *Emotional Communities*, 196.

25. A note on terminology: I use the designation "Second Great Awakening," even though efforts to catalog both its chronology and scope are notoriously imprecise. Still, it is possible to make useful observations even while acknowledging the concept's slipperiness. On the need to re-periodize American religious history, see, for example, James D. Bratt, "The Reorientation of American Protestantism, 1835-1845," *Church History* 67, no. 1 (1998): 52-82. For a still-indispensable effort to bring some conceptual sense to our slippery term, see Donald G. Mathews, "The Second Great Awakening as an Organizing Process, 1780-1830: An Hypothesis," *American Quarterly* 21, no. 1 (1969): 23-43.

26. Byron Cecil Lambert, *The Rise of the Anti-mission Baptists: Sources and Leaders, 1800-1840* (New York: Arno Press, 1980); Anne C. Loveland, *Southern Evangelicals and the Social Order, 1800-1860* (Baton Rouge: Louisiana State University Press, 1980), 65-90; Bratt, "Religious Anti-revivalism in Antebellum America"; James D. Bratt, *Antirevivalism in Antebellum America: A Collection of Religious Voices* (New Brunswick, N.J.: Rutgers University Press, 2006); Bradley J. Longfield, *The Presbyterian Controversy: Fundamentalists, Modernists, and Moderates* (New York: Oxford University Press, 1991); Richard T. Hughes and C. Leonard Allen, eds., *Illusions of Innocence: Protestant Primitivism in America, 1630-1875* (Chicago: University of Chicago Press, 1988); Richard T. Hughes, ed., *The American Quest for the Primitive Church* (Urbana: University of Illinois Press, 1988).

27. "The triumph of Arminianism ... over Calvinism was the crucial ideological reorientation brought about by the Second Great Awakening," writes Richard Carwardine

in "Charles Sellers's 'Antinomians' and 'Arminians': Methodists and the Market Revolution," in *God and Mammon: Protestants, Money, and the Market, 1790–1860*, ed. Mark A. Noll (New York: Oxford University Press, 2002), 87. For a transnational overview of the subject, see Daniel Walker Howe, "The Decline of Calvinism: An Approach to Its Study," *Comparative Studies in Society and History* 14, no. 3 (1972): 306–72. For a comprehensive survey of the intellectual tradition of American Calvinism, see Noll, *America's God*. For the specific case of Southern Baptists, see Paul Harvey, *Redeeming the South: Religious Cultures and Racial Identities among Southern Baptists, 1865–1925* (Chapel Hill: University of North Carolina Press, 1997), 152–54.

28. Harry L. Poe, "The History of the Anti-missionary Baptists," *Chronicle* 2, no. 2 (1939): 64. Poe, who drew his data from the U.S. Census, divided the Primitives into three groups: Two-Seed-in-the-Spirit Predestinarian Baptists, Colored Primitive Baptists, and, finally, "plain old" Primitive Baptists, by which he meant white Primitive Baptists.

29. Frank S. Mead and Samuel S. Hill, eds., *Handbook of Denominations in the United States*, 11th ed. (Nashville: Abingdon Press, 2001). Here numbers and nomenclature can become confusing. Mead and Hill estimated that these 72,000 Primitive Baptists were spread across about 1,000 churches in 1995. They estimated another 300 to 400 Reformed or Sovereign Grace Baptist churches, though they provided no membership estimates. Reformed or Sovereign Grace Baptists hold to orthodox Calvinistic doctrines, just as Primitives do, though they do not consider themselves Primitive Baptists. Finally, Mead and Hill reported that the National Primitive Baptist Convention (NPBC), the umbrella organization of black Primitive Baptist churches, boasted a membership of approximately 1 million members and 1,530 churches. These numbers seem improbably high. In 1980, the NPBC claimed 250,000 members, according to the eighth edition of Mead and Hill's book. This estimate also seems too large, though at least it has the virtue of possessing a small measure of plausibility. More conservative estimates have appeared in Association of Statisticians of American Religious Bodies, *Religious Congregations and Membership in the United States 2000: An Enumeration by Region, State and County Based on Data Reported for 149 Religious Bodies* (Nashville, Tenn.: Glenmary Research Center, 2002). This study found 547 NPBC churches with 53,630 members and an estimated 66,452 adherents. This study's membership numbers for other Primitive Baptist subdenominations were incomplete. On the lack of solid membership statistics for NPBC churches, see Robert G. Gardner, *National Primitive Baptists in Georgia* (Macon: Georgia Baptist Historical Society, 2004), 42–44.

30. Loyal Jones and Howard Dorgan, among others, have used the "Old-Time Baptist" category to distinguish several central Appalachian Baptist subdenominations from their "mainline" counterparts. See, especially, Jones, *Faith and Meaning in the Southern Uplands* (Urbana: University of Illinois Press, 1999); and Dorgan, *In the Hands of a Happy God: The "No-Hellers" of Central Appalachia* (Knoxville: University of Tennessee Press, 1997), 8–11. Also see Dorgan's earlier books, *The Old Regular Baptists of Central Appalachia: Brothers and Sisters in Hope* (Knoxville: University of Tennessee Press, 1989) and *Giving Glory to God in Appalachia: Worship Practices of Six Baptist Subdenominations* (Knoxville: University of Tennessee Press, 1987); and Deborah Vansau McCauley, *Appalachian Mountain Religion: A History* (Urbana: University of Illinois Press, 1995).

31. W. J. Cash, *The Mind of the South* (New York: Knopf, 1941; repr., New York: Vintage, 1991), 81 (page citations are to the reprint edition). A magnificent exception to the popular and scholarly tendency to flatten Calvin and Calvinism is Thomas J. Davis, ed., *John Calvin's American Legacy* (New York: Oxford University Press, 2010).

32. Cushing Biggs Hassell and Sylvester Hassell, *History of the Church of God, from the Creation to A.D. 1885; Including Especially the History of the Kehukee Primitive Baptist Association* (Middletown, N.Y.: Gilbert Beebe's Sons, 1886), 748; Tarboro Primitive Baptist Church Record Book, 2 January 1830, DMR; *Minutes of the Cumberland Baptist Association: Convened at Friendship Meeting-house, Davidson County, Ten.* (Franklin, Tenn.: The Review, 1835), 7; A. J. Coleman, "Circular Letter," *PB*, 2 May 1846, 69; Edward S. Duke, letter to the editor, *PB*, 12 May 1838, 129–30; Smith Hansbrough, letter to the editor, *PB*, 14 April 1838, 108; Sandra D. Hayslette, "Missions, Markets, and Men: A Baptist Contest of Values in Tarboro, North Carolina, 1800–1835" (M.A. thesis, University of North Carolina at Chapel Hill, 1995); Heyrman, *Southern Cross*; McCurry, *Masters of Small Worlds*.

33. For examples of these arguments, see Eugene D. Genovese, *Roll, Jordan, Roll: The World the Slaves Made* (New York: Vintage Books, 1976), 287; Mechal Sobel, *Trabelin' On: The Slave Journey to an Afro-Baptist Faith* (Westport, Conn.: Greenwood Press, 1979), 244; Bertram Wyatt-Brown, *The Shaping of Southern Culture: Honor, Grace, and War, 1760s–1890s* (Chapel Hill: University of North Carolina Press, 2001), 112; Hatch, *Democratization of American Christianity*, 171; and Randy J. Sparks, *On Jordan's Stormy Banks: Evangelicalism in Mississippi, 1773–1876* (Athens: University of Georgia Press, 1994), 118. Sparks attributes the preponderance of pro-slavery southern Presbyterian ministers to their theology "because Calvinism was free of the Arminian doctrines of equality." The outstanding exception to the assumption of African Americans' aversion to Calvinism is Erskine Clarke, *Our Southern Zion: A History of Calvinism in the South Carolina Low Country, 1690–1990* (Tuscaloosa: University of Alabama Press, 1996). Meanwhile, there is a burgeoning literature on religion and Reconstruction, though here, too, the Primitives have been ignored. Daniel W. Stowell's *Rebuilding Zion: The Religious Reconstruction of the South, 1863–1877* (New York: Oxford University Press, 1998) remains the touchstone text, but see Edward J. Blum and W. Scott Poole, eds., *Vale of Tears: New Essays on Religion and Reconstruction* (Macon, Ga.: Mercer University Press, 2005), for more recent contributions. John M. Giggie's splendid *After Redemption: Jim Crow and the Transformation of African American Religion in the Delta, 1875–1915* (New York: Oxford University Press, 2008) offers the most persuasive case for how many southern African Americans reinvented their religious lives along denominational, spiritual, and consumer lines during the late nineteenth and early twentieth centuries.

Chapter One

1. Lemuel Burkitt and Jesse Read, *A Concise History of the Kehukee Baptist Association: From Its Original Rise to the Present Time* (Halifax, N.C.: A. Hodge, 1803), 138–55 (quotes from 146, 141, 154).

2. Ibid., 138, 154. As early as 1767, the churches within the bounds of the United (née Kehukee) Baptist Association "began earnestly to desire a revival of religion" and

so set aside two days for fasting and prayer to God. The association took similar measures in 1785 and, once again, ten years later (ibid., 61, 75, 114–15). For the full sweep of the Great Revival, see John B. Boles, *The Great Revival: Beginnings of the Bible Belt* (1972; Lexington: University Press of Kentucky, 1996).

3. "Address to the Particular Baptist Churches of the 'Old School' in the United States," *ST*, 3 July 1833, 246; Cushing Biggs Hassell and Sylvester Hassell, *History of the Church of God, from the Creation to A.D. 1885; Including Especially the History of the Kehukee Primitive Baptist Association* (Middletown, N.Y.: Gilbert Beebe's Sons, 1886), 717.

4. Revivalists of all stripes used the new measures, though they have been most closely associated with Charles Grandison Finney, who, in 1835, spelled out both his revival techniques and anti-Calvinist theology in *Lectures on the Revival of Religion*. See Charles Grandison Finney, *Lectures on Revivals of Religion*, ed. William G. McLoughlin (Cambridge: Belknap Press of Harvard University Press, 1960).

5. I generally follow the Primitive Baptists' terminology because it reflects the way they bifurcated antebellum America's heterogeneous religious landscape. However, where appropriate, I discuss various inter- and intradenominational distinctions. Needless to say, the Primitives' terminology shoves together under one umbrella an array of Baptist sects whose members might have been amused or, most probably, outraged to be standing shoulder-to-shoulder with those whose beliefs they considered heterodox. And yet the Primitives' terminology was not entirely inaccurate. In antebellum America, many Baptists, and indeed many Protestants, embraced a new ethos that was revivalistic, missionary, and leery of Calvinist theology.

6. Rhys Isaac, *The Transformation of Virginia, 1740–1790* (Chapel Hill: University of North Carolina Press, 1982), 164.

7. Ibid., 159–77 (quote from 164). Donald G. Mathews's *Religion in the Old South* (Chicago: University of Chicago Press, 1977) still makes the best case for understanding early evangelicalism in the South as a social movement. Mathews argues that Separate Baptists, in particular, radicalized that movement.

Many historians have questioned what the historian Jewel L. Spangler describes as "the oppositional narrative" that runs through Isaac's and Mathews's landmark works. Studies by Spangler, Charles Irons, Janet Moore Lindeman, Monica Najar, Randolph Ferguson Scully, and Scott Stephan all question how estranged early southern evangelicals really were from planter culture. I follow Isaac's basic account here because it closely tracks nineteenth-century Baptists' understanding of their denomination's history. See Spangler's *Virginians Reborn: Anglican Monopoly, Evangelical Dissent, and the Rise of the Baptists in the Late Eighteenth Century* (Charlottesville: University of Virginia Press, 2008) and her reply to a review of *Virginians Reborn*: Spangler to H-SHEAR Discussion Network, 14 July 2009, <http://h-net.msu.edu/cgi-bin/logbrowse.pl?trx=vx&list=H-SHEAR&month=0907&week=b&msg=HR2QhNKC4B-GQ%2BvZT1vUtag> (25 July 2009).

8. Burkitt and Read, *Concise History of the Kehukee*, 32, 38–39; William Fristoe, *A Concise History of the Ketocton Baptist Association....* (Staunton, Va.: William Gilman Lyford, 1808; repr., San Antonio, Tex.: Primitive Baptist Heritage Corporation, 2002), 22 (page citations are to the reprint edition). Monica Najar, *Evangelizing the South:*

A Social History of Church and State in Early America (New York: Oxford University Press, 2008), 33-34, cautions against overstating the differences between Separate and Particular/Regular Baptists.

9. Fristoe, *Concise History of the Ketocton*, 74-79 (quote from 74); Burkitt and Read, *Concise History of the Kehukee*, 55-57.

10. Fristoe, *Concise History of the Ketocton*, 85; Burkitt and Read, *Concise History of the Kehukee*, 57 (italics in the original); Hassell and Hassell, *History of the Church of God*, 577.

11. Burkitt and Read, *Concise History of the Kehukee*, 32, 21 (italics in original); Fristoe, *Concise History of the Ketocton*, 21.

12. Ruth H. Bloch, *Visionary Republic: Millennial Themes in American Thought, 1756-1800* (New York: Cambridge University Press, 1985).

13. Nathan O. Hatch, *The Democratization of American Christianity* (New Haven, Conn.: Yale University Press, 1989), 13; Christine Leigh Heyrman, *Southern Cross: The Beginnings of the Bible Belt* (New York: Knopf, 1997), 78-82.

14. Peter Cartwright, *Autobiography of Peter Cartwright: The Backwoods Preacher*, ed. W. P. Strickland (New York: Carlton and Porter, 1857), 79, 46; Boles, *Great Revival*, 125, 102 (page citations are to the 1996 edition).

15. Jon Butler, *Awash in a Sea of Faith: Christianizing the American People* (Cambridge, Mass.: Harvard University Press, 1990), 216-18; Robert H. Abzug, *Cosmos Crumbling: American Reform and the Religious Imagination* (New York: Oxford University Press, 1994).

16. David Benedict, *Fifty Years among the Baptists* (New York: Sheldon and Company, 1860), 111, 183; Mk 16:15 and Mt 28:19; George Winfred Hervey, *The Story of Baptist Missions in Foreign Lands: From the Time of Carey to the Present Date* (St. Louis: Chancy R. Barnes, 1884), xvii, xv, xvi.

17. Adiel Sherwood, "The Identity of Primitive and Modern Missions: A Discourse," *Southern Baptist Preacher; Or, Sermons by Living Baptist Ministers in the South* 1, no. 4 (1840): 63 (italics in the original); James B. Taylor, *Lives of Virginia Baptist Ministers*, 2nd ed. (Richmond, Va.: Yale and Wyatt, 1838), 433-35; Benedict, *Fifty Years*, 111-16 (quote from 114).

18. Benedict, *Fifty Years*, 118-25 (quotes from 118 and 124); Hervey, *Baptist Missions*, 193-94. Benedict mentioned that the end of Rice's "laborious, peculiar, and earthly career" came "in South Carolina, in 1836, at the age of fifty-three." James Taylor lauded Rice but conceded that "as a financier he was not skilled." See Taylor, *Lives of Virginia Baptist Ministers*, 436.

19. Benedict, *Fifty Years*, 238, 431.

20. Hervey, *Baptist Missions*, xv; Benedict, *Fifty Years*, 217-18.

21. James Osbourn, *A Religious Devil Detected; or, Apollyon's Soliloquies Overheard by a Listener, and the Depths of Satan Exposed* (Baltimore: Toy, 1834), 150.

22. See, for example, Hezekiah West, letter to the editor, *ST*, 11 December 1833, 5.

23. Quoted in Paul Brewster, *Andrew Fuller: Model Pastor-Theologian* (Nashville, Tenn.: B and H Publishing, 2010), 67.

24. Gilbert Beebe, "Remarks on Religious Revivals," *ST*, 15 April 1905, 247 (originally published in June 1862).

25. These were Lemuel Burkitt and Jesse Read's 1803 account and Joseph Biggs's 1834 revision, a work written in the immediate wake of the schism. Joseph Biggs, Lemuel Burkitt, and Jesse Read, *A Concise History of the Kehukee Baptist Association, from Its Original Rise to the Present Time* (Tarboro, N.C.: G. Howard, 1834).

26. Hassell and Hassell, *History of the Church of God*, 578, 587.

27. Ibid., 721.

28. Ibid., 586.

29. Ibid., 579.

30. Ibid., 717.

31. Ibid., 721; Beebe, "Remarks on Religious Revivals," 248; Hassell and Hassell, *History of the Church of God*, 334.

32. Hassell and Hassell, *History of the Church of God*, 722, 738, 754, 723, 744, 737. "Wire-worker" was Victorian-era slang for a scheming politician. See Richard H. Thornton and Louise Hanley, *An American Glossary: Being an Attempt to Illustrate Certain Americanisms upon Historical Principles* (London: Francis, 1900), 949.

33. Richard Hofstadter, *The Paranoid Style in American Politics, and Other Essays* (New York: Knopf, 1965).

34. Hassell and Hassell, *History of the Church of God*, 622.

35. Ibid., 582; John Taylor, *Thoughts on Missions* (Franklin County, Ky., 1820), 6; Joshua Lawrence, writing in an 1831 issue of the *Church Advocate*, quoted in Dan B. Wimberly, *Frontier Religion: Elder Daniel Parker, His Religious and Political Life* (Austin, Tex.: Eakin Press, 2002), 83; John Taylor, *Thoughts on Missions*, 10. Republicanism was ubiquitous among American Protestants. A confluence of republican political ideology, commonsense philosophy, and evangelical Protestantism shaped what Mark A. Noll has described as the American intellectual synthesis. Primitive Baptists' self-image could fit comfortably within the generous confines of Noll's term, but Primitives were considerably more skeptical of the senses than many nineteenth-century Protestants. See Noll, *America's God: From Jonathan Edwards to Abraham Lincoln* (New York: Oxford University Press, 2002).

36. Benjamin Griffin, *History of the Primitive Baptists of Mississippi....* (Jackson, Miss.: Barksdale and Jones, 1853), 245; John M. Watson, *The Old Baptist Test; or Bible Signs of the Lord's People* (Nashville, Tenn.: Republican Banner Press, 1855), 55–56; Tarboro Primitive Baptist Church Record Book, 31 October 1829, DMR; Hassell and Hassell, *History of the Church of God*, 333.

37. Peck quoted in Harry L. Poe, "The History of the Anti-missionary Baptists," *Chronicle* 2, no. 2 (1939): 54; John Frederick Mallett Journal, DMR (spelling and punctuation in the original); "The North Carolina Whig's Memorial and Remonstrance," *North Carolina Baptist Interpreter*, 4 January 1834, 12; Benedict, *Fifty Years*, 134; "Circular Letter," in *Minutes of the Sandy Creek Baptist Association, Convened at Rocky Springs Meeting House, Chatham County, North Carolina, on the 17th, 28th and 29th Days of October, A.D. 1832* (Pittsborough, N.C.: Henry Ward, 1832), 15; Samuel Boykin, *History of the Baptist Denomination in Georgia: With Biographical Compendium and Portrait Gallery of Baptist Ministers and Other Georgia Baptists* (Atlanta, Ga.: J. P. Harrison and Co., 1881), 172; Hatch, *Democratization of American Christianity*, 202, 205; Beth Barton Schweiger, *The Gospel Working Up: Progress and the Pulpit*

in Nineteenth Century Virginia (New York: Oxford University Press, 2000), 6. John Frederick Mallett's remarks in his journal appear to be written in early 1854. At about this time, Mallett was shifting his religious identification from Methodist to Campbellite Baptist. His sentiments here reflected widely held missionary Baptist opinions, and, indeed, Mallett found friendly audiences at the missionary Baptist churches in eastern North Carolina.

38. On the issues of stereotype and cultural durability, I have been guided by Robert Cantwell's work; see especially his *Ethnomimesis: Folklife and the Representation of Culture* (Chapel Hill: University of North Carolina Press, 1993), 150–84; and James L. Peacock and Ruel W. Tyson, *Pilgrims of Paradox: Calvinism and Experience among the Primitive Baptists of the Blue Ridge* (Washington, D.C.: Smithsonian Institution Press, 1989).

39. Some Baptists were aware of this process. For example, the minutes from an 1846 meeting of the pro-missions Florida Baptist Association noted that schism seemed to be forcing Baptists on either side of the divide into increasingly severe versions of their positions: "It is unfortunate for the people of God that when they disagree on certain points of doctrine . . . they become perfect antipodes to each other." Quoted in John G. Crowley, *Primitive Baptists of the Wiregrass South: 1815 to the Present* (Gainesville: University Press of Florida, 1998), 79. For similar observation from the Primitive Baptist side of the ledger, see Watson, *Old Baptist Test*, 189–90.

40. "Obituary. Gilbert Beebe," *NYT*, 3 May 1881; Gilbert Beebe, "2 Timothy IV. 3, 4," *ST*, 10 October 1856.

41. Beebe, "Remarks on Religious Revivals," 248; Gilbert Beebe to Zelotes Grenell, 27 December 1830, in Levi Osborn Grenelle, *Life and Labors of Elder Zelotes Grenell: For Sixty-Four Years an Eminently Successful Baptist Minister, 1818–1882* (n.p. [New Jersey?]: North Jersey Baptist Association, 1885), 184 (punctuation as in the original).

42. William G. McLoughlin, *Soul Liberty: The Baptists' Struggle in New England, 1630–1833* (Hanover, N.H.: University Press of New England, 1991), 3; Sydney E. Ahlstrom, *A Religious History of the American People* (New Haven, Conn.: Yale University Press, 1972), 721; Bertram Wyatt-Brown, *The Shaping of Southern Culture: Honor, Grace, and War, 1760s–1890s* (Chapel Hill: University of North Carolina Press, 2001), 134–35.

Chapter Two

1. Thomas Hill Sr., letter to the editor, *PB*, 23 October 1841, 314, 316; ibid., 13 November 1841; ibid., 27 November 1841.

2. Edmund Sears Morgan, *Visible Saints: The History of a Puritan Idea* (New York: New York University Press, 1963); Patricia Caldwell, *The Puritan Conversion Narrative: The Beginnings of American Expression* (New York: Cambridge University Press, 1983); Peter G. Stromberg, *Language and Self-Transformation: A Study of the Christian Conversion Narrative* (New York: Cambridge University Press, 1993); Rodger M. Payne, *The Self and the Sacred: Conversion and Autobiography in Early American Protestantism* (Knoxville: University of Tennessee Press, 1998). "Conversion morphology" was Edmund Morgan's coinage.

3. James R. Mathis, *The Making of the Primitive Baptists: A Cultural and Intellectual History of the Anti-mission Movement, 1800–1840* (New York: Routledge, 2004), 127–47.

4. This succinct definition of sincerity comes from Lionel Trilling, *Sincerity and Authenticity* (Cambridge, Mass.: Harvard University Press, 1972), 2.

5. Sarah Ann Hollister, "From Sister Hollister to Sister Mather, after Reading Her Experience, as Published in a Late Number of the *Monitor*," *CDA* 3 (1840): 266–69 (quotes from 267).

6. John M. Watson, *The Old Baptist Test; or Bible Signs of the Lord's People* (Nashville, Tenn.: Republican Banner Press, 1855), 21 (see also 1 Jn 5:10); Lick Fork Primitive Baptist Church Record Book, January 1824, BHC; Peter L. Branstetter, "The Life of Elder Peter Branstetter—Experience and Call to the Ministry," 9 June 1887, Primitive Baptist Online, <http://primitivebaptist.info/mambo//content/view/936/36/> (14 September 2006). The distinction between prayer and watching was a common one. See, for instance, Martha A. Walker, letter to the editor, *PB*, 28 August 1840, 298–99. Though Primitive Baptists would disavow the language of intent and would deny that they had any ability to influence their otherworldly fate, the practice of watching seems to have been designed to catch sin before it metastasized or even to prevent its growth in the first place.

7. S. A. Elkins, "The Life and Writings of Elder Peter Branstetter: Character Sketch," December 1891, Primitive Baptist Online, <http://primitivebaptist.info/mambo//content/view/937/36/> (14 September 2006).

8. Joshua Lawrence, "Victorious Grace: Being a Mere Glance of His Experience," *PB*, 23 October 1841, 311.

9. Hollister, "From Sister Hollister," 268.

10. Rebecca Anna Phillips, *Led by a Way I Knew Not: Being the Christian Experience, and Reasons for Leaving the Missionary Baptists, and Uniting with the Primitive Baptists, with an Exposition of the Issues Dividing Them ... Together with Supplementary Articles on Scriptural Subjects* (Pulaski City, Va.: Hurst, 1901), 58; Rebecca Anna Phillips, *The Experience of R. Anna Phillips, of Rome, Georgia, and Her Reasons for Uniting with the Primitive Baptists* (Wilson, N.C.: P. D. Gold, 1875); Phillips, *Led by a Way I Knew Not*, 1.

11. Donald G. Mathews, *Religion in the Old South* (Chicago: University of Chicago Press, 1977), 215. Mathews contrasted southern whites' experience of being "broken down" under preaching with southern blacks' experience of being lifted up.

12. Mary Beckley Bristow, "Diary of Miss Mary B. Bristow: 1844–1863, Containing a Partial Record of Activities of Sardis Baptist Church, Licking Association in Kentucky," UKY.

13. See, for example, William Scarborough's letter to his brother, Daniel, who expressed astonishment that William had joined the Primitive Baptists. William Scarborough wrote: "I read the Scripture prayerfully and attentively and knowing from my own feelings if I am a child of god it is free grace alone and unmerited favor on my part for I tryed my own strength till I thought every other man on earth had a better chance for heaven then myself." William Scarborough to Daniel Scarborough, 7 December 1839, William Scarborough Papers, Private Collection #906, State Archives of North Carolina, Raleigh.

14. Hill, letter to the editor, 23 October 1841, 314, 316; ibid., 13 November 1841, 333.

15. J. Taylor Moore, *A Biography of the Late Elder Thos. P. Dudley* (Occoquan, Va.[?]: Printed at the Sectarian Printing Office by Wm. M. Smoot[?], 1891), 24–25. Moore was quoting from Dudley's 1851 letters to the *Signs of the Times*.

16. Joshua Lawrence, "Victorious Grace: Being a Mere Glance of His Experience," *PB*, 9 October 1841, 299, 301, 302; ibid., Joshua Lawrence, "Victorious Grace: Being a Mere Glance of His Experience," *PB*, 27 November 1841, 340.

17. Arnold Bolch Jr., letter to the editor, *CDA* 1 (1837): 151.

18. R. D. Hart, "Biography of Elder Joshua Lawrence," *PB*, 28 October 1843.

19. J. H. Purifoy, "Autobiography," *GM* 10, no. 8 (August 1888): 343–44.

20. Ibid.

21. Silas H. Durand, *Fragments: Autobiography and Later Writings* (Philadelphia: Biddle Press, 1920), 77. Durand originally penned this piece, "Thoughts in Sickness," in 1900.

22. Wesley quoted in Mark A. Noll, *America's God: From Jonathan Edwards to Abraham Lincoln* (New York: Oxford University Press, 2002), 335.

23. Leigh Eric Schmidt, *Hearing Things: Religion, Illusion, and the American Enlightenment* (Cambridge, Mass.: Harvard University Press, 2000), 38–77 (quote from 47); Christine Leigh Heyrman, *Southern Cross: The Beginnings of the Bible Belt* (New York: Knopf, 1997), 34; John Corrigan, *Business of the Heart: Religion and Emotion in the Nineteenth Century* (Berkeley: University of California Press, 2002), 81. Also see Richard Rabinowitz, *The Spiritual Self in Everyday Life: The Transformation of Personal Religious Experience in Nineteenth-Century New England* (Boston: Northeastern University Press, 1989), 98, on what he calls the "distinctive cognitive style" fostered by new-measures revivalism.

24. Joseph Biggs, letter to the editor, *PB*, 9 January 1836, 10; "Address to the Particular Baptist Churches of the 'Old School' in the United States," *ST*, 3 July 1833, 246; Edward Beecher, "The Nature, Importance, and Means of Eminent Holiness throughout the Church," *American National Preacher* 10, nos. 1 and 2 (1835): 222; Mark Bennett, letter to the editor, *PB*, 13 February 1836, 42. Bennett's missive was an uncommon example of a Primitive Baptist directly engaging one of the doyens of northern establishment Protestantism.

25. John Respess, "The Experience of a Sinner," *GM* 13, no. 8 (August 1891): 321. This is one part of Respess's twelve-part serialized autobiography. Respess was born in 1831 in Upson County, Georgia. For similar observations, see H. C. Lee, "H. C. Lee: Experience and Death," *GM* 13, no. 4 (April 1891): 161. Lee, who was born in 1813, had spent his youth "bound in sorrow." God appeared to him, though "doubts and fears," he wrote, "often disturbed my mind." These formative experiences eventually drew him toward the Primitive Baptists, about whom he knew little if anything. "I had never heard an experience related, or seen any person baptized, and I was fearful that I was deceived, and did not wish to deceive others," he wrote. "I never had the pleasure of attending meeting often, as there was no church near us."

26. Joseph B. Lewis, letter to the editor, *PB*, 26 February 1842, 55–56; Hill, letter to the editor, 13 November 1841, 333. Many Primitives described scenes similar to Hill's at the Little Pigeon River. See, for example, Isaac N. Vanmeter, letter to

the editor, *GM* 7, no. 3 (March 1885): 113-19; and Branstetter, "Life of Elder Peter Branstetter."

27. David Jacks, letter to the editor, *PB*, 10 March 1838, 68; A. J. Coleman, letter to the editor, ibid., 23 September 1843, 286; Samuel Clark, letter to the editor, ibid., 23 January 1841, 26.

28. Hill, letter to the editor, 27 November 1841, 341.

29. Finney quoted in Noll, *America's God*, 307.

30. Ps 22:6, 22:1. This kind of double action makes me skeptical of Bertram Wyatt-Brown's claim that the Primitives' focus on human depravity and inability indicates that they were more concerned with justice than with love. It seems to me that these two categories were, as they say, inextricably linked. Primitives craved God's love precisely because they knew he was just to condemn them. See Wyatt-Brown, *The Shaping of Southern Culture: Honor, Grace, and War, 1760s-1890s* (Chapel Hill: University of North Carolina Press, 2001), 126.

31. Lee Hanks, "The Conflicts of an Orphan," Primitive Baptist Online, 1 March 1886, <http://primitivebaptist.info/mambo//content/view/124/36/> (2 February 2007); Benjamin Lloyd, *The Primitive Hymns, Spiritual Songs, and Sacred Poems: Regularly Selected, Classified and Set in Order and Adapted to Social Singing and All Occasions of Divine Worship* (Greenville, Ala.: published for the proprietor, 1841), 294; Gilbert Beebe, *The Baptist Hymn Book: Comprising a Choice Collection of Psalms, Hymns and Spiritual Songs Adapted to the Faith and Order of the Old School, or Primitive Baptists in the United States of America*, 2nd stereotype ed. (Middletown, N.Y.: office of the "Signs of the Times," 1859), 614. Hanks originally published his narrative in 1886 in the *Primitive Monitor*. Hanks was born in Pittsylvania County, Virginia, in 1861.

32. Joshua Lawrence, "Victorious Grace: Being a Mere Glance of His Experience," *PB*, 11 December 1841, 357.

33. Watson, *Old Baptist Test*, 20, 195; Amans Veritatis, "A Difference between the Spirit of Christ and Mere Party Zeal," *CDA* 1 (1837): 6.

34. Dan B. Wimberly, *Frontier Religion: Elder Daniel Parker, His Religious and Political Life* (Austin, Tex.: Eakin Press, 2002), vii-xvii, 1-25 (quote from 15); Nathan O. Hatch, *The Democratization of American Christianity* (New Haven, Conn.: Yale University Press, 1989), 178.

35. Parker first outlined his thoughts on Two Seedism in 1826 in a pair of pamphlets, *Views on the Two Seeds* and *A Supplement or Explanation of My Views on the Two Seeds*.

36. Wimberly, *Frontier Religion*, 151; G. M. Thompson to Jesse C. Knight, 16 November 1857, B. F. Knight Papers, DMR; unnamed Parker critic quoted in Wimberly, *Frontier Religion*, 136. The "American Manichaeanism" epithet was Alexander Campbell's, but it was a sentiment shared by Parker's Primitive Baptist critics.

37. Jeffrey Wayne Taylor, *The Formation of the Primitive Baptist Movement* (Kitchener, Ont.: Pandora Press, 2004), 139; William Warren Sweet, *The Baptists, 1783-1830: A Collection of Source Material* (New York: Cooper Square, 1964).

38. Wimberly, *Frontier Religion*, 73.

39. Cushing Biggs Hassell Diary, 11 December 1848, CBH, SHC; Bolch, letter to the editor; Joseph King, letter to the editor, *PB*, 23 April 1836; Wm. Eblen, letter to the

editor, *PB*, 14 May 1836; *Minutes of the Cumberland Baptist Association: Convened at Friendship Meeting-house, Davidson County, Ten.* (Franklin, Tenn.: The Review, 1835), 7; Joshua Lawrence, letter to the editor, *PB*, 23 January 1836.

40. Joshua Lawrence, *A Patriotic Discourse: Delivered by the Rev. Joshua Lawrence, at the Old Church in Tarborough, North Carolina, on Sunday, the 4th of July, 1830* (Tarborough, N.C.: Free Press, 1830), 14.

41. Shadrach Mustain, letter to the editor, *PB*, 10 February 1844, 46.

42. Brush Creek Meeting House Record Book, 30 April 1853, PBL.

Chapter Three

1. C. B. Hassell, letter to the editor, *ST*, 24 September 1834, 308.

2. 2 Pt 2:1; Mt 20:28; Kenneth Moore Startup, *The Root of All Evil: The Protestant Clergy and the Economic Mind of the Old South* (Athens: University of Georgia Press, 1997).

3. John Taylor, *Thoughts on Missions* (Franklin County, Ky., 1820), 4; editorial, *PB*, 9 January 1836, 8.

4. Keith Robert Burich, "The Primitive Baptist Schism in North Carolina: A Study of the Professionalization of the Baptist Ministry" (M.A. thesis, University of North Carolina at Chapel Hill, 1973). More recently, James R. Mathis examined two churches in Muscogee County, Georgia, in 1850. He concluded that missionary Baptists "came from only a slightly higher social status" than Primitives, and that Primitives were "not drawn from the bottom of society . . . but were a decidedly middle class group." See Mathis, *The Making of the Primitive Baptists: A Cultural and Intellectual History of the Anti-mission Movement, 1800–1840* (New York: Routledge, 2004), 121–24.

I cross-referenced names in the Tarboro church record book with information gleaned from census schedules, abstracts of wills, and marriage records. Tarboro Primitive Baptist Church Record Book, DMR; David B. Gammon, ed., *Abstracts of Wills of Edgecombe County, North Carolina* (Raleigh, N.C.: D. B. Gammon, 1992); Ruth Smith Williams, ed., *Marriages of Early Edgecombe County, North Carolina, 1773–1868* (Rocky Mount, N.C.: Dixie Letter Service, 1958); Stephen E. Bradley Jr., ed., *The 1800 and 1810 Federal Censuses: Edgecombe County, North Carolina* (South Boston, Va.: S .E. Bradley, 1989) and *The 1830 Federal Census: Edgecombe County, North Carolina* (South Boston, Va.: S. E. Bradley, 1987); Dorothy Williams Potter, ed., *1820 Federal Census of North Carolina*, vol. 19 (Tullahoma, Tenn.: Dorothy Williams Potter, 1972). The definition of yeoman farmer household comes from Stephanie McCurry, *Masters of Small Worlds: Yeoman Households, Gender Relations, and the Political Culture of the Antebellum South Carolina Low Country* (New York: Oxford University Press, 1995), 47–55.

5. Ira Durwood Hudgins, "The Anti-missionary Controversy among Baptists," *Chronicle* 14, no. 4 (1951); Bertram Wyatt-Brown, "The Antimission Movement in the Jacksonian South: A Study in Regional Folk Culture," *Journal of Southern History* 36, no. 4 (1970); T. Scott Miyakawa, *Protestants and Pioneers: Individualism and Conformity on the American Frontier* (Chicago: University of Chicago Press, 1964); William Warren Sweet, ed., *The Baptists, 1783–1830: A Collection of Source Material* (New York: Cooper Square, 1964); John G. Crowley, *Primitive Baptists of the Wiregrass*

South: 1815 to the Present (Gainesville: University Press of Florida, 1998). The quote comes from Wyatt-Brown, *The Shaping of Southern Culture: Honor, Grace, and War, 1760s-1890s* (Chapel Hill: University of North Carolina Press, 2001), 134-35. John B. Boles, *Religion in Antebellum Kentucky* (Lexington: University Press of Kentucky, 1995), 137, has made a similar point. Antebellum Primitive Baptists in Kentucky "are important because they were an intense microcosm of the larger Baptist—and southern—society," Boles wrote. "As their remote mountain valley communities were to the rest of Kentucky, so the rural, agricultural South was to the rapidly changing, urbanizing, industrializing North with its shifting views on slavery. Much of southern history may be see as a religiocultural reaction to the emergent North."

6. Cushing Biggs Hassell and Sylvester Hassell, *History of the Church of God, from the Creation to A.D. 1885; Including Especially the History of the Kehukee Primitive Baptist Association* (Middletown, N.Y.: Gilbert Beebe's Sons, 1886), 55; William Garrard and Cushing Biggs Hassell, *Friendly Greetings across the Water, or the Love Letters of Elders Garrard and Hassell* (New York: Chatterton and Crist, 1847), 18.

7. "Close Communion," *PB*, 9 January 1836, 14 (this article was a reprint of the 1834 circular letter from the Little River Association); C. B. Hassell, "The Salvation of the Righteous Is of the Lord," ibid., 26 March 1836, 85; Joshua Lawrence, letter to the editor, ibid., 27 February 1836, 50; Joshua Lawrence, letter to the editor, 9 January 1836, 4. The image of evangelicals hustling their way into heaven by steam, a common one in Old Baptist circles and, perhaps, in the culture at large, appeared a few years later in Nathaniel Hawthorne's 1843 allegory "The Celestial Railroad," in which naive pilgrims eagerly let Mr. Smooth-it-away lead them by train and steamboat to their doom. Hassell and his son Sylvester were fond of Hawthorne's satirization of what they saw as modern religion's foolish optimism. The story appears at the end of the Hassells' *History of the Church of God*, serving as an aesthetic coda to the larger work's symphony of facts, narrative streams, and arguments.

8. S. W. [?] Outterbridge, Spring Green Church (Flat Swamp, Martin Co., N.C.), to the Kehukee Association, 21 August 1869, Bryant Bennett Papers, DMR; "The Mystery of Faith," *PB*, 14 May 1836, 144. For similar sentiments about the crucifixion-as-debt-payment, see, for example, hymn 342 in James Osbourn, *North Carolina Sonnets, or A Selection of Choice Hymns for the Use of Old School Baptists: Compiled by the Recommendation of the Kehukee Association* (Baltimore: John D. Toy, 1844), 197.

9. John Clark, letter to the editor, *PB*, 14 May 1836, 135; James Osbourn, letter to the editor, ibid., 13 January 1844, 3; James Osbourn, "An Address to the Mayo Baptist Association, in the State of North Carolina, and to All Sister Associations with Whom She Corresponds," *ST*, 5 June 1833, 209; Lawrence, letter to the editor, 9 January 1836, 6; Garrard and Hassell, *Friendly Greetings*, 8.

10. "The Two Covenants," *PB*, 3 October 1835, 5-8. For a similar account of this wholly "divine transaction," see Trust, "The Final Salvation of the Redeemed Not Doubtful, but Certain," *CDA* 1 (1837): 114-17.

11. Cushing Biggs Hassell, "Auto-Biography," 23-24, 47, 58, CBH. For similar sentiments (God's involvement in everything as being a happy fact) from another Primitive believer, see, for instance, "A Conversation on the Question," *CDA* 1 (1837): 81-84. The motivational force of Calvinism was, of course, one of Max Weber's primary concerns

in *The Protestant Ethic and the Spirit of Capitalism*, trans. Talcott Parsons (New York: Scribner, 1958).

12. Hassell, "Auto-Biography," 58. As the years wore on, a few Primitive Baptist preachers, with a dampened sense of irony, openly grumbled about what they believed were their close-fisted flocks. See John M. Watson, *The Old Baptist Test; or Bible Signs of the Lord's People* (Nashville, Tenn.: Republican Banner Press, 1855), 51–53; and P. D. Gold, *A Treatise on the Book of Joshua* (Wilson, N.C.: Zion's Landmark, 1889), 116.

13. Hassell, "Auto-Biography," 49; Hassell's undated notebook, MS 51, Hassell Family Papers, BHC.

14. Cushing Biggs Hassell, appendix to diary, December 1853–June 1859, box 2, vol. 20, folder 22, CBH; Cushing Biggs Hassell Diary, 24 April 1847, 103, ibid.

15. Hassell, "Auto-Biography," 57–58.

16. Ibid., 57–59; Weber, *Protestant Ethic*; Daniel T. Rogers, *The Work Ethic in Industrial America: 1850–1920* (Chicago: University of Chicago Press, 1974).

17. Hassell, "Auto-Biography," 39, 41, 46–47, 49. Hassell's decision, albeit a temporary one, to eliminate his reliance on credit was a common one for antebellum entrepreneurs scarred by steep losses or business failure. See Edward J. Balleisen, *Navigating Failure: Bankruptcy and Commercial Society in Antebellum America* (Chapel Hill: University of North Carolina Press, 2001), 16, 200–201.

18. Hassell Diary, 27 October 1849, 317; 15 May 1849, 275. In a similar entry from 2 May 1849, Hassell linked his "barrenness of soul" to his "close connection with the world of secular matters."

19. Ibid., 27 October 1849, 276.

20. Ibid., 12 July 1849, 292; 27 October 1849, 317.

21. Ibid., 14 June 1850, 358. In a January 1852 church meeting, Hassell identified himself as "poor" and "now made public" his opinion that preachers ought to accept donations and that churches should contemplate establishing a separate fund as a "gift" (he refused to call it a salary) to their minister. Ibid., 10 January 1852, 465. But according to Hassell's own records, he had started accepting donations for his preaching in May 1850. It is difficult to resolve this discrepancy. It may be, however, that Hassell did, in fact, begin accepting donations in May 1850 for most of his preaching but that he refused to do so at his home church of Skewarkey, where he was ordained and had "avowed his intention of receiving nothing as a pecuniary compensation" when he first took charge of the church. During these years, Hassell regularly preached at several Primitive Baptist churches near his home in Williamston, North Carolina. He also embarked on preaching tours through the state's eastern and central counties. For records of donations made to Hassell, see his booklet "Ordinations, Baptisms, Donations," box 3, vol. 26, folder 28, CBH.

22. Hassell Diary, 14 June 1850, 358; 4 July 1850, 363; 10 April 1851, 414; 11 April 1851, 414; 21 June 1851, 429; 11 June 1851, 426–27.

23. Ibid., 6 November 1851, 454. The historian Frank J. Byrne argues that "sentiment" and a "spirit of camaraderie" characterized relationships between merchants and their clerks in the old South. See Byrne, *Becoming Bourgeois: Merchant Culture in the South, 1820–1865* (Lexington: University Press of Kentucky, 2006), 38. C. B. Hassell's counting room, however, proved an unusually inhospitable place, for suspicion and

blame stained Hassell's relationships with the men he employed. He pointed his finger at his clerk when his business soured in the mid-1830s. He fired a second clerk who enjoyed himself too much after hours.

24. Hassell and Hassell, *History of the Church of God*, 929; Hassell Diary, 27 December 1851, 462; 10 January 1852, 465.

25. Hassell Diary, 11 May 1852, 847; 17 June 1852, 854.

26. Ibid., 17 June 1852, 854; 31 December 1852, 889.

27. Ibid., 6 May 1852, 486; 3 May 1852, 485.

28. Ibid., 4 January 1852, 464; Rv 18:4.

29. Joshua Lawrence, "Victorious Grace: Being a Mere Glance of His Experience," *PB*, 27 November 1841, 337. This is one of several visions Lawrence related in his spiritual autobiography. Though this vision came upon him while he was asleep, Lawrence did not consider it a dream. A mere "wandering of the thoughts," dreams left "but little impression on the mind, or feelings." Visions, by contrast, permanently shaped subsequent experience. For Lawrence's complete discussion of the differences between visions and dreams, see the third published installment of his spiritual autobiography: "Victorious Grace: Being a Mere Glance of His Experience," *PB*, 13 November 1841, 324. The *Primitive Baptist* serialized Lawrence's autobiography over five issues. Lawrence wrote the original manuscript in 1812; it resides in the Joshua Lawrence Papers, SHC. Many thanks to Sandra Hayslette, whose "Missions, Markets, and Men: A Baptist Contest of Values in Tarboro, North Carolina, 1800–1835" (M.A. thesis, University of North Carolina at Chapel Hill, 1995) broached the question of the gendered dimensions of the Primitive Baptist movement. I follow Hayslette in describing Joshua Lawrence's patriarchal bent, but we differ significantly in our conclusions.

30. Lawrence, "Victorious Grace," 27 November 1841, 338. The phrase "family religion" comes from Donald Mathews, who uses it to describe evangelicals' particular emphasis on the family as the center of religious life. I, too, use it in that sense, but I also want to emphasize the extent to which evangelicals and Primitive Baptists saw the church itself as a family. Donald G. Mathews, *Religion in the Old South* (Chicago: University of Chicago Press, 1977), 44–45, 97–101.

31. Joshua Lawrence, letter to the editor, 27 February 1836, 55.

32. Joshua Lawrence, *The American Telescope, by a Clodhopper, of North Carolina* (Philadelphia: printed for the author, 1825), 6, 8; Joshua Lawrence, letter to the editor, *PB*, 13 February 1836, 35. That missionaries personally profited from their endeavors was a persistent theme of Primitive Baptist writing. The specimen issue of the *Primitive Baptist*, for instance, featured a table purporting to show the considerable salaries and fees paid to the agents of the North Carolina Baptist Society for Foreign and Domestic Missions. See "Extract from the 'Minutes of the North Carolina Baptist Society for Foreign and Domestic Missions, convened at Haywood's meeting house, Franklin county, May 22, 1824,'" *PB*, 3 October 1835, 3. The conventions of the anti-missionary polemic usually did not allow for distinctions to be drawn between missionaries and missions-supporting clergy. But we can do what they chose not to do. We can see that the Primitives' notion of the wealthy circuit rider was off base. In 1840, for instance, Methodist circuit riders had a yearly income of $400 plus payment for "traveling and table" expenses. On the other hand, the Primitives' habitual concern with well-to-do

preachers was not unfounded. In southern towns, at least, pastors by 1860 boasted an average wealth of $10,600 as opposed to the $2,500 nationwide average for free adult men. There were, however, key denominational tends, with Episcopalians and Presbyterians near the top of the ranks and Baptists and Methodists toward the bottom. See E. Brooks Holifield, *The Gentlemen Theologians: American Theology in Southern Culture, 1795-1860* (Durham: Duke University Press, 1978), 28-30.

33. Lawrence, letter to the editor, 27 February 1836, 53; Joshua Lawrence, *A Patriotic Discourse: Delivered by the Rev. Joshua Lawrence, at the Old Church in Tarborough, North Carolina, on Sunday, the 4th of July, 1830* (Tarborough, N.C.: Free Press, 1830), 14; Joshua Lawrence, "Teeth to Teeth: Tom Thumb Tugging with the Wolves for the Sheepskin," *PB*, 27 May 1837, 148. The relevant Bible passages are Gn 3:1-19; 1 Kgs 11:3-13; Jgs 16:4-20; 2 Tm 3:6; and Ex 32:1-35. The "silly women" image circulated widely in Primitive Baptist circles. See, for example, "Reasons for Roundly Asserting That the Popular Institutions Are Anti-Christian," *PB*, 3 October 1835, 12.

34. Joshua Lawrence, "Teeth to Teeth: Tom Thumb Tugging with the Wolves for the Sheepskin," *PB*, 28 January 1837, 21-22; Lawrence, *American Telescope*, 9; Lawrence, "Teeth to Teeth," 27 May 1837, 150. For similar accusations made by others, see Kemuel C. Gilbert, letter to the editor, *PB*, 26 March 1836, 82.

35. See Mary P. Ryan, *Cradle of the Middle Class: The Family in Oneida County, New York, 1790-1865* (Cambridge: Cambridge University Press, 1981), 75-104, on the women's presence and influence in evangelical churches. Mathews, *Religion in the Old South*, 47, estimated that the ratio of women to men in southern evangelical churches was 65 to 35. For additional information about women's majority presence in evangelical churches in the early nineteenth century, see Christine Leigh Heyrman, *Southern Cross: The Beginnings of the Bible Belt* (New York: Knopf, 1997), especially 311-12n13. McCurry conducted a systematic analysis of gender ratios in evangelical churches in antebellum-era low country South Carolina. In McCurry's sample of ten evangelical Baptist churches, women composed 59.4 percent of the total membership. McCurry looked at one Primitive Baptist church, which had only a one-woman majority. See McCurry, *Masters of Small Worlds*, 162-63.

36. Mathews, *Religion in the Old South*, 111. See McCurry, *Masters of Small Worlds*, especially 171-207, for a more skeptical view about the place of southern evangelical women. McCurry insists that southern evangelical women, unlike their northern counterparts, never developed a positive, public identity. Instead, secular gender norms and hierarchies continually triumphed over any egalitarian tendencies within the churches or their theologies. McCurry sees her research as, in part, a corrective to the scholarship on northern evangelical women—scholarship that, she argues, has too often been interpreted as having national, rather than regional, implications. Heyrman, *Southern Cross*, 117-205, argues that after 1800, southern evangelicals gradually tempered and even erased the egalitarian aspects of church life in order "to cultivate the South's masters."

37. Ann Douglas, *The Feminization of American Culture* (New York: Knopf, 1977); "Proposals for Publishing a Semi-monthly paper, Called 'Signs of the Times,'" *ST*, 28 November 1832, 16.

38. Joshua Lawrence, "Teeth to Teeth: Tom Thumb Tugging with the Wolves for the Sheepskin," *PB*, 9 September 1837, 259; Joshua Lawrence, letter to the editor, ibid., 23 January 1836, 18; Joshua Lawrence, "Circular Letter," ibid., 24 November 1838, 341. Other Primitives, too, availed themselves of the passage in 1 Pt 2:2 that compares new believers in Christ to "newborn babes" who "desire the sincere milk of the word." See Wilson Thompson, *The Autobiography of Elder Wilson Thompson Embracing a Sketch of His Life, Travels, & Ministerial Labors, in Which Is Included a Concise History of the Old Order of Regular Baptist Churches* (Cincinnati: Moore, Wilstach and Baldwin, 1867), 400; "Circular Letter: Of the Kehukee Association, of 1836," *PB*, 26 November 1836, 338; and Vachal D. Whatley, letter to the editor, *PB*, 22 May 1841, 152.

39. Lawrence, letter to the editor, 23 January 1836, 18; Lawrence, "Teeth to Teeth," 9 September 1837, 259. As we have seen, C. B. Hassell used a similar metaphor—the dry breast—to describe Episcopal preaching.

40. Hassell, "Auto-Biography," 58; Lawrence, letter to the editor, 23 January 1836, 18; "Ministerial Support," *PB*, 3 October 1835.

41. Esther Barlow, letter to the editor, *CDA* 6 (1843): 185.

42. Gold, *Treatise*, 116; Watson, *Old Baptist Test*, 51–53.

43. Lawrence first inherited wealth. His father left him two male slaves and several tracts of land. Lawrence's marriage brought him an additional pair of slaves. By 1841 Lawrence held land in three North Carolina counties, oversaw a workforce of at least twenty slaves, and supplemented his plantation's profits from cotton, corn, and pork with large catches of shad from the nearby creek. See Gammon, *Abstracts of Wills*; and Bradley, *1800 and 1810 Federal Censuses*.

44. Lawrence, "Victorious Grace," 23 October 1841, 312. Lawrence might have had other reasons to worry about being an impostor. Lawrence's early ministry coincided with a series of spectacular revivals sweeping the South, and his preaching met with similar success. He was ordained in 1801 by two leading lights of the revival in the Kehukee Association, Lemuel Burkitt and Jesse Read. Within two years, Lawrence's efforts added more than one hundred names to the rolls at the Baptist church near the falls of the Tar River. At that time, the revivals in the Kehukee Association featured techniques that Lawrence and his fellow Primitives would later find abhorrent. Preachers, for instance, asked sinners eager for salvation to leave their seats and come toward the pulpit where they became a focus of intensified preaching. See Lemuel Burkitt and Jesse Read, *A Concise History of the Kehukee Baptist Association: From Its Original Rise to the Present Time* (Halifax, N.C.: A. Hodge, 1803), 146. Lawrence, too, backed the Kehukee Association's early involvement with missions, a fact he never acknowledged during his years leading the Primitives' anti-missionary efforts. Lawrence's enemies, in addition to noting his blistering rhetoric, sometimes made this connection, though they often got some of the details wrong. One missionary Baptist, for example, suggested that Lawrence was a "disappointed, vexed man" whose supposed failures as a missionary caused him to turn against the cause with an "envenomed vituperation." See Obadiah Echols, "Controversial Record," *Christian Index* 7, no. 13 (1832): 198.

45. The slogan "Come out of her, my people" (taken from Rv 18:4) emblazoned the masthead of each issue of the *Primitive Baptist*, the Tarborough-based biweekly in which Lawrence's writings most frequently appeared. The magazine's readers wrote

approvingly of its motto and echoed its language. See, for instance, Gray Haggard, letter to the editor, *PB*, 27 February 1836, 61; and Rowell Reese, letter to the editor, ibid., 27 February 1836, 63. Also see the circular letter "Close Communion."

46. James W. Cook, *The Arts of Deception: Playing with Fraud in the Age of Barnum* (Cambridge, Mass.: Harvard University Press, 2001). There is a distinct possibility that Barnum and Joshua Lawrence met. The story is just a historical bauble, but why not tell it? In his autobiography, Barnum writes of visiting a Baptist church at "Rocky Mount Falls, North Carolina," on a Sunday morning in November 1836. Barnum does not mention Lawrence, but Lawrence pastored a church there and it was his home church. As Barnum tells it, he—Barnum—entertained a post-service crowd of about 300 with a forty-five-minute stem-winder. And what was his subject? "The outside show of things is of very small account. We must look to realities and not to appearances." Barnum apparently knew his audience. See P. T. Barnum, *Struggles and Triumphs: Or, Forty Years' Recollections of P. T. Barnum* (London: Sampson Low, Son, and Marston, 1869), 88–89.

47. Garnett Jones, letter to the editor, *ST*, 12 November 1834, 359; T. J. Jackson Lears, *Something for Nothing: Luck in America* (New York: Viking, 2003). "Culture of control" is Lears's coinage.

Chapter Four

1. Annie Marion MacLean, "A Town in Florida," in *The Negro Church: Report of a Social Study Made under the Direction of Atlanta University; Together with the Proceedings of the Eighth Conference for the Study of the Negro Problems, Held at Atlanta University, May 26th, 1903*, ed. W. E. B. Du Bois (Atlanta: Atlanta University Press, 1903), 67.

2. Ibid., 64–68; MacLean was not the only perplexed white outsider to compare the ring shout to an Indian dance. In his Civil War diary, Thomas Wentworth Higginson, an abolitionist, a Unitarian minister, and eventually a Union colonel in a regiment staffed by escaped slaves, described the ring shouts he witnessed on the South Carolina Sea Islands as "half pow-wow, half prayer meeting." See Higginson quoted in Dena J. Epstein, *Sinful Tunes and Spirituals: Black Folk Music to the Civil War* (Urbana: University of Illinois Press, 1977), 280. DeLand had been founded thirty years earlier by Henry A. DeLand, a baking soda manufacturer from western New York, who believed the rolling pinelands and congenial climate would make the region a healthy year-round settlement. See Pleasant Daniel Gold, *History of Volusia County, Florida: Also Biographies of Prominent People of Volusia County* (De Land, Fla.: E. O. Painter Printing, 1927), 111–17; DeLand's population in 1900 was 1,449. See Volusia County Heritage, "City of Deland," <http://volusia.org/history/deland.htm> (9 July 2011); W. E. B. Du Bois, *The Negro Church: Report of a Social Study Made under the Direction of Atlanta University; Together with the Proceedings of the Eighth Conference for the Study of the Negro Problems, Held at Atlanta University, May 26th, 1903* (Atlanta: Atlanta University Press, 1903), ii.

3. Paul Harvey, *Redeeming the South: Religious Cultures and Racial Identities among Southern Baptists, 1865–1925* (Chapel Hill: University of North Carolina Press,

1997), 228. For historians' general assumption that Calvinism was inimical to African Americans, see the discussion in n. 30 to the introduction of *Strangers Below*.

4. *Tenth Annual Session of the Mount Olive Primitive Baptist Association* (Georgia, 1912).

5. U.S. Bureau of the Census, *Religious Bodies: 1916—Separate Denominations: History, Description, and Statistics* (Washington, D.C.: Government Printing Office, 1919), 147; *Minutes of the Sixteenth Annual Session of the Mt. Ramah Primitive Baptist Association* (Americus, Ga.: Americus Printing Co., 1905); Robert G. Gardner, *National Primitive Baptists in Georgia* (Macon: Georgia Baptist Historical Society, 2004), 34; William H. Gaston, "Associational," *HG*, 6 January 1894; National Primitive Baptist Convention of America, *Souvenir and Official Programme of the National Primitive Bapt. Convention America* (n.p.: National Primitive Baptist Convention of America, 1908), 43. Little more than three decades after its founding, the Zion Primitive Baptist Church in Key West owned more than $15,000 of property and paid its preacher an annual salary drawn from the rent it collected from the tenement houses it possessed.

6. Joseph Kelly Turner and John Luther Bridgers, *History of Edgecombe County, North Carolina* (Raleigh, N.C.: Edwards and Broughton, 1920), 427. Sometimes even after a white-run association had regularly dismissed black believers so they might form an association of their own, whites itched to reassert their authority. For example, in 1889, white Primitives in the Fisher's River Association in northwestern North Carolina "appointed a committee to visit the colored association, and impart such instruction to them in behalf of this association as it might find necessary." Jesse A. Ashburn, *History of the Fisher's River Primitive Baptist Association from Its Organization in 1832 to 1904* (Laurel Fork, Va.: F. P. Branscome, 1905), 86–87.

7. Cushing Biggs Hassell and Sylvester Hassell, *History of the Church of God, from the Creation to A.D. 1885; Including Especially the History of the Kehukee Primitive Baptist Association* (Middletown, N.Y.: Gilbert Beebe's Sons, 1886), 810, 353. At the 1873 annual meeting of the Kehukee Primitive Baptist Association, whites formally decided that African Americans should not "be dismissed to form churches of their color, to which all of them might become attached." See ibid., 809–10.

8. Sylvester Hassell, "A Marvel of Divine Grace," *Messenger of Peace* 45, no. 1 (1919): 11–13; ibid., 45, no. 2 (1919): 32. The narrative purports to be the first-person testimony of James Hinton, an illiterate black Primitive Baptist elder. It was first made available by the white Primitive leader Sylvester Hassell, who claimed to have written down Hinton's account "in very nearly his own simple and expressive language." See "Marvel of Divine Grace," no. 1, 11. The narrative was first published in the 3 September 1864 issue of the *Primitive Baptist*. It was subsequently reprinted in the *Gospel Messenger* in 1917 and 1922, in the issues of the *Messenger of Peace* cited immediately above, and as a separate booklet also published through the offices of the *Messenger of Peace* in 1919. Hassell's handwritten manuscript from 1864 appears in his commonplace book, which can be found in the Cushing Biggs Hassell Papers, DMR. Despite Hassell's intervention, there are good reasons to think that the narrative is not purely a work of white ventriloquism. Hinton's conversion story, for instance, sparkles with an ebullience that is, first, almost entirely absent from white Primitive narratives and, second, only partially attributable to white fantasies of innate black contentment.

9. Hassell and Hassell, *History of the Church of God*, 827; John G. Crowley, *Primitive Baptists of the Wiregrass South: 1815 to the Present* (Gainesville: University Press of Florida, 1998), 103–4; E. I. Wiggens, *The History of the Absolute Mt. Enon Association* (n.p.: 1922[?]), Primitive Baptist Online, <http://primitivebaptist.info/mambo//content/view/658/70/> (12 May 2011); Turner and Bridgers, *Edgecombe*, 430–31.

10. Bethlehem Primitive Baptist Church Record Book, 2 July 1870, 3 July 1870, 31 December 1870, 2 September 1871, 2 May 1874, 3 January 1875, 1 February 1879, 2 February 1881, 2 September 1876, 1 February 1879 (emphasis in original), PBL.

11. Ibid., 5 March 1881, 5 November 1881, 3 December 1887, 6 March 1880, 5 April 1873, 5 June 1880, 5 November 1881, 4 March 1882, 6 March 1880; Quantico Primitive Baptist Church Record Book, 12 September 1869, 2 February 1882, PBL.

12. Katharine L. Dvorak, *An African-American Exodus: The Segregation of the Southern Churches* (Brooklyn: Carlson, 1991); William E. Montgomery, *Under Their Own Vine and Fig Tree: The African-American Church in the South, 1865–1900* (Baton Rouge: Louisiana State University Press, 1994); Evelyn Brooks Higginbotham, *Righteous Discontent: The Women's Movement in the Black Baptist Church, 1880–1920* (Cambridge, Mass.: Harvard University Press, 1994); Daniel W. Stowell, *Rebuilding Zion: The Religious Reconstruction of the South, 1863–1877* (New York: Oxford University Press, 1998); James Melvin Washington, *Frustrated Fellowship: The Black Baptist Quest for Social Power* (Macon, Ga.: Mercer University Press, 1986).

Bequeathed to us by an earlier generation of sociologists and historians, the categories of "white church" and especially "black church" are giving way to richer historical portraits marked by intraracial dissent and interracial exchange. See Paul Harvey, *Freedom's Coming: Religious Culture and the Shaping of the South from the Civil War through the Civil Rights Era* (Chapel Hill: University of North Carolina Press, 2005). James B. Bennett, *Religion and the Rise of Jim Crow in New Orleans* (Princeton, N.J.: Princeton University Press, 2005), and John M. Giggie, *After Redemption: Jim Crow and the Transformation of African American Religion in the Delta, 1875–1915* (New York: Oxford University Press, 2008), push back against the standard historiography. Laurie F. Maffly-Kipp, "The Burdens of Church History," *Church History* 82, no. 2 (June 2013): 353–67, also challenges historians to move beyond instrumental and material reasons in their explanations of the importance of the church to African Americans.

13. Bethlehem Primitive Baptist Church Record Book, 1 October 1910; "Summary of Quantico Baptist Church Cemetery," Mycemetery.org, <http://mycemetery.org/exhibits/show/quanticochurch> (22 May 2012).

14. Hosea Holcombe, *A History of the Rise and Progress of the Baptists in Alabama: With a Miniature History of the Denomination from the Apostolic Age Down to the Present Time, Interspersed with Anecdotes Original and Selected, and Concluded with an Address to the Baptists of Alabama* (Philadelphia: King and Baird, 1840), 111; Wayne Flynt, *Alabama Baptists: Southern Baptists in the Heart of Dixie* (Tuscaloosa: University of Alabama Press, 1998), 49; I. M. Allen, ed., *The Triennial Baptist Register: No. 2—1836* (Philadelphia: Baptist General Tract Society, 1836), 204–11; Holcombe, *Baptists in Alabama*, 111; Charles Octavius Boothe, *The Cyclopedia of the Colored Baptists of Alabama: Their Leaders and Their Work* (Birmingham: Alabama Publishing Company, 1895), 24–25. African Huntsville joined the Flint River Association in

1821. About nine years later, a second black Baptist church, African Cottonfort, joined the association.

15. H. C., "Alabama," *NYT*, 12 December 1874; "Neighborhood News and Gossip," *HG*, 12 November 1881; J. J. Smith, "More about the Baptist Association," *HG*, 21 September 1889; Boothe, *Cyclopedia*, 25. The editors at the *Huntsville Gazette*, the city's African American newspaper, often could not be bothered to tack on the word "Primitive" when referring to St. Bartley's Primitive Baptist Church. To them, it was simply the Baptist church.

16. H. C., "Alabama"; "Affairs in Alabama," *NYT*, 21 August 1865. Visitors to Huntsville had long been fascinated by both the spring and the black Primitives' baptisms. As early as 1818, for example, Anne Royall enthusiastically described the spring as "a great natural curiosity." Virginia Clay-Clopton remembered the baptisms during the 1860s as "a sight never to be forgotten." The *New York Times* correspondent in 1865 had marveled at "the vast ebony multitude" that thronged Huntsville for the mass baptisms. Other black churches occasionally held baptisms at the spring, but these were irregular and minor affairs, carried on at dawn and devoid of the Primitives' pageantry. Anne Newport Royall, *Letters from Alabama on Various Subjects: To Which Is Added, an Appendix, Containing Remarks on Sundry Members of the 20th & 21st Congress, and Other High Characters, &c. &c. at the Seat of Government* (Washington, D.C., 1830), 44; Virginia Clay-Clopton, *A Belle of the Fifties: Memoirs of Mrs. Clay of Alabama, Covering Social and Political Life in Washington and the South, 1853-66* (New York: Doubleday, Page, 1904), 162-63; *HG*, 25 May 1889; *HG*, 21 June 1884.

17. H. C., "Alabama."

18. "Big Spring," *HG*, 2 June 1894; "Matters Municipal," *HG*, 7 May 1887; Solonite, "Excursions," *HG*, 19 June 1886; "The Gazette Hears That," *HG*, 22 November 1890; Alan C. Wright, *Huntsville in Vintage Postcards* (Charleston, S.C.: Arcadia, 2000), 24.

19. "Affairs in the South," *NYT*, 17 August 1865; "Affairs in Alabama"; *Souvenir Program of the 100th Anniversary of the Indian Creek P. B. Association*, 1970, St. Bartley's Clipping File, Local History Collection, Huntsville–Madison County Public Library Special Collections, Huntsville, Ala.

20. "Neighborhood News and Gossip," *HG*, 25 February 1882; "The Old Cemetery," *HG*, 25 March 1882; "Wants Him Beaten Because He Put a Fence around the Colored Cemetery," *HG*, 4 April 1885; "Desecration of the Graves of Our Dead," *HG*, 23 July 1887.

21. Daniel S. Dupre, *Transforming the Cotton Frontier: Madison County, Alabama, 1800-1840* (Baton Rouge: Louisiana State University Press, 1997), 127-29; H. C., "Alabama."

22. "A Tribute of Respect," *HJ*, 2 April 1897; U.S. Bureau of the Census, *Tenth Census of the United States*, 1880, Huntsville, Madison County, Alabama, series T9, roll 22, p. 380D, s.v. "Charles H. Ware"; Charles H. Ware, no. 1276, 15 June 1872, U.S. Department of Treasury, *Registers of Signatures of Depositors in Branches of the Freedman's Savings and Trust Company, 1865-1874*, Huntsville Branch, Microfilm Publication M816, roll 1 (Washington, D.C.: National Archives and Records Administration); "A Brilliant Tin Wedding," *HG*, 31 January 1885; "City Affairs," *HG*, 18 April 1885.

23. Walter Lynwood Fleming, *Civil War and Reconstruction in Alabama* (New York: Columbia University Press, 1905), 456; John Watson Alvord, *Fourth Semi-annual Report on Schools for Freedmen, July 1, 1867* (Washington, D.C.: Government Printing Office, 1867), 41. Nominally, Freedmen's Bureau agents and missionaries in the employ of various Christian aid societies established most of the schools, but it was the freedpeople themselves who initiated and seized educational opportunities wherever they could find them. See Heather Andrea Williams, *Self-Taught: African American Education in Slavery and Freedom* (Chapel Hill: University of North Carolina Press, 2005); Robert Sherer, *Subordination or Liberation? The Development and Conflicting Theories of Black Education in Nineteenth Century Alabama* (Tuscaloosa: University of Alabama Press, 1977), 3.

24. Alvord, *Fourth Semi-annual Report*, 41; William H. Gaston, Federal Military Pension Record, National Archives and Records Administration, Washington, D.C.; William H. Gaston, no. 54, 19 October 1867, U.S. Department of Treasury, *Registers of Signatures of Depositors*; U.S. Bureau of the Census, *Ninth Census of the United States*, 1870, Huntsville, Madison County, Alabama, series M593, roll 27, p. 394A, s.v. "William Gaston"; "The Educational Meeting," *HG*, 30 August 1884; "Neighborhood News and Gossip," *HG*, 20 May 1882; "Night and Day School," *HG*, 21 October 1882; William H. Gaston, "Education!," *HG*, 27 August 1887.

25. William H. Gaston, "Educational and Industrial Meeting," *HG*, 27 September 1884, 3; *Official Proceedings of the National Republican Conventions of 1868, 1872, 1876, and 1880* (Minneapolis: Charles W. Johnson, 1903), 184; "Notice," *HG*, 11 November 1882; "School House Movement," *HG*, 27 June 1891; "The Teachers' Meeting," *HG*, 3 April 1886; William H. Gaston, "Pension and Bounty Claims," *HG*, 17 February 1883; "Local Notes," *HG*, 3 February 1894; "Alderman Gaston Moves for a Colored School House," *HG*, 11 April 1885. On county teachers' institutes in Alabama, see Sherer, *Subordination or Liberation?*, 17–22.

26. William H. Gaston, "The Freedmans Suffrage," *HG*, 17 November 1883; "Personal," ibid., 9 August 1890; "Central Ala. Academy Commencement," ibid., 23 May 1891; "Triana," ibid., 11 August 1883; "City Affairs"; "A Success," *HJ*, 9 August 1895; "For Justice of the Peace," *HJ*, 3 April 1896; J. R. Scales, "Wait for the Wagon," *HJ*, 10 April 1896; "Educational Meeting," *HG*, 23 August 1884.

27. Samuel Brazile, William H. Gaston, and James C. Hobbs, "Baptist Educational Meeting," *HG*, 25 July 1885; William H. Gaston and J. R. Scales, "Primitive Baptist Educational Meeting," ibid., 19 September 1885. The Freedmen's Aid Society, an arm of the Methodist Episcopal Church (North), organized Rust in 1866.

28. Jack Daw, "All Is Vanity," *HG*, 28 January 1882; "Colored Societies and Education," ibid., 28 January 1882; "Lease of the Green Academy Lot," ibid., 20 May 1882.

29. "The Educational Meeting."

30. Louis R. Harlan, *Booker T. Washington: The Making of a Black Leader, 1856–1901* (New York: Oxford University Press, 1975), 169; Adam Fairclough, *A Class of Their Own: Black Teachers in the Segregated South* (Cambridge, Mass.: Harvard University Press, 2007), 84; William J. Simmons, *Men of Mark: Eminent, Progressive and Rising* (Cleveland, Ohio: G. M. Rewell and Company, 1887), 390–93; Sherer, *Subordination or Liberation?*, 32–44; August Meier, *Negro Thought in America, 1880–1915: Racial*

Ideologies in the Age of Booker T. Washington (Ann Arbor: University of Michigan Press, 1963); Booker T. Washington to Timothy Thomas Fortune, 11 September 1899 in Louis R. Harlan and Raymond W. Smock, eds., *The Booker T. Washington Papers: 1899-1900*, vol. 5 (Urbana: University of Illinois Press, 1976), 203; Gaston, "Educational and Industrial Meeting."

31. "A Grave Matter," *HG*, 2 May 1885; U.S. Bureau of the Census, *Twelfth Census of the United States*, 1900, Huntsville, Madison County, Alabama, series T623, roll 28, p. 31A, s.v. "Blount McCray"; Alabama Public Service Commission, *Eighth Annual Report of the Railroad Commissioners of Alabama for the Year Ending June 30, 1888* (Nashville, Tenn.: Marshall and Bruce, 1888), 259; "In Mass Meeting," *HG*, 23 May 1885. The spelling of McCravy's last name varied depending upon the source. Census records list him and his wife, Mary, under "McCray," while the *Huntsville Gazette* used the spelling "McCravy."

32. Samuel Bolden, James C. Hobbs, and B. L. Chapman, "What We Have Seen!," *HG*, 3 September 1887; "Primitive Baptists' Appeal," ibid., 7 December 1889 (emphasis added).

33. "Rally Day at Primitive Baptist Church," ibid., 7 July 1888; Bartley Harris and William H. Gaston, "Primitive Baptist Church," ibid., 28 July 1888; William H. Gaston, "Huntsville Baptist Seminary," ibid., 7 September 1889; Samuel Bolden, James C. Hobbs, and William H. Gaston, "A Rousing Educational Meeting," ibid., 22 September 1888; William H. Gaston, "Primitive Baptist," ibid., 28 September 1889.

34. James D. Anderson, *The Education of Blacks in the South, 1860-1935* (Chapel Hill: University of North Carolina Press, 1988); H. Williams, *Self-Taught*; Sherer, *Subordination or Liberation?*, 146-47, 149-50n4; Higginbotham, *Righteous Discontent*, 10, 16; Montgomery, *Under Their Own Vine and Fig Tree*. Sherer first pointed out that Booker T. Washington "was outside the mainstream of black educational thought" in the nineteenth-century South. Anderson later concurred. Washington, he argued "was virtually alone in urging that prime emphasis be put on industrial rather than classical liberal education" (67).

35. National Primitive Baptist Convention of America, *Souvenir and Official Programme*, 3, 14.

36. U.S. Congress, House, *Annual Reports of the Department of Interior for the Fiscal Year Ended June 30, 1898: Report of the Commissioner of Education*, vol. 2, 55th Cong., 3rd sess., 1899, H. Doc. 5, at 2488.

37. National Primitive Baptist Convention of America, *Souvenir and Official Programme*, 44, 36, 47, 39, 37.

38. Ibid., 15, 48, 51, 1; Roxanne McKnight, "Mexia Once Home to Historic Black College," *Mexia News*, 25 February 2012; "Places in Peril Lists Thomaston Colored Institute," *Linden (Ala.) Democrat-Reporter*, 24 May 2012, 1. The names and places of these various African American Primitive Baptist academies were as follows: the Griffin Industrial and Theological Seminary (Tallahassee, Fla.); the National Industrial and Theological College (Winston-Salem, N.C.); the St. Paul Industrial College (Mexia, Tex.); the Thomaston Academy (Marengo County, Ala.); the Bogue Chitto Institute (Dallas County, Ala.); and the Tennessee Valley Primitive Baptist Institute (Lawrence County, Ala.).

39. U.S. Bureau of the Census, *Twelfth Census of the United States*, 1900, Jacksonville, Duval County, Florida, series T623, roll 167, p. 5A, s.v. "Clarence Sams"; National Primitive Baptist Convention of America, *Souvenir and Official Programme*, 35, 40, 36, 46.

40. Crowley, *Primitive Baptists of the Wiregrass South*, 104; see also the listing for the Sunday school running out of Eustis's "Primitive Baptist Church (colored)—Egypt" in the *Orange County Gazetteer and Business Directory*, vol. 1 (Jacksonville, Fla.: John R. Richards and Co., 1887), 19; Primitive Baptist General State Convention of Florida, *Primitive Baptist Manual: Containing a Complete, Comprehensive Guide to the Doctrines, Discipline and Usages of the Primitive (Old School) Baptist Church* (DeLand, Fla.: News Publishing Co., 1904); J. E. A. Keeler, "The Colored People's Department," *Ocala Evening Star*, 9 March 1905; Albert Emanuel, "About the Colored People," *Daytona Gazette-News*, 16 March 1901, 30 March 1901, 13 April 1901; "The Gossip of the Week," *Daytona Gazette-News*, 6 April 1901.

41. National Primitive Baptist Convention of America, *Souvenir and Official Programme*, 3, 14.

42. Primitive Baptist General State Convention of Florida, *Primitive Baptist Manual*, 9–11, 77–79.

43. Rom 16:1; Phil 4:3; Primitive Baptist General State Convention of Florida, *Primitive Baptist Manual*, 26; Tera W. Hunter, *To 'Joy My Freedom: Southern Black Women's Lives and Labors after the Civil War* (Cambridge, Mass.: Harvard University Press, 1997).

44. National Primitive Baptist Convention of America, *Souvenir and Official Programme*, 35, 40, 25, 16.

45. Sterling Stuckey, *Slave Culture: Nationalist Theory and the Foundations of Black America* (New York: Oxford University Press, 1987), 12, 95; Michael Angelo Gomez, *Exchanging Our Country Marks: The Transformation of African Identities in the Colonial and Antebellum South* (Chapel Hill: University of North Carolina Press, 1998), 149, 4; Samuel A. Floyd Jr., "Ring Shout! Literary Studies, Historical Studies, and Black Music Inquiry," *Black Music Research Journal* 11, no. 2 (1991): 266; Albert J. Raboteau, *Slave Religion: The "Invisible Institution" in the Antebellum South*, updated ed. (New York: Oxford University Press, 2004), 73.

46. *Mississippi: Saints and Sinners: From before the Blues and Gospel*, Rounder 11661-1824-2, 1999, compact disc; Joseph Spence, *Glory*, Rounder CD 2096, 1990, compact disc; Viv Broughton, *Black Gospel: An Illustrated History of the Gospel Sound* (Poole, Dorset, England: Blandford Press, 1985), 50; Samuel C. Adams, Jr., "Changing Negro Life in the Delta," in *Lost Delta Found: Rediscovering the Fisk University-Library of Congress Coahoma County Study, 1941–1942*, ed. Robert Gordon and Bruce Nemerov (Nashville, Tenn.: Vanderbilt University Press, 2005), 235; Lewis Wade Jones, "The Mississippi Delta," in *Lost Delta Found: Rediscovering the Fisk University-Library of Congress Coahoma County Study, 1941–1942*, ed. Robert Gordon and Bruce Nemerov (Nashville, Tenn.: Vanderbilt University Press, 2005), 47; Art Rosenbaum, *Shout Because You're Free: The African American Ring Shout Tradition in Coastal Georgia* (Athens: University of Georgia Press, 1998), 121; interview with Rev. C. H. Savage included with *Mississippi: Saints and Sinners*; The McIntosh County Shouters, "The

McIntosh County Shouters," <http://shoutforfreedom.synthasite.com/> (7 May 2012); McIntosh County Shouters, *Slave Shout Songs from the Coast of Georgia*, Folkways FE 4344, 1984, 33 1/3 rpm; Rosenbaum, *Shout Because You're Free*, 122-24.

47. The silence of the St. Annis Primitives about the origins of "Rocking Daniel" might well have been strategic. African Americans, both slave and free, have often been hesitant to discuss the meanings of the ring shout with white outsiders. See, for example, Stuckey, *Slave Culture*, 24.

48. Bessie Jones and Bess Lomax Hawes, *Step It Down: Games, Plays, Songs, and Stories from the Afro-American Heritage* (New York: Harper and Row, 1972; repr., Athens: University of Georgia Press, 1987), 143-46 (page citations are to the reprint edition); Sister Rosetta Tharpe, *Complete Recorded Works in Chronological Order: Vol. 1, 1938-1941*, Document DOCD-5334, 1996, compact disc. "Rock Daniel" was originally recorded in 1941.

Chapter Five

1. W. J. Cash, *The Mind of the South* (New York: Knopf, 1941; reprint, New York: Vintage, 1991), 81 (page citations are to the reprint edition).

2. Sydney E. Ahlstrom, *A Religious History of the American People* (New Haven, Conn.: Yale University Press, 1972), 722.

3. Catharine E. Beecher, *Common Sense Applied to Religion; Or, The Bible and the People* (New York: Harper and Brothers, 1857), xxvi (italics in original); Nathan O. Hatch, *The Democratization of American Christianity* (New Haven, Conn.: Yale University Press, 1989), 173; Mark A. Noll, *America's God: From Jonathan Edwards to Abraham Lincoln* (New York: Oxford University Press, 2002), 294.

4. Thomas Hill Sr., letter to the editor, *PB*, 13 November 1841, 314, 316; Mary Beckley Bristow, "Diary of Miss Mary B. Bristow: 1844-1863, Containing a Partial Record of Activities of Sardis Baptist Church, Licking Association in Kentucky," UKY; Lee Hanks, "The Conflicts of an Orphan," 1 March 1886, Primitive Baptist Online, <http://primitivebaptist.info/mambo//content/view/124/36/> (2 February 2007); Sarah Ann Hollister, "From Sister Hollister to Sister Mather, after Reading Her Experience, as Published in a Late Number of the *Monitor*," *CDA* 3 (1840); Joshua Lawrence, "Victorious Grace: Being a Mere Glance of His Experience," *PB*, 23 October 1841, 311; J. H. Purifoy, "Autobiography," *GM* 10, no. 8 (August 1888).

5. John Pankake and Paul Nelson, *Little Sandy Review*, no. 12 (1961); Bob Dylan, *Chronicles: Volume One* (New York: Simon and Schuster, 2004), 72. Pankake and Nelson met Holcomb at the 1961 University of Chicago Folk Festival. Another attendee at the early 1960s folk festivals in Hyde Park recalled that Holcomb "was like nothing I'd ever heard before" and that his performance left him "speechless." See Art Thielme, "RE: A Quote from Roscoe Holcomb," 24 April 2004, <http://www.mudcat.org/thread.cfm?threadid=69113> (28 January 2008).

6. Pankake and Nelson, *Little Sandy Review*; quoted in John Cohen, notes to *An Untamed Sense of Control*, Smithsonian Folkways SFW 40144, 2003, compact disc.

7. Review of *Shady Grove: Old Time Music from North Carolina, Kentucky, and Virginia*, *Sing Out!* 43, no. 2 (1998): 161; Al Riess, "Recordings: Roscoe Holcomb—'An

Untamed Sense of Control,'" *Dirty Linen*, October–November 2003, 56; Cohen, notes to *Untamed Sense of Control*; "Off the Beaten Track," review of *The High Lonesome Sound*, *Sing Out!* 43, no. 1 (1998): 126; Ted Anthony, *Chasing the Rising Sun: The Journey of an American Song* (New York: Simon and Schuster, 2007), 96.

8. John Cohen, "Field Trip—Kentucky," *Sing Out!* 10, no. 2 (1960): 13–15.

9. Benjamin Filene, *Romancing the Folk: Public Memory and American Roots Music* (Chapel Hill: University of North Carolina Press, 2000); *Remembering the High Lonesome*, Mini DV, dir. Tom Davenport and Barry Dornfeld, Tom Davenport, 2003.

10. John Cohen, notes to *Mountain Music of Kentucky*, Folkways FA 2317, 1960, 33 1/3 rpm.

11. John Cohen, "There Is No Eye: A Photo Essay," *Sing Out!* 45, no. 4 (2001): 30; James Agee and Walker Evans, *Let Us Now Praise Famous Men: Three Tenant Families* (Boston: Houghton Mifflin, 1941); Cohen, notes to *Mountain Music of Kentucky*; Cohen, Notes to *Untamed Sense of Control*.

12. Richard Rinzler, notes to *Friends of Old Time Music*, Folkways, FA 2390, 1964, 33 1/3 rpm; Cohen quoted in Philip F. Gura, "Southern Roots and Branches: Forty Years of the New Lost City Ramblers," *Southern Cultures* 6, no. 4 (2000): 58–81. Ralph Rinzler and Richard Rinzler were cousins.

13. Pierre Bourdieu, "The Production of Belief: Contribution to an Economy of Symbolic Goods," in *The Field of Cultural Production: Essays on Art and Literature*, ed. Randal Johnson (New York: Columbia University Press, 1993), 95. I first came across this passage and these ideas in Julia S. Ardery's endlessly fascinating and insightful book *The Temptation: Edgar Tolson and the Genesis of Twentieth-Century Folk Art* (Chapel Hill: University of North Carolina Press, 1998).

14. Cohen, notes to *Untamed Sense of Control*.

15. Quoted in Cohen, notes to *The High Lonesome Sound*, Folkways FA 2368, 1965, 33 1/3 rpm (my emphasis).

16. There is a Brobdingnagian literature on the social construction of the folk and folklore. Some of the works that have been most useful to me are Raymond Williams, *The Country and the City* (New York: Oxford University Press, 1973); David E. Whisnant, *All That Is Native and Fine: The Politics of Culture in an American Region* (Chapel Hill: University of North Carolina Press, 1983); Robert Cantwell, *When We Were Good: The Folk Revival* (Cambridge, Mass.: Harvard University Press, 1996); and W. T. Lhamon, *Raising Cain: Blackface Performance from Jim Crow to Hip Hop* (Cambridge, Mass.: Harvard University Press, 1998).

17. Neil V. Rosenberg, *Bluegrass: A History* (Urbana: University of Illinois Press, 1985), 174 (emphasis in original).

18. Robert Cantwell, *Bluegrass Breakdown: The Making of the Old Southern Sound* (Urbana: University of Illinois Press, 1984; repr., New York: Da Capo Press, 1992), 242 (page citations are to the reprint edition); Monroe quote on 165.

19. Bill Monroe and His Blue Grass Boys, "No Letter in the Mail," *The Father of Bluegrass Music*, Camden CAL 719, 1962, 33 1/3 rpm; Bill Monroe and His Blue Grass Boys, "What Is a Home without Love?," *All the Classic Releases: 1937–1949*, JSP 7712, 2003, compact disc; Bill Monroe and His Bluegrass Boys, "Come Back to Me in My Dreams," *The Essential Bill Monroe and His Bluegrass Boys: 1945–1949*, Columbia

C2K 52478, 1992, compact disc; Bill Monroe, "Roane County Prison," *The Best of Bill Monroe*, MCA 2 4090, 1975, 33 1/3 rpm.

20. Cantwell, *Bluegrass Breakdown*, 243 (emphasis in original).

21. Bill Monroe and His Blue Grass Boys, "I'm on My Way to the Old Home," *Bill Monroe Sings Country Songs*, Vocalion VL 3702, 1962, 33 1/3 rpm.

22. Cohen, notes to *Untamed Sense of Control*; quoted in Cohen, notes to *High Lonesome Sound*.

23. Cantwell, *Bluegrass Breakdown*, 209; quoted in John Cohen, notes to *The Music of Roscoe Holcomb and Wade Ward*, Folkways FA 2363, 1962, 33 1/3 rpm; Roscoe Holcomb, "Across the Rocky Mountain," *Mountain Music of Kentucky*, Folkways FA 2317, 1960, 33 1/3 rpm.

24. Josiah Henry Combs, *Folk-Songs of the Southern United States (Folk-Songs Du Midi Des Etats-Unis)*, ed. D. K. Wilgus (Austin: University of Texas Press, 1967), 88; *Gaelic Psalms from Lewis*, Tangent TNGM 120, 1975, 33 1/3 rpm; Nicholas Temperley, "The Old Way of Singing: Its Origins and Development," *Journal of the American Musicological Society* 34, no. 3 (1981): 511–44; Nicholas Temperley, "The Old Way of Singing," *Musical Times* 120, no. 1641 (1979): 943–47; Jean Ritchie, *Folk Songs of the Southern Appalachians as Sung by Jean Ritchie*, 2nd ed. (Lexington: University Press of Kentucky, 1997), 44. On Old Way singing among the Old Regular Baptists, see William H. Tallmadge, "Baptist Monophonic and Heterophonic Hymnody in Southern Appalachia," *Anuario Interamericano de Investigacion Musical* 11 (1975): 106–36.

25. Quoted in Sammie Ann Wicks, "A Belated Salute to the 'Old Way' of 'Snaking' the Voice on Its (ca.) 345th Birthday," *Popular Music* 8, no. 1 (1989): 59–96; Temperley, "Origins and Development," 537. Wicks's article provides a brilliant historical summary and analysis of the vocal style underpinning Primitive Baptist and Old Regular Baptist singing. This article helped me listen to Holcomb and Stanley with a fresh appreciation of their music's roots in centuries-old musical and religious folkways.

26. Quoted in Cohen, notes to *Untamed Sense of Control*; Cohen, notes to *Roscoe Holcomb and Wade Ward*. The anecdote from Ritchie comes via Robert Cantwell (personal communication).

27. Cohen, notes to *Roscoe Holcomb and Wade Ward*.

28. Roscoe Holcomb, "Wandering Boy," *The High Lonesome Sound*, Folkways FA 2368, 1965, 33 1/3 rpm; John Cohen, notes to *Close to Home*, Folkways FA 2374, 1975, 33 1/3 rpm; *The High Lonesome Sound*, 16mm, dir. John Cohen, Audio-Brandon Films, 1963.

29. Quoted in Jeff Todd Titon, notes to *Old Regular Baptists: Lined-Out Hymnody from Southeastern Kentucky*, Smithsonian Folkways SFW 40106, 1997, compact disc; Sammie Ann Wicks, "Life and Meaning: Singing, Praying, and the Word among the Old Regular Baptists of Eastern Kentucky" (Ph.D. diss., University of Texas at Austin, 1983), 173.

30. Robert Shelton, "Folk Singers from the 'Source,'" *NYT*, 24 April 1966; John Cohen, notes to *Back Roads to Cold Mountain*, Smithsonian Folkways SFW 40149, 2004, compact disc.

31. What follows is but a sampling of such description. One reviewer claimed that the Stanley Brothers' sound "was the very embodiment of haunting mountain sorrow" and

that Ralph's voice was "positively otherworldly." In a different piece, this same reviewer explained that Ralph's tenor "lends an appropriately ghostly quality to old and new songs of loneliness, despair, and fundamental religious faith." Country music historian Bill Malone has written of Ralph's "haunting, almost sepulchral voice." A writer in the 1970s reflected on Stanley's "haunting" lead vocals and also imagined that an a cappella rendition of "Village Church Yard" had "moss hanging all over it." The liner notes to the best-selling *O Brother, Where Art Thou?* soundtrack picked up all these cues. There, Robert Oermann hailed the Stanley Brothers' "haunting 1955 version of 'Angel Band,'" and Ralph Stanley's capsule biography noted that "his haunting tenor voice" had been described as "otherworldly" by the *New York Times*. Mark Greenberg, "Off the Beaten Track," review of *Ralph Stanley and the Clinch Mountain Boys, 1971-1973, Sing Out!* 40, no. 4 (1996): 132; Bill C. Malone quoted in John Wright, *Traveling the High Way Home: Ralph Stanley and the World of Traditional Bluegrass Music* (Urbana: University of Illinois Press, 1993), 15; Walter V. Saunders, notes to *Ralph Stanley and the Clinch Mountain Boys, 1971-1973*, Rebel REB-4001, 1995, compact disc; Robert K. Oermann, Notes to *O Brother, Where Art Thou?*, Mercury 088 170-069-2, 2000, compact disc. Saunders's contributions above originally appeared as record reviews in *Bluegrass Unlimited* during the mid-1970s.

32. Christopher Gray, "O Brother: Down from the Mountain and into Wal-Mart," *Austin Chronicle*, 19 July 2002, <http://www.austinchronicle.com/gyrobase/Issue/story?oid=oid%3A97586> (7 July 2008); David Germain, "New 'O Brother' Set Serves Up More Old-Timey Music," Associated Press, *Yahoo! News*, 22 August 2011, <http://news.yahoo.com/o-brother-set-serves-more-old-timey-music-095857364.html> (23 August 2011); Aaron A. Fox, "'Alternative' to What? *O Brother*, September 11, and the Politics of Country Music," in *Country Music Goes to War*, ed. Charles K. Wolfe and James E. Akenson (Lexington: University Press of Kentucky, 2005), 164–91. Fox's essay is the keenest of the bunch, pulling together old threads to make something new.

33. Alan Lomax, "Bluegrass Background: Folk Music with Overdrive," *Esquire*, October 1959, 108.

34. Quoted in J. Wright, *Traveling the High Way Home*, 74. In terms of instrumental virtuosity and the Stanley sound, one immediately thinks of guitarist George Shuffler's innovative cross-picking technique featured in the 1960s editions of the Stanley Brothers' bands. Stanley himself began featuring clawhammer playing on his records not long after his brother Carter died. See, for example, Ralph Stanley, *A Man and His Music*, Rebel SLP 153, 1974, 33 1/3 rpm, whose first six cuts feature clawhammer banjo. Stanley continued to demonstrate his clawhammer technique at each of his concerts for the next several decades.

35. J. Wright, *Traveling the High Way Home*, 70 (my emphasis).

36. Beverly Bush Patterson, *The Sound of the Dove: Singing in Appalachian Primitive Baptist Churches* (Urbana: University of Illinois Press, 1995); Wicks, "Belated Salute," 66–67. For recordings of Primitive Baptist singing, see, for instance, Walter Evans, *Old Hymns Lined and Led by Elder Walter Evans*, Sovereign Grace 6057 and 6058, 196-[?]. Sovereign Grace Recordings, based in Cincinnati, Ohio, also issued a second album of hymns sung by Evans and his congregation at the Little River Primitive Baptist Church in Sparta, North Carolina.

37. J. Wright, *Traveling the High Way Home*, 71. Also see similar comments by Stanley quoted in Nicholas Dawidoff, *In the Country of Country: A Journey to the Roots of American Music* (New York: Vintage Books, 1998), 93.

38. J. Wright, *Traveling the High Way Home*, 69; Ralph Stanley and the Clinch Mountain Boys, "You're Drifting On," *Cry from the Cross*, Rebel SLP 1499, 1971, 33 1/3 rpm.

39. J. Wright, *Traveling the High Way Home*, 70; Dawidoff, *In the Country of Country*, 90; Ralph Stanley and Eddie Dean, *Man of Constant Sorrow: My Life and Times* (New York: Penguin, 2009), 1–2; Patterson, *Sound of the Dove*, 33, 166, 197. It is important to note that Patterson's informants also referred to their music as "the joyful sound." In his work with white and black Primitive congregations, Brett Sutton notes that members described their hymns as "lonesome and sad." Brett Sutton, notes to *Primitive Baptist Hymns of the Blue Ridge*, University of North Carolina Press 39088, 1982, 33 1/3 rpm.

40. H. Richard Niebuhr, *Christ and Culture* (New York: Harper and Row, 1951), 68.

41. Wicks, "Belated Salute," 67; Stanley and Dean, *Man of Constant Sorrow*, 13; Greg Urban, "Ritual Wailing in Amerindian Brazil," *American Anthropologist* 90 (1988): 385–400; Steven Feld, "Wept Thoughts: The Voicing of Kaluli Memories," in *South Pacific Oral Traditions*, ed. Ruth Finnegan and Margaret Orben (Bloomington: Indiana University Press, 1995), 85–108.

42. Patterson, *Sound of the Dove*, 196–97.

43. These excerpts of lyrics come, respectively, from the songs "Death Is Only a Dream," "Angel Band," "Man of Constant Sorrow," "I'll Not Be a Stranger," and "I Hold a Clear Title."

44. David Gates, "Constant Sorrow: The Long Road of Ralph Stanley," *New Yorker*, 20 August 2001; Stanley and Dean, *Man of Constant Sorrow*, 394; Howard Dorgan, *In the Hands of a Happy God: The "No-Hellers" of Central Appalachia* (Knoxville: University of Tennessee Press, 1997). Gates does not mention that Hale Creek is a Universalist church. J. Wright, *Traveling the High Way Home*, refers to Stanley's "Old Regular Baptist heritage," but nowhere have I found Stanley describing himself as an Old Regular. He has consistently described himself and his parents as Primitive Baptists. The evidence for Stanley's membership in a Universalist congregation comes from the man himself in his autobiography.

45. 1 Pt 2:9.

46. Lorraine Ali and David Gates, "Looking Grim at the Grammys: Ralph Stanley's Performance of 'O Death' Wasn't the Only Ominous Note," *Newsweek*, 11 March 2002, 60.

47. Fox, "'Alternative' to What?," 184–88. Whatever one thinks of Stanley as a symbol of whiteness, it is worth noting that "O Death" exists in both black and white church traditions. In 1959, Bessie Jones, an African American singer from the Georgia Sea Islands, recorded an a capella version that offers a full portion of gospel swing in place of Stanley's twistings. See Jones, "O Death," *Georgia Sea Islands, Volume 1*, Prestige International INT-DS-25001, 1961, 33 1/3 rpm.

48. Stanley and Dean, *Man of Constant Sorrow*, 296, 3.

49. This drama is even more vivid in other versions of the song in which the singer, after pleading for more time on earth "to fix my heart, to change my mind" is told by

Death, who speaks like God with predestinary powers, that "your heart is fixed, your mind is bound." The singer at last admits that "as long as God in heaven shall dwell / My soul, my soul, shall scream in hell." See, for example, Hazel Dickens, David Patrick Kelly, and Bobby McMillen, "Conversation with Death," *Songcatcher: Music from and Inspired by the Motion Picture*, Vanguard CD 79586-2, 2001, compact disc.

50. An Out-Cast, letter to the editor, *ST*, 12 November 1834; Temperley, "Origins and Development," 511; Wesley Berg, "Hymns of the Old Colony Mennonites and the Old Way of Singing." *Musical Quarterly* 80, no. 1 (1996): 77–117.

Epilogue

1. Beth Barton Schweiger, "Max Weber in Mt. Airy, Or, Revivals and Social Theory in the Early South," in *Religion in the American South: Protestants and Others in History and Culture*, ed. Beth Barton Schweiger and Donald G. Mathews (Chapel Hill: University of North Carolina Press, 2004), 54. More recently, Monica Najar has insisted that the organizing processes Schweiger limned originated with eighteenth-century evangelicals who "left their mark on southern society less through the volume of their conversions than through the institutional structures that they introduced into the region's civil and religious life." See Najar, *Evangelizing the South: A Social History of Church and State in Early America* (New York: Oxford University Press, 2008), 4.

2. Candy Gunther Brown, *The Word in the World: Evangelical Writing, Publishing, and Reading in America, 1789–1880* (Chapel Hill: University of North Carolina Press, 2004); Randall J. Stephens, *The Fire Spreads: Holiness and Pentecostalism in the American South* (Cambridge, Mass.: Harvard University Press, 2008), 25. "Passion-exciter" was one of the many names that Primitives had for missionary Baptists. See Joseph Kelly Turner and John Luther Bridgers, *History of Edgecombe County, North Carolina* (Raleigh, N.C.: Edwards and Broughton, 1920), 417.

3. James D. Bratt, "Religious Anti-revivalism in Antebellum America," *Journal of the Early Republic* 24, no. 1 (2004): 68.

4. George Santayana, *The Life of Reason: Or, the Phases of Human Progress* (New York: Scribner's, 1905), 13; Gilbert Beebe, "Remarks on Religious Revivals," *ST*, 15 April 1905 (originally published in June 1862); Job E. W. Smith (the "man" from the Alabama River Association, holding his Bible) quoted in John G. Crowley, *Primitive Baptists of the Wiregrass South: 1815 to the Present* (Gainesville: University Press of Florida, 1998), 114. Smith was engaged in the "means" controversy that simmered in Primitive associations nationwide in the mid- to late nineteenth century. Like Smith, most Primitives landed in the anti-means camp, which argued that the gospel was not a means used by God to regenerate or save the elect. Other Primitives, however, insisted that the gospel was, of course, a means used by God to save lost souls.

5. C. F. Sams, "The Negro Primitive Baptist Church in America: Its Work and Progress," in *The United Negro: His Problems and His Progress: Containing the Addresses and Proceedings [of] the Negro Young People's Christian and Educational Congress, Held August 6–11, 1902*, ed. I. Garland Penn and J. W. E. Bowen (Atlanta: D. E. Luther Publishing Co., 1902), 547–48.

Bibliography

Music discussed in this book can be heard at the author's website: strangers below.net.

Manuscript Collections

Chapel Hill, North Carolina
    North Carolina Collection, Louis Round Wilson Special Collections Library,
        University of North Carolina at Chapel Hill
        North Carolina Collection Biographical Clipping File, 1976–1989
    Southern Historical Collection, Louis Round Wilson Special Collections Library,
        University of North Carolina at Chapel Hill
        Brett Sutton and Peter Hartman Collection, 1976
        Cushing Biggs Hassell Papers, 1809–1880
        Joshua Lawrence Papers, 1812, 1826
        Morattock Primitive Baptist Church Records, 1798–1868
Durham, North Carolina
    David M. Rubenstein Rare Book and Manuscript Library, Duke University
        B. F. Knight Papers, 1840–1866
        Bryant Bennett Papers, 1767–1902
        Cushing Biggs Hassell Papers, 1814–1926
        John Frederick Mallett Journal, 1853–1884
        Tarboro Primitive Baptist Church Record Book, 1819–1850
Elon, North Carolina
    Primitive Baptist Library
        Bethlehem Primitive Baptist Church Record Book, 1870–1914
        Brush Creek Meeting House Record Book, 1833–1869
        Bush Arbor Primitive Baptist Church Records, 1806–1841
        Frying Pan Springs Church Record Book, 1828–1879
        Linches Creek Church Record Book, 1799–1856
        Quantico Primitive Baptist Church Record Book, 1865–1882
Huntsville, Alabama
    Huntsville-Madison County Public Library Special Collections
        St. Bartley's Clipping File, Local History Collection
            Souvenir Program of the 100th Anniversary of the Indian Creek P. B.
                Association, Huntsville, Ala., 1970
Lexington, Kentucky
    Special Collections Library, University of Kentucky

Mary Beckley Bristow, "Diary of Miss Mary B. Bristow: 1844–1863, Containing a Partial Record of Activities of Sardis Baptist Church, Licking Association in Kentucky"

Raleigh, North Carolina
   State Archives of North Carolina
      William Scarborough Papers, Private Collection #906

Winston-Salem, North Carolina
   Baptist Historical Collection, Wake Forest University
      Abbott's Creek Baptist Church Records, 1832–1989
      Abbott's Creek Primitive Baptist Church Records, 1783–1944
      Gilliam's Primitive Baptist Church Record Book, 1824–1837
      Hassell Family Papers
      Lick Fork Primitive Baptist Church Record Book, 1791–1828
      Skewarkey Baptist Church Records, 1786–1845
   Special Collections and Archives, Wake Forest University
      Samuel and Sarah Wait Papers, 1813–1975

Newspapers and Periodicals

Austin Chronicle
Christian Doctrinal Advocate and Spiritual Monitor
Christian Index
Daytona Gazette-News
Dirty Linen
Gospel Messenger
Huntsville Gazette
Huntsville Journal
Little Sandy Review
Messenger of Peace
Newsweek
New York Times
North Carolina Baptist Interpreter
Ocala Evening Star
Old-Time Herald
Primitive Baptist
Signs of the Times
Sing Out!

Sound Recordings

American Folk and Country Music Festival. Bear Family BCD 16849, 2006, compact disc. Originally recorded in 1966.

Evans, Walter. *Old Hymns Lined and Led by Elder Walter Evans.* Sovereign Grace 6057 and 6058, 196-[?], 33 1/3 rpm.

Gaelic Psalms from Lewis. Tangent TNGM 120, 1975, 33 1/3 rpm. Recorded between 1955 and 1974 in Lewis by the School of Scottish Studies.

Georgia Sea Islands, Volume 1. Prestige International INT-DS-25001, 1961, 33 1/3 rpm.

Holcomb, Roscoe. *The High Lonesome Sound.* Folkways FA 2368, 1965, 33 1/3 rpm.

Holcomb, Roscoe, and Wade Ward. *The Music of Roscoe Holcomb and Wade Ward.* Folkways FA 2363, 1962, 33 1/3 rpm.

McIntosh County Shouters. *Slave Shout Songs from the Coast of Georgia.* Folkways FE 4344, 1984, 33 1/3 rpm.

Mississippi: Saints and Sinners: From before the Blues and Gospel. Rounder 11661-1824-2, 1999, compact disc. Original field recordings produced and recorded between 1936 and 1942.

Monroe, Bill. *The Best of Bill Monroe.* MCA 2 4090, 1975, 33 1/3 rpm.

Monroe, Bill, and His Blue Grass Boys. *All the Classic Releases: 1937–1949*. JSP 7712, 2003, compact disc.

———. *Bill Monroe Sings Country Songs*. Vocalion VL 3702, 1962, 33 1/3 rpm.

———. *The Essential Bill Monroe and His Bluegrass Boys: 1945–1949*. Columbia C2K 52478, 1992, compact disc.

———. *The Father of Bluegrass Music*. Camden CAL 719, 1962, 33 1/3 rpm.

Mountain Music of Kentucky. Folkways FA 2317, 1960, 33 1/3 rpm.

O Brother, Where Art Thou? Mercury 088 170-069-2, 2000, compact disc.

Songcatcher: Music from and Inspired by the Motion Picture. Vanguard CD 79586-2, 2001, compact disc.

Spence, Joseph. *Glory*. Rounder CD 2096, 1990, compact disc. Originally recorded between March 1978 and June 1989.

Stanley, Ralph. *A Man and His Music*. Rebel SLP 153, 1974, 33 1/3 rpm.

Stanley, Ralph, and the Clinch Mountain Boys. *Cry from the Cross*. Rebel SLP 1499, 1971, 33 1/3 rpm.

———. *Old Country Church*. Rebel SLP-1508, 1972, 33 1/3 rpm.

The Stanley Brothers. *Old Time Camp Meeting*. King 750, 1961, 33 1/3 rpm.

Tharpe, Sister Rosetta. *Complete Recorded Works in Chronological Order: Vol. 1, 1938–1941*. Document DOCD-5334, 1996, compact disc. Originally recorded in 1941.

Films

The High Lonesome Sound. 16 mm. Directed by John Cohen. Audio-Brandon Films, 1963.

Remembering the High Lonesome. Mini DV. Directed by Tom Davenport and Barry Dornfeld. Tom Davenport, 2003.

Primary Sources

"Address to the Particular Baptist Churches of the 'Old School' in the United States." *Signs of the Times*, 3 July 1833, 241–49.

"Affairs in Alabama." *New York Times*, 21 August 1865, 8.

"Affairs in the South." *New York Times*, 17 August 1865, 1.

Agee, James, and Walker Evans. *Let Us Now Praise Famous Men: Three Tenant Families*. Boston: Houghton Mifflin, 1941.

Alabama Public Service Commission. *Eighth Annual Report of the Railroad Commissioners of Alabama for the Year Ending June 30, 1888*. Nashville, Tenn.: Marshall and Bruce, 1888.

"Alderman Gaston Moves for a Colored School House." *Huntsville Gazette*, 11 April 1885, 3.

Ali, Lorraine, and David Gates. "Looking Grim at the Grammys: Ralph Stanley's Performance of 'O Death' Wasn't the Only Ominous Note." *Newsweek*, 11 March 2002, 60.

Allen, I. M., ed. *The Triennial Baptist Register: No. 2—1836*. Philadelphia: Baptist General Tract Society, 1836.

Alvord, John Watson. *Fourth Semi-annual Report on Schools for Freedmen, July 1, 1867.* Washington, D.C.: Government Printing Office, 1867.

Ashburn, Jesse A. *History of the Fisher's River Primitive Baptist Association from Its Organization in 1832 to 1904.* Laurel Fork, Va.: F. P. Branscome, 1905.

Barlow, Esther. Letter to the editor. *Christian Doctrinal Advocate and Spiritual Monitor* 6 (1843): 182–85.

Barnum, P. T. *Struggles and Triumphs: Or, Forty Years' Recollections of P. T. Barnum.* London: Sampson Low, Son, and Marston, 1869.

Beebe, Gilbert. *The Baptist Hymn Book: Comprising a Choice Collection of Psalms, Hymns and Spiritual Songs Adapted to the Faith and Order of the Old School, or Primitive Baptists in the United States of America.* 2nd stereotype ed. Middletown, N.Y.: office of the "Signs of the Times," 1859.

———. "Remarks on Religious Revivals." *Signs of the Times,* 15 April 1905.

———. "2 Timothy IV. 3, 4," *Signs of the Times,* 10 October 1856.

Beecher, Catharine E. *Common Sense Applied to Religion; Or, The Bible and the People.* New York: Harper and Brothers, 1857.

Beecher, Edward. "The Nature, Importance, and Means of Eminent Holiness throughout the Church." *American National Preacher* 10, nos. 1 and 2 (1835): 217–24.

Benedict, David. *Fifty Years among the Baptists.* New York: Sheldon and Company, 1860.

Bennett, Mark. Letter to the editor. *Primitive Baptist,* 13 February 1836, 42.

Biggs, Joseph. Letter to the editor. *Primitive Baptist,* 9 January 1836, 9–10.

Biggs, Joseph, Lemuel Burkitt, and Jesse Read. *A Concise History of the Kehukee Baptist Association, from Its Original Rise to the Present Time.* Tarboro, N.C.: G. Howard, 1834.

"Big Spring." *Huntsville Gazette,* 2 June 1894, 2.

Bolch, Arnold, Jr. Letter to the editor. *Christian Doctrinal Advocate and Spiritual Monitor* 1 (1837): 151–52.

Bolden, Samuel, James C. Hobbs, and B. L. Chapman. "What We Have Seen!" *Huntsville Gazette,* 3 September 1887, 2.

Bolden, Samuel, James C. Hobbs, and William H. Gaston. "A Rousing Educational Meeting." *Huntsville Gazette,* 22 September 1888, 3.

Boothe, Charles Octavius. *The Cyclopedia of the Colored Baptists of Alabama: Their Leaders and Their Work.* Birmingham: Alabama Publishing Company, 1895.

Boykin, Samuel. *History of the Baptist Denomination in Georgia: With Biographical Compendium and Portrait Gallery of Baptist Ministers and Other Georgia Baptists.* Atlanta, Ga.: J. P. Harrison and Co., 1881.

Branstetter, Peter L. "The Life of Elder Peter Branstetter—Experience and Call to the Ministry," 9 June 1887. Primitive Baptist Online. <http://primitivebaptist.info/mambo//content/view/936/36/>. 14 September 2006.

Brazile, Samuel, William H. Gaston, and James C. Hobbs. "Baptist Educational Meeting." *Huntsville Gazette,* 25 July 1885, 3.

"A Brilliant Tin Wedding." *Huntsville Gazette,* 31 January 1885, 3.

Burkitt, Lemuel, and Jesse Read. *A Concise History of the Kehukee Baptist Association: From Its Original Rise to the Present Time.* Halifax, N.C.: A. Hodge, 1803.

Cartwright, Peter. *Autobiography of Peter Cartwright: The Backwoods Preacher.* Edited by W. P. Strickland. New York: Carlton and Porter, 1857.

"Central Ala. Academy Commencement." *Huntsville Gazette*, 23 May 1891, 3.

"Circular Letter." In *Minutes of the Sandy Creek Baptist Association, Convened at Rocky Springs Meeting House, Chatham County, North Carolina, on the 17th, 28th and 29th Days of October, A.D. 1832.* Pittsborough, N.C.: Henry Ward, 1832.

"Circular Letter: Of the Kehukee Association, of 1836." *Primitive Baptist*, 26 November 1836, 337–42.

"City Affairs." *Huntsville Gazette*, 18 April 1885, 3.

Clark, John. Letter to the editor. *Primitive Baptist*, 14 May 1836, 135–36.

Clark, Samuel. Letter to the editor. *Primitive Baptist*, 23 January 1841, 26.

Clay-Clopton, Virginia. *A Belle of the Fifties: Memoirs of Mrs. Clay of Alabama, Covering Social and Political Life in Washington and the South, 1853–66.* New York: Doubleday, Page, 1904.

"Close Communion." *Primitive Baptist*, 9 January 1836, 11–16.

Cohen, John. "Field Trip—Kentucky." *Sing Out!* 10, no. 2 (1960): 13–15.

———. Notes to *Back Roads to Cold Mountain*. Smithsonian Folkways SFW 40149, 2004, compact disc.

———. Notes to *Close to Home*. Folkways FA 2374, 1975, 33 1/3 rpm.

———. Notes to *The High Lonesome Sound*. Folkways FA 2368, 1965, 33 1/3 rpm.

———. Notes to *Mountain Music of Kentucky*. Folkways FA 2317, 1960, 33 1/3 rpm.

———. Notes to *The Music of Roscoe Holcomb and Wade Ward*. Folkways FA 2363, 1962, 33 1/3 rpm.

———. Notes to *An Untamed Sense of Control*. Smithsonian Folkways SFW 40144, 2003, compact disc.

———. "There Is No Eye: A Photo Essay." *Sing Out!* 45, no. 4 (2001): 30–31.

Coleman, A. J. "Circular Letter." *Primitive Baptist*, 2 May 1846, 67–71.

———. Letter to the editor. *Primitive Baptist*, 23 September 1843, 286.

"Colored Societies and Education." *Huntsville Gazette*, 28 January 1882, 2.

"A Conversation on the Question." *Christian Doctrinal Advocate and Spiritual Monitor* 1 (1837): 81–84.

Daw, Jack. "All Is Vanity." *Huntsville Gazette*, 28 January 1882, 3.

"Desecration of the Graves of Our Dead." *Huntsville Gazette*, 23 July 1887, 3.

Du Bois, W. E. B., ed. *The Negro Church: Report of a Social Study Made under the Direction of Atlanta University; Together with the Proceedings of the Eighth Conference for the Study of the Negro Problems, Held at Atlanta University, May 26th, 1903.* Atlanta: Atlanta University Press, 1903.

Duke, Edward S. Letter to the editor. *Primitive Baptist*, 12 May 1838, 129–32.

Durand, Silas H. *Fragments: Autobiography and Later Writings*. Philadelphia: Biddle Press, 1920.

Durand, Silas H., and P. G. Lester. *Hymn and Tune Book for Use in Old School or Primitive Baptist Churches*. Greenfield, Ind.: D. H. Goble, 1886.

Dylan, Bob. *Chronicles: Volume One*. New York: Simon and Schuster, 2004.

Eblen, Wm. Letter to the editor. *Primitive Baptist*, 14 May 1836, 142.

Echols, Obadiah. "Controversial Record." *Christian Index* 7, no. 13 (1832): 198–200.

Editorial. *Primitive Baptist*. 9 January 1836, 8.

"Educational Meeting." *Huntsville Gazette*, 23 August 1884, 3.

"The Educational Meeting." *Huntsville Gazette*, 30 August 1884, 3.

Elkins, S. A. "The Life and Writings of Elder Peter Branstetter: Character Sketch," December 1891. Primitive Baptist Online. <http://primitivebaptist.info/mambo//content/view/937/36/>. 14 September 2006.

Emanuel, Albert. "About the Colored People." *Daytona Gazette-News*, 16 March 1901, 4.

———. "About the Colored People." *Daytona Gazette-News*, 30 March 1901, 2.

———. "About the Colored People." *Daytona Gazette-News*, 13 April 1901, 4.

Emerson, Ralph Waldo. "Nature." In *Nature*, 5–9. Boston: James Munroe and Company, 1849.

"Extract from the 'Minutes of the North Carolina Baptist Society for Foreign and Domestic Missions, convened at Haywood's meeting house, Franklin county, May 22, 1824.'" *Primitive Baptist*, 3 October 1835, 3.

Finney, Charles Grandison. *Lectures on Revivals of Religion*. Edited by William G. McLoughlin. Cambridge: Belknap Press of Harvard University Press, 1960.

"For Justice of the Peace." *Huntsville Journal*, 3 April 1896, 2.

Fristoe, William. *A Concise History of the Ketocton Baptist Association: Wherein a Description Is Given of Her Constitution, Progress and Increase, the Intention in Associating, the Doctrines Holden by Her, Reasons for the Names of Regular and Separate Baptists, an Account of the Death of Sundries, the Constitution and Order of Churches, the Manner of Administering Baptism, of the Ordination of Ministers, Bounds of the Association, the Doctrines Preached, Providing for the Ministry, Annual Meetings, the Number of Ministers, of Persecution, the Mode of Redress, of Circular Letters, Objections to the Baptists Replied to, of Good Works, and of Her Civil Policy*. Staunton, Va.: William Gilman Lyford, 1808. Reprint, San Antonio, Tex.: Primitive Baptist Heritage Corporation, 2002.

Garrard, William, and Cushing Biggs Hassell. *Friendly Greetings across the Water, or the Love Letters of Elders Garrard and Hassell*. New York: Chatterton and Crist, 1847.

Gaston, William H. "Associational." *Huntsville Gazette*, 6 January 1894, 2.

———. "Education!" *Huntsville Gazette*, 27 August 1887, 3.

———. "Educational and Industrial Meeting." *Huntsville Gazette*, 27 September 1884, 3.

———. "The Freedmans Suffrage." *Huntsville Gazette*, 17 November 1883, 8.

———. "Huntsville Baptist Seminary." *Huntsville Gazette*, 7 September 1889, 3.

———. "Pension and Bounty Claims." *Huntsville Gazette*, 17 February 1883, 3.

———. "Primitive Baptist." *Huntsville Gazette*, 28 September 1889, 2.

Gaston, William H., and J. R. Scales. "Primitive Baptist Educational Meeting." *Huntsville Gazette*, 19 September 1885, 3.

"The Gazette Hears That." *Huntsville Gazette*, 22 November 1890, 3.

Germain, David. "New 'O Brother' Set Serves Up More Old-Timey Music." Associated Press. *Yahoo! News*, 22 August 2011, <http://news.yahoo.com/o-brother-set-serves-more-old-timey-music-095857364.html>. 23 August 2011.

Gilbert, Kemuel C. Letter to the editor. *Primitive Baptist*, 26 March 1836, 81–83.

Gold, P. D. *A Treatise on the Book of Joshua*. Wilson, N.C.: Zion's Landmark, 1889.

"The Gossip of the Week." *Daytona Gazette-News*, 6 April 1901, 3.

"A Grave Matter." *Huntsville Gazette*, 2 May 1885, 3.

Gray, Christopher. "O Brother: Down from the Mountain and into Wal-Mart." *Austin Chronicle*, 19 July 2002. <http://www.austinchronicle.com/gyrobase/Issue/story?oid=oid%3A97586>. 7 July 2008.

Greenberg, Mark. "Off the Beaten Track." Review of *Ralph Stanley and the Clinch Mountain Boys, 1971-1973*. *Sing Out!* 40, no. 4 (1996): 132-33.

Grenelle, Levi Osborn. *Life and Labors of Elder Zelotes Grenell: For Sixty-Four Years an Eminently Successful Baptist Minister, 1818-1882*. N.p. [New Jersey?]: North New Jersey Baptist Association, 1885.

Griffin, Benjamin. *History of the Primitive Baptists of Mississippi, from the First Settlement by the Americans. Up to the Middle of the XIXth Century; Containing a Brief Allusion to the Course, Doctrines, and Practice of the Christian Church from Jerusalem to America; Also, the Doctrine and Practice of Modern Missionaries, from the Days of Andrew Fuller, and a Brief Notice of D. Benedict's Late History of the Baptists; Concluded with an Address to the General Reader*. Jackson, Miss.: Barksdale and Jones, 1853.

H. C. "Alabama." *New York Times*, 12 December 1874, 1.

Haggard, Gray. Letter to the editor. *Primitive Baptist*, 27 February 1836, 61-62.

Hanks, Lee. "The Conflicts of an Orphan." 1 March 1866. Primitive Baptist Online. <http://primitivebaptist.info/mambo//content/view/124/36/>. 2 February 2007.

Hansbrough, Smith. Letter to the editor. *Primitive Baptist*, 14 April 1838, 107-9.

Harris, Bartley, and William H. Gaston. "Primitive Baptist Church." *Huntsville Gazette*, 28 July 1888, 3.

Hart, R. D. "Biography of Elder Joshua Lawrence." *Primitive Baptist*, 28 October 1843, 312-16.

Hassell, C. B. Letter to the editor. *Signs of the Times*, 24 September 1834, 307-8.

———. "The Salvation of the Righteous Is of the Lord." *Primitive Baptist*, 26 March 1836, 85-86.

Hassell, Cushing Biggs, and Sylvester Hassell. *History of the Church of God, from the Creation to A.D. 1885; Including Especially the History of the Kehukee Primitive Baptist Association*. Middletown, N.Y.: Gilbert Beebe's Sons, 1886.

Hassell, Sylvester. "A Marvel of Divine Grace." *Messenger of Peace* 45, no. 1 (1919): 11-13.

———. "A Marvel of Divine Grace." *Messenger of Peace* 45, no. 2 (1919): 32-33.

Hervey, George Winfred. *The Story of Baptist Missions in Foreign Lands: From the Time of Carey to the Present Date*. St. Louis: Chancy R. Barnes, 1884.

Hill, Thomas, Sr. Letter to the editor. *Primitive Baptist*, 23 October 1841, 313-16.

———. Letter to the editor. *Primitive Baptist*, 13 November 1841, 332-35.

———. Letter to the editor. *Primitive Baptist*, 27 November 1841, 341-42.

Holcombe, Hosea. *A History of the Rise and Progress of the Baptists in Alabama: With a Miniature History of the Denomination from the Apostolic Age Down to the Present Time, Interspersed with Anecdotes Original and Selected, and Concluded with an Address to the Baptists of Alabama*. Philadelphia: King and Baird, 1840.

Hollister, Sarah Ann. "From Sister Hollister to Sister Mather, after Reading Her Experience, as Published in a Late Number of the *Monitor*." *Christian Doctrinal Advocate and Spiritual Monitor* 3 (1840): 266-69.

Howell, Robert Boyte C. *The Early Baptists of Virginia*. Philadelphia: The Bible and Publication Society, 1857.

———. "Missions and Anti-missions in Tennessee." *Baptist Memorial and Monthly Record* 4, no. 11 (November 1845): 305-9.

"In Mass Meeting." *Huntsville Gazette*, 23 May 1885, 3.

Jacks, David. Letter to the editor. *Primitive Baptist*, 10 March 1838, 68.

Jones, Garnett. Letter to the editor. *Signs of the Times*, 12 November 1834, 359.

Keeler, J. E. A. "The Colored People's Department." *Ocala Evening Star*, 9 March 1905, 4.

King, Joseph. Letter to the editor. *Primitive Baptist*, 23 April 1836, 127.

Lawrence, Joshua. *The American Telescope, by a Clodhopper, of North Carolina*. Philadelphia: printed for the author, 1825.

———. "Circular Letter." *Primitive Baptist*, 24 November 1838, 332-48.

———. "Declaration of the Reformed Baptist Churches in the State of North Carolina." *Primitive Baptist*, 14 May 1842, 129-33.

———. Letter to the editor. *Primitive Baptist*, 9 January 1836, 1-7.

———. Letter to the editor. *Primitive Baptist*, 23 January 1836, 17-23.

———. Letter to the editor. *Primitive Baptist*, 13 February 1836, 33-45.

———. Letter to the editor. *Primitive Baptist*, 27 February 1836, 49-57.

———. *A Patriotic Discourse: Delivered by the Rev. Joshua Lawrence, at the Old Church in Tarborough, North Carolina, on Sunday, the 4th of July, 1830*. Tarborough, N.C.: Free Press, 1830.

———. "Teeth to Teeth: Tom Thumb Tugging with the Wolves for the Sheepskin." *Primitive Baptist*, 28 January 1837, 7-25.

———. "Teeth to Teeth: Tom Thumb Tugging with the Wolves for the Sheepskin." *Primitive Baptist*, 27 May 1837, 145-53.

———. "Teeth to Teeth: Tom Thumb Tugging with the Wolves for the Sheepskin." *Primitive Baptist*, 9 September 1837, 257-64.

———. "Victorious Grace: Being a Mere Glance of His Experience." *Primitive Baptist*, 9 October 1841, 297-303.

———. "Victorious Grace: Being a Mere Glance of His Experience." *Primitive Baptist*, 23 October 1841, 305-12.

———. "Victorious Grace: Being a Mere Glance of His Experience." *Primitive Baptist*, 13 November 1841, 321-28.

———. "Victorious Grace: Being a Mere Glance of His Experience." *Primitive Baptist*, 27 November 1841, 337-41.

———. "Victorious Grace: Being a Mere Glance of His Experience." *Primitive Baptist*, 11 December 1841, 353-58.

"Lease of the Green Academy Lot." *Huntsville Gazette*, 20 May 1882, 3.

Lee, H. C. "H. C. Lee: Experience and Death." *Gospel Messenger* 13, no. 4 (April 1891): 161-62.

Lewis, Joseph B. Letter to the editor. *Primitive Baptist*, 26 February 1842, 55–56.

Lloyd, Benjamin. *The Primitive Hymns, Spiritual Songs, and Sacred Poems: Regularly Selected, Classified and Set in Order and Adapted to Social Singing and All Occasions of Divine Worship*. Greenville, Ala.: published for the proprietor, 1841.

"Local Notes." *Huntsville Gazette*, 3 February 1894, 3.

Lomax, Alan. "Bluegrass Background: Folk Music with Overdrive." *Esquire*, October 1959, 108.

MacLean, Annie Marion. "A Town in Florida." In *The Negro Church: Report of a Social Study Made under the Direction of Atlanta University; Together with the Proceedings of the Eighth Conference for the Study of the Negro Problems, Held at Atlanta University, May 26th, 1903*, edited by W. E. B. Du Bois, 64–68. Atlanta: Atlanta University Press, 1903.

"Matters Municipal." *Huntsville Gazette*, 7 May 1887, 3.

McIntosh County Shouters. "The McIntosh County Shouters." <http://shoutforfreedom.synthasite.com/>. 7 May 2012.

"Ministerial Support." *Primitive Baptist*, 3 October 1835, 4–5.

Minutes of the Cumberland Baptist Association: Convened at Friendship Meetinghouse, Davidson County, Ten. Franklin, Tenn.: The Review, 1835.

Minutes of the Sixteenth Annual Session of the Mt. Ramah Primitive Baptist Association. Americus, Ga.: Americus Printing Co., 1905.

Moore, J. Taylor. *A Biography of the Late Elder Thos. P. Dudley*. Occoquan, Va.[?]: Printed at the Sectarian Printing Office by Wm. M. Smoot[?], 1891.

Mustain, Shadrach. Letter to the editor. *Primitive Baptist*, 10 February 1844, 46–47.

"The Mystery of Faith," *Primitive Baptist*, 13 February 1836, 48.

"The Mystery of Faith," *Primitive Baptist*, 14 May 1836, 144.

National Primitive Baptist Convention of America. *Souvenir and Official Programme of the National Primitive Bapt. Convention America*. N.p.: National Primitive Baptist Convention of America, 1908.

"Neighborhood News and Gossip." *Huntsville Gazette*, 12 November 1881, 3.

"Neighborhood News and Gossip." *Huntsville Gazette*, 25 February 1882, 3.

"Neighborhood News and Gossip." *Huntsville Gazette*, 20 May 1882, 3.

Newman, Albert Henry. *A History of the Baptist Churches in the United States*. New York: Christian Literature Company, 1894.

Newport, Richard M. "Imposition Exposed." *Signs of the Times*, 2 April 1834, 134–37.

"Night and Day School." *Huntsville Gazette*, 21 October 1882, 3.

"The North Carolina Whig's Memorial and Remonstrance." *North Carolina Baptist Interpreter*, 4 January 1834, 11–12.

"Notice." *Huntsville Gazette*, 11 November 1882, 3.

"Obituary. Gilbert Beebe." *New York Times*, 3 May 1881, 5.

Oermann, Robert. Notes to *O Brother, Where Art Thou?* Mercury 088 170-069-2, 2000, compact disc.

Official Proceedings of the National Republican Conventions of 1868, 1872, 1876, and 1880. Minneapolis: Charles W. Johnson, 1903.

"Off the Beaten Track." Review of *The High Lonesome Sound*. *Sing Out!* 43, no. 1 (1998): 122–25, 160.

"The Old Cemetery." *Huntsville Gazette*, 25 March 1882, 3.

Orange County Gazetteer and Business Directory. Vol. 1. Jacksonville, Fla.: John R. Richards and Co., 1887.

Osbourn, James. "An Address to the Mayo Baptist Association, in the State of North Carolina, and to All Sister Associations with Whom She Corresponds." *Signs of the Times*, 5 June 1833, 209–16.

———. Letter to the editor. *Primitive Baptist*, 13 January 1844, 1–3.

———. *North Carolina Sonnets, or A Selection of Choice Hymns for the Use of Old School Baptists : Compiled by the Recommendation of the Kehukee Association*. Baltimore: John D. Toy, 1844.

———. *Old School Sonnets, or a Selection of Choice Hymns, for the Use of the Old School Baptists*. Baltimore: John D. Toy, 1836.

———. *A Religious Devil Detected; or, Apollyon's Soliloquies Overheard by a Listener, and the Depths of Satan Exposed*. Baltimore: Toy, 1834.

An Out-Cast. Letter to the editor. *Signs of the Times*, 12 November 1834, 356.

Pankake, John, and Paul Nelson. *Little Sandy Review*, no. 12 (1961).

"Personal." *Huntsville Gazette*, 9 August 1890, 3.

Phillips, Rebecca Anna. *The Experience of R. Anna Phillips, of Rome, Georgia, and Her Reasons for Uniting with the Primitive Baptists*. Wilson, N.C.: P. D. Gold, 1875.

———. *Led by a Way I Knew Not: Being the Christian Experience, and Reasons for Leaving the Missionary Baptists, and Uniting with the Primitive Baptists, with an Exposition of the Issues Dividing Them . . . Together with Supplementary Articles on Scriptural Subjects*. Pulaski City, Va.: Hurst, 1901.

Primitive Baptist General State Convention of Florida. *Primitive Baptist Manual: Containing a Complete, Comprehensive Guide to the Doctrines, Discipline and Usages of the Primitive (Old School) Baptist Church*. DeLand, Fla.: News Publishing Company, 1904.

"Primitive Baptists' Appeal." *Huntsville Gazette*, 7 December 1889, 3.

"Proposals for Publishing a Semi-monthly paper, Called 'Signs of the Times.'" *Signs of the Times*, 28 November 1832, 16.

Purifoy, J. H. "Autobiography." *Gospel Messenger* 10, no. 8 (August 1888): 341–48.

"Rally Day at Primitive Baptist Church." *Huntsville Gazette*, 7 July 1888, 3.

"Reasons for Roundly Asserting That the Popular Institutions Are Anti-Christian." *Primitive Baptist*, 3 October 1835, 9–12.

Reese, Rowell. Letter to the editor. *Primitive Baptist*, 27 February 1836, 62–63.

Respess, John. "The Experience of a Sinner." *Gospel Messenger* 13, no. 8 (August 1891): 320–23.

Review of *Shady Grove: Old Time Music from North Carolina, Kentucky, and Virginia*. *Sing Out!* 43, no. 2 (1998): 161.

Riess, Al. "Recordings: Roscoe Holcomb—'An Untamed Sense of Control.'" *Dirty Linen*, October–November 2003, 56.

Riley, Benjamin Franklin. *A History of the Baptists in the Southern States East of the Mississippi*. Philadelphia: American Baptist Publication Society, 1898.

Rinzler, Richard. Notes to *Friends of Old Time Music*. Folkways FA 2390, 1964, 33 1/3 rpm.

Royall, Anne Newport. *Letters from Alabama on Various Subjects: To Which Is Added, an Appendix, Containing Remarks on Sundry Members of the 20th & 21st Congress, and Other High Characters, &c. &c. at the Seat of Government*. Washington, D.C., 1830.

Sammons, Wiley W. *Identity of the True Baptist Church: Doctrine, Precept & Practice from 1701-1971 in West Tennessee, North Carolina and Alabama*. Collierville, Tenn.: n.p., 1971.

Sams, C. F. "The Negro Primitive Baptist Church in America: Its Work and Progress." In *The United Negro: His Problems and His Progress: Containing the Addresses and Proceedings [of] the Negro Young People's Christian and Educational Congress, Held August 6-11, 1902*, edited by I. Garland Penn and J. W. E. Bowen, 547-48. Atlanta: D. E. Luther Publishing Co., 1902.

Santayana, George. *The Life of Reason: Or, the Phases of Human Progress*. New York: Scribner's, 1905.

Saunders, Walter V. Notes to *Ralph Stanley and the Clinch Mountain Boys, 1971-1973*. Rebel REB-4001, 1995, compact disc.

Scales, J. R. "Wait for the Wagon." *Huntsville Journal*, 10 April 1896, 2.

"School House Movement." *Huntsville Gazette*, 27 June 1891, 3.

Sheets, Henry. *A History of the Liberty Baptist Association: From Its Organization in 1832 to 1906, Containing Much History Incidentally Connected with This Body; Also There Is Presented Quite an Extended Account of the "Split" in Baptist Ranks Showing Who Are the "Primitive Baptists," Together with Side-Lights on the "Split."* Raleigh, N.C.: Edwards and Broughton Printing Co., 1907.

Shelton, Robert. "Folk Singers from the 'Source.'" *New York Times*, 24 April 1966, 22.

Sherwood, Adiel. "The Identity of Primitive and Modern Missions: A Discourse." *Southern Baptist Preacher; Or, Sermons by Living Baptist Ministers in the South* 1, no. 4 (1840): 53-66.

Simmons, William J. *Men of Mark: Eminent, Progressive and Rising*. Cleveland, Ohio: G. M. Rewell and Company, 1887.

Smith, J. J. "More about the Baptist Association." *Huntsville Gazette*, 21 September 1889, 3.

Solonite. "Excursions." *Huntsville Gazette*, 19 June 1886, 2.

Stanley, Ralph, and Eddie Dean. *Man of Constant Sorrow: My Life and Times*. New York: Penguin, 2009.

Stott, William T. *Indiana Baptist History, 1798-1908*. N.p., 1908.

"A Success." *Huntsville Journal*, 9 August 1895, 3.

"Summary of Quantico Baptist Church Cemetery." Mycemetery.org. <http://mycemetery.org/exhibits/show/quanticochurch>. 22 May 2012.

Sutton, Brett. Notes to *Primitive Baptist Hymns of the Blue Ridge*. University of North Carolina Press 39088, 1982, 33 1/3 rpm.

Taylor, James B. *Lives of Virginia Baptist Ministers*. 2nd ed. Richmond, Va.: Yale and Wyatt, 1838.

Taylor, John. *Thoughts on Missions.* Franklin County, Ky., 1820.

"The Teachers' Meeting." *Huntsville Gazette,* 3 April 1886, 3.

Tenth Annual Session of the Mount Olive Primitive Baptist Association. Georgia, 1912.

Thielme, Art. "RE: A Quote from Roscoe Holcomb." 24 April 2004. <http://www.mudcat.org/thread.cfm?threadid=69113>. 28 January 2008.

Thompson, Wilson. *The Autobiography of Elder Wilson Thompson Embracing a Sketch of His Life, Travels, & Ministerial Labors, in Which Is Included a Concise History of the Old Order of Regular Baptist Churches.* Cincinnati: Moore, Wilstach and Baldwin, 1867.

Titon, Jeff Todd. Notes to *Old Regular Baptists: Lined-Out Hymnody from Southeastern Kentucky.* Smithsonian Folkways SFW 40106, 1997, compact disc.

"Triana." *Huntsville Gazette,* 11 August 1883, 3.

"A Tribute of Respect." *Huntsville Journal,* 2 April 1897, 2.

Trott, Samuel. "Union of Christ with the Church." In *A Compilation of Elder Samuel Trott's Writings: Copied from the "Signs of the Times" Embracing a Period from 1832-1862,* edited by Marc Jacobsson, 39-43. Salisbury, Md.: Welsh Tract Publications, 1999.

Trust. "The Final Salvation of the Redeemed Not Doubtful, but Certain." *Christian Doctrinal Advocate and Spiritual Monitor* 1 (1837): 114-17.

Turner, Joseph Kelly, and John Luther Bridgers. *History of Edgecombe County, North Carolina.* Raleigh, N.C.: Edwards and Broughton, 1920.

"The Two Covenants." *Primitive Baptist,* 3 October 1835, 5-8.

"The Two Covenants." *Primitive Baptist,* 9 January 1836, 10-11.

U.S. Bureau of the Census. *Ninth Census of the United States.* Population Schedules. 1870. Huntsville, Madison County, Alabama. Microfilm M593. Washington, D.C.: National Archives and Records Administration.

U.S. Bureau of the Census. *Religious Bodies: 1916—Separate Denominations: History, Description, and Statistics.* Washington, D.C.: Government Printing Office, 1919.

U.S. Bureau of the Census. *Tenth Census of the United States.* Population Schedules. 1880. Huntsville, Madison County, Alabama. Microfilm T9. Washington, D.C.: National Archives and Records Administration.

U.S. Bureau of the Census. *Twelfth Census of the United States.* Population Schedules. 1900. Huntsville, Madison County, Alabama. Microfilm T623. Washington, D.C.: National Archives and Records Administration.

U.S. Congress. House. *Annual Reports of the Department of Interior for the Fiscal Year Ended June 30, 1898: Report of the Commissioner of Education,* vol. 2. 55th Cong., 3rd sess., 1899, H. Doc. 5.

U.S. Department of Treasury. *Registers of Signatures of Depositors in Branches of the Freedman's Savings and Trust Company, 1865-1874.* Huntsville Branch. Microfilm Publication M816, roll 1. Washington, D.C.: National Archives and Records Administration.

Vanmeter, Isaac N. Letter to the editor. *Gospel Messenger* 7, no. 3 (March 1885): 113-19.

Veritatis, Amans. "A Difference between the Spirit of Christ and Mere Party Zeal." *Christian Doctrinal Advocate and Spiritual Monitor* 1 (1837): 5–8.

Volusia County Heritage. "City of DeLand." <http://volusia.org/history/deland.htm>. 9 July 2011.

Walker, Martha A. Letter to the editor. *Primitive Baptist*, 28 August 1840, 298–99.

"Wants Him Beaten Because He Put a Fence around the Colored Cemetery." *Huntsville Gazette*, 4 April 1885, 3.

Watson, John M. *The Old Baptist Test; or Bible Signs of the Lord's People*. Nashville, Tenn.: Republican Banner Press, 1855.

West, Hezekiah. Letter to the editor. *Signs of the Times*, 11 December 1833, 4–7.

Whatley, Vachal D. Letter to the editor. *Primitive Baptist*, 22 May 1841, 151–52.

Wiggens, E. I. *The History of the Absolute Mt. Enon Association*. N.p.: 1922[?]. Primitive Baptist Online, <http://primitivebaptist.info/mambo//content/view/658/70/>. 12 May 2011.

Wright, Alan C. *Huntsville in Vintage Postcards*. Charleston, S.C.: Arcadia, 2000.

Wright, John. *Traveling the High Way Home: Ralph Stanley and the World of Traditional Bluegrass Music*. Urbana: University of Illinois Press, 1993.

Secondary Sources

Abu-Lughod, Lila. *Veiled Sentiments: Honor and Poetry in a Bedouin Society*. Berkeley: University of California Press, 1986.

Abzug, Robert H. *Cosmos Crumbling: American Reform and the Religious Imagination*. New York: Oxford University Press, 1994.

Adams, Samuel C., Jr. "Changing Negro Life in the Delta." In *Lost Delta Found: Rediscovering the Fisk University–Library of Congress Coahoma County Study, 1941–1942*, edited by Robert Gordon and Bruce Nemerov, 225–90. Nashville, Tenn.: Vanderbilt University Press, 2005.

Ahlstrom, Sydney E. *A Religious History of the American People*. New Haven, Conn.: Yale University Press, 1972.

Albaugh, Gaylord P. "Anti-missionary Movement in the United States." In *An Encyclopedia of Religion*, edited by Vergilius Ferm, 27–28. New York: Philosophical Library, 1945.

Anderson, James D. *The Education of Blacks in the South, 1860–1935*. Chapel Hill: University of North Carolina Press, 1988.

Anthony, Ted. *Chasing the Rising Sun: The Journey of an American Song*. New York: Simon and Schuster, 2007.

Ardery, Julia S. *The Temptation: Edgar Tolson and the Genesis of Twentieth-Century Folk Art*. Chapel Hill: University of North Carolina Press, 1998.

Association of Statisticians of American Religious Bodies. *Religious Congregations and Membership in the United States 2000: An Enumeration by Region, State and County Based on Data Reported for 149 Religious Bodies*. Nashville, Tenn.: Glenmary Research Center, 2002.

Balleisen, Edward J. *Navigating Failure: Bankruptcy and Commercial Society in Antebellum America*. Chapel Hill: University of North Carolina Press, 2001.

Bender, Courtney. "Practicing Religions." In *The Cambridge Companion to Religious Studies*, edited by Robert A. Orsi, 273–95. New York: Cambridge University Press, 2012.

Bennett, James B. *Religion and the Rise of Jim Crow in New Orleans*. Princeton, N.J.: Princeton University Press, 2005.

Berg, Wesley. "Hymns of the Old Colony Mennonites and the Old Way of Singing." *Musical Quarterly* 80, no. 1 (1996): 77–117.

Bloch, Ruth H. *Visionary Republic: Millennial Themes in American Thought, 1756–1800*. New York: Cambridge University Press, 1985.

Blum, Edward J., and W. Scott Poole, eds. *Vale of Tears: New Essays on Religion and Reconstruction*. Macon, Ga.: Mercer University Press, 2005.

Boles, John B. *The Great Revival: Beginnings of the Bible Belt*. Lexington: University Press of Kentucky, 1996. First published in 1972 as *The Great Revival, 1787–1805: The Origins of the Southern Evangelical Mind*.

———. *Religion in Antebellum Kentucky*. Lexington: University Press of Kentucky, 1995.

Bourdieu, Pierre. "The Production of Belief: Contribution to an Economy of Symbolic Goods." In *The Field of Cultural Production: Essays on Art and Literature*, edited by Randal Johnson, 74–111. New York: Columbia University Press, 1993.

Brackney, William H. *The Baptists*. New York: Greenwood Press, 1988.

Bradley, Stephen E., Jr., ed. *The 1800 and 1810 Federal Censuses: Edgecombe County, North Carolina*. South Boston, Va.: S. E. Bradley, 1989.

———. *The 1830 Federal Census: Edgecombe County, North Carolina*. South Boston, Va.: S. E. Bradley, 1987.

Bratt, James D. "Religious Anti-revivalism in Antebellum America." *Journal of the Early Republic* 24, no. 1 (2004): 65–106.

———. "The Reorientation of American Protestantism, 1835–1845." *Church History* 67, no. 1 (1998): 52–82.

———, ed. *Antirevivalism in Antebellum America: A Collection of Religious Voices*. New Brunswick, N.J: Rutgers University Press, 2006.

Brauer, Jerald C. "Revivalism Revisited." *Journal of Religion* 77, no. 2 (1997): 268–77.

Brewster, Paul. *Andrew Fuller: Model Pastor-Theologian*. Nashville, Tenn.: B and H Publishing, 2010.

Broughton, Viv. *Black Gospel: An Illustrated History of the Gospel Sound*. Poole, Dorset, England: Blandford Press, 1985.

Brown, Candy Gunther. *The Word in the World: Evangelical Writing, Publishing, and Reading in America, 1789–1880*. Chapel Hill: University of North Carolina Press, 2004.

Burich, Keith Robert. "The Primitive Baptist Schism in North Carolina: A Study of the Professionalization of the Baptist Ministry." M.A. thesis, University of North Carolina at Chapel Hill, 1973.

Butler, Jon. *Awash in a Sea of Faith: Christianizing the American People*. Cambridge, Mass.: Harvard University Press, 1990.

Byrne, Frank J. *Becoming Bourgeois: Merchant Culture in the South, 1820–1865*. Lexington: University Press of Kentucky, 2006.

Caldwell, Patricia. *The Puritan Conversion Narrative: The Beginnings of American Expression*. New York: Cambridge University Press, 1983.

Cantwell, Robert. *Bluegrass Breakdown: The Making of the Old Southern Sound*. Urbana: University of Illinois Press, 1984. Reprint, New York: Da Capo Press, 1992.

———. *Ethnomimesis: Folklife and the Representation of Culture*. Chapel Hill: University of North Carolina Press, 1993.

———. *When We Were Good: The Folk Revival*. Cambridge, Mass.: Harvard University Press, 1996.

Carwardine, Richard. "Charles Sellers's 'Antinomians' and 'Arminians': Methodists and the Market Revolution." In *God and Mammon: Protestants, Money, and the Market, 1790-1860*, edited by Mark A. Noll, 75-98. New York: Oxford University Press, 2002.

Cash, W. J. *The Mind of the South*. New York: Knopf, 1941. Reprint, New York: Vintage Books, 1991.

Clarke, Erskine. *Our Southern Zion: A History of Calvinism in the South Carolina Low Country, 1690-1990*. Tuscaloosa: University of Alabama Press, 1996.

Combs, Josiah Henry. *Folk-Songs of the Southern United States (Folk-Songs du Midi des Etats-Unis)*. Edited by D. K. Wilgus. Austin: University of Texas Press, 1967.

Cook, James W. *The Arts of Deception: Playing with Fraud in the Age of Barnum*. Cambridge, Mass.: Harvard University Press, 2001.

Corrigan, John. *Business of the Heart: Religion and Emotion in the Nineteenth Century*. Berkeley: University of California Press, 2002.

Crowley, John G. *Primitive Baptists of the Wiregrass South: 1815 to the Present*. Gainesville: University Press of Florida, 1998.

———. "The Primitive or Old School Baptists." In *The Baptist River: Essays on Many Tributaries of a Diverse Tradition*, edited by W. Glenn Jonas Jr., 158-81. Macon, Ga.: Mercer University Press, 2006.

Davis, Thomas J., ed. *John Calvin's American Legacy*. New York: Oxford University Press, 2010.

Dawidoff, Nicholas. *In the Country of Country: A Journey to the Roots of American Music*. New York: Vintage Books, 1998.

Dochuk, Darren. *From Bible Belt to Sunbelt: Plain-Folk Religion, Grassroots Politics, and the Rise of Evangelical Conservatism*. New York: W. W. Norton, 2010.

Dorgan, Howard. *Giving Glory to God in Appalachia: Worship Practices of Six Baptist Subdenominations*. Knoxville: University of Tennessee Press, 1987.

———. *In the Hands of a Happy God: The "No-Hellers" of Central Appalachia*. Knoxville: University of Tennessee Press, 1997.

———. *The Old Regular Baptists of Central Appalachia: Brothers and Sisters in Hope*. Knoxville: University of Tennessee Press, 1989.

Douglas, Ann. *The Feminization of American Culture*. New York: Knopf, 1977.

Dupre, Daniel S. *Transforming the Cotton Frontier: Madison County, Alabama, 1800-1840*. Baton Rouge: Louisiana State University Press, 1997.

Dvorak, Katharine L. *An African-American Exodus: The Segregation of the Southern Churches*. Brooklyn: Carlson, 1991.

Elias, Norbert. *The Civilizing Process: The History of Manners*. New York: Urizen Books, 1978.

Epstein, Dena J. *Sinful Tunes and Spirituals: Black Folk Music to the Civil War*. Urbana: University of Illinois Press, 1977.

Eustace, Nicole. *Passion Is the Gale: Emotion, Power, and the Coming of the American Revolution*. Chapel Hill: University of North Carolina Press, 2008.

Eustace, Nicole, Eugenia Lean, Julie Livingston, Jan Plamper, William M. Reddy, and Barbara H. Rosenwein. "AHR Conversation: The Historical Study of Emotions." *American Historical Review* 117, no. 5 (December 2012): 1487–1531.

Fairclough, Adam. *A Class of Their Own: Black Teachers in the Segregated South*. Cambridge, Mass.: Harvard University Press, 2007.

Feld, Steven. "Wept Thoughts: The Voicing of Kaluli Memories." In *South Pacific Oral Traditions*, edited by Ruth Finnegan and Margaret Orben, 85–108. Bloomington: Indiana University Press, 1995.

Filene, Benjamin. *Romancing the Folk: Public Memory and American Roots Music*. Chapel Hill: University of North Carolina Press, 2000.

Fleming, Walter Lynwood. *Civil War and Reconstruction in Alabama*. New York: Columbia University Press, 1905.

Floyd, Samuel A., Jr. "Ring Shout! Literary Studies, Historical Studies, and Black Music Inquiry." *Black Music Research Journal* 11, no. 2 (1991): 265–87.

Flynt, Wayne. *Alabama Baptists: Southern Baptists in the Heart of Dixie*. Tuscaloosa: University of Alabama Press, 1998.

Foster, Charles I. *An Errand of Mercy: The Evangelical United Front, 1790–1837*. Chapel Hill: University of North Carolina Press, 1960.

Fox, Aaron A. "'Alternative' to What? *O Brother*, September 11, and the Politics of Country Music." In *Country Music Goes to War*, edited by Charles K. Wolfe and James E. Akenson, 164–91. Lexington: University Press of Kentucky, 2005.

Gammon, David B., ed. *Abstracts of Wills of Edgecombe County, North Carolina*. Vols. 3–4. Raleigh: D. B. Gammon, 1992.

Gardner, Robert G. *National Primitive Baptists in Georgia*. Macon: Georgia Baptist Historical Society, 2004.

Gates, David. "Constant Sorrow: The Long Road of Ralph Stanley." *New Yorker*, 20 August 2001, 88–94.

Genovese, Eugene D. *Roll, Jordan, Roll: The World the Slaves Made*. New York: Vintage Books, 1976.

Giggie, John M. *After Redemption: Jim Crow and the Transformation of African American Religion in the Delta, 1875–1915*. New York: Oxford University Press, 2008.

Gold, Pleasant Daniel. *History of Volusia County, Florida: Also Biographies of Prominent People of Volusia County*. De Land, Fla.: E. O. Painter Printing, 1927.

Gomez, Michael Angelo. *Exchanging Our Country Marks: The Transformation of African Identities in the Colonial and Antebellum South*. Chapel Hill: University of North Carolina Press, 1998.

Gura, Philip F. "Southern Roots and Branches: Forty Years of the New Lost City Ramblers." *Southern Cultures* 6, no. 4 (2000): 58–81.

Harlan, Louis R. *Booker T. Washington: The Making of a Black Leader, 1856-1901.* New York: Oxford University Press, 1975.

Harlan, Louis R., and Raymond W. Smock, eds. *The Booker T. Washington Papers: 1899-1900.* Vol. 5. Urbana: University of Illinois Press, 1976.

Harvey, Paul. *Freedom's Coming: Religious Culture and the Shaping of the South from the Civil War through the Civil Rights Era.* Chapel Hill: University of North Carolina Press, 2005.

———. *Redeeming the South: Religious Cultures and Racial Identities among Southern Baptists, 1865-1925.* Chapel Hill: University of North Carolina Press, 1997.

Hatch, Nathan O. *The Democratization of American Christianity.* New Haven, Conn.: Yale University Press, 1989.

Hayslette, Sandra D. "Missions, Markets, and Men: A Baptist Contest of Values in Tarboro, North Carolina, 1800-1835." M.A. thesis, University of North Carolina at Chapel Hill, 1995.

Heyrman, Christine Leigh. *Southern Cross: The Beginnings of the Bible Belt.* New York: Knopf, 1997.

Higginbotham, Evelyn Brooks. *Righteous Discontent: The Women's Movement in the Black Baptist Church, 1880-1920.* Cambridge, Mass.: Harvard University Press, 1994.

Hochschild, Arlie Russell. *The Managed Heart: Commercialization of Human Feeling.* Berkeley: University of California Press, 1983.

Hofstadter, Richard. *The Paranoid Style in American Politics, and Other Essays.* New York: Knopf, 1965.

Holifield, E. Brooks. *The Gentlemen Theologians: American Theology in Southern Culture, 1795-1860.* Durham: Duke University Press, 1978.

Howe, Daniel Walker. "The Decline of Calvinism: An Approach to Its Study." *Comparative Studies in Society and History* 14, no. 3 (1972): 306-72.

———. "The Market Revolution and the Shaping of Identity in Whig-Jacksonian America." In *The Market Revolution in America: Social, Political, and Religious Expressions, 1800-1880,* edited by Melvyn Stokes and Stephen Conway, 259-81. Charlottesville: University Press of Virginia, 1996.

———. *What Hath God Wrought: The Transformation of America, 1815-1848.* New York: Oxford University Press, 2007.

Hudgins, Ira Durwood. "The Anti-missionary Controversy among Baptists." *Chronicle* 14, no. 4 (1951): 147-63.

Hughes, Richard T., ed. *The American Quest for the Primitive Church.* Urbana: University of Illinois Press, 1988.

Hughes, Richard T., and C. Leonard Allen, eds. *Illusions of Innocence: Protestant Primitivism in America, 1630-1875.* Chicago: University of Chicago Press, 1988.

Hunter, Tera W. *To 'Joy My Freedom: Southern Black Women's Lives and Labors after the Civil War.* Cambridge, Mass.: Harvard University Press, 1997.

Isaac, Rhys. *The Transformation of Virginia, 1740-1790.* Chapel Hill: University of North Carolina Press, 1982.

Johnson, Curtis D. "Supply-Side and Demand-Side Revivalism? Evaluating the Social Influences on New York State Evangelism in the 1830s." *Social Science History* 19, no. 1 (1995): 1-30.

Johnson, Paul E. "Democracy, Patriarchy, and American Revivals, 1780–1830." *Journal of Social History* 24, no. 4 (1991): 843–50.

———. *A Shopkeeper's Millennium: Society and Revivals in Rochester, New York, 1815–1837*. New York: Hill and Wang, 1978.

Jones, Bessie, and Bess Lomax Hawes. *Step It Down: Games, Plays, Songs, and Stories from the Afro-American Heritage*. New York: Harper and Row, 1972. Reprint, Athens: University of Georgia Press, 1987.

Jones, Lewis Wade. "The Mississippi Delta." In *Lost Delta Found: Rediscovering the Fisk University-Library of Congress Coahoma County Study, 1941–1942*, edited by Robert Gordon and Bruce Nemerov, 31–49. Nashville, Tenn.: Vanderbilt University Press, 2005.

Jones, Loyal. *Faith and Meaning in the Southern Uplands*. Urbana: University of Illinois Press, 1999.

Lambert, Byron Cecil. *The Rise of the Anti-mission Baptists: Sources and Leaders, 1800–1840*. New York: Arno Press, 1980.

Lears, T. J. Jackson. *Something for Nothing: Luck in America*. New York: Viking, 2003.

Lepore, Jill. "Vast Designs: How America Came of Age." *New Yorker*, 29 October 2007, 88–92.

Lhamon, W. T. *Raising Cain: Blackface Performance from Jim Crow to Hip Hop*. Cambridge, Mass.: Harvard University Press, 1998.

Longfield, Bradley J. *The Presbyterian Controversy: Fundamentalists, Modernists, and Moderates*. New York: Oxford University Press, 1991.

Loveland, Anne C. *Southern Evangelicals and the Social Order, 1800–1860*. Baton Rouge: Louisiana State University Press, 1980.

Lutz, Catherine. *Unnatural Emotions: Everyday Sentiments on a Micronesian Atoll and Their Challenge to Western Theory*. Chicago: University of Chicago Press, 1988.

Maffly-Kipp, Laurie F. "The Burdens of Church History." *Church History* 82, no. 2 (June 2013): 353–67.

Mathews, Donald G. *Religion in the Old South*. Chicago: University of Chicago Press, 1977.

———. "The Second Great Awakening as an Organizing Process, 1780–1830: An Hypothesis." *American Quarterly* 21, no. 1 (1969): 23–43.

Mathis, James R. *The Making of the Primitive Baptists: A Cultural and Intellectual History of the Anti-mission Movement, 1800–1840*. New York: Routledge, 2004.

McCauley, Deborah Vansau. *Appalachian Mountain Religion: A History*. Urbana: University of Illinois Press, 1995.

McCurry, Stephanie. *Masters of Small Worlds: Yeoman Households, Gender Relations, and the Political Culture of the Antebellum South Carolina Low Country*. New York: Oxford University Press, 1995.

McKnight, Roxanne. "Mexia Once Home to Historic Black College." *Mexia News*, 25 February 2012.

McLoughlin, William G. *Soul Liberty: The Baptists' Struggle in New England, 1630–1833*. Hanover, N.H.: University Press of New England, 1991.

Mead, Frank S., and Samuel S. Hill, eds. *Handbook of Denominations in the United States*. 11th ed. Nashville, Tenn.: Abingdon Press, 2001.

Meier, August. *Negro Thought in America, 1880–1915: Racial Ideologies in the Age of Booker T. Washington.* Ann Arbor: University of Michigan Press, 1963.

Miyakawa, T. Scott. *Protestants and Pioneers: Individualism and Conformity on the American Frontier.* Chicago: University of Chicago Press, 1964.

Montgomery, William E. *Under Their Own Vine and Fig Tree: The African-American Church in the South, 1865–1900.* Baton Rouge: Louisiana State University Press, 1994.

Morgan, Edmund Sears. *Visible Saints: The History of a Puritan Idea.* New York: New York University Press, 1963.

Mulder, Philip N. *A Controversial Spirit: Evangelical Awakenings in the South.* New York: Oxford University Press, 2002.

Najar, Monica. *Evangelizing the South: A Social History of Church and State in Early America.* New York: Oxford University Press, 2008.

Newsome, Jerry. "'Primitive Baptists': A Study in Name Formation or What's in a Word." *Viewpoints: Georgia Baptist History* 6 (1978): 63–70.

Niebuhr, H. Richard. *Christ and Culture.* New York: Harper and Row, 1951.

Noll, Mark A. *America's God: From Jonathan Edwards to Abraham Lincoln.* New York: Oxford University Press, 2002.

Orsi, Robert. "Everyday Miracles: The Study of Lived Religion." In *Lived Religion in America: Toward a History of Practice*, edited by David D. Hall, 3–21. Princeton, N.J.: Princeton University Press, 1997.

Patterson, Beverly Bush. *The Sound of the Dove: Singing in Appalachian Primitive Baptist Churches.* Urbana: University of Illinois Press, 1995.

Payne, Rodger M. *The Self and the Sacred: Conversion and Autobiography in Early American Protestantism.* Knoxville: University of Tennessee Press, 1998.

Peacock, James L., and Ruel W. Tyson. *Pilgrims of Paradox: Calvinism and Experience among the Primitive Baptists of the Blue Ridge.* Washington, D.C.: Smithsonian Institution Press, 1989.

"Places in Peril Lists Thomaston Colored Institute." *Linden (Ala.) Democrat-Reporter*, 24 May 2012.

Plamper, Jan. "The History of Emotions: An Interview with William Reddy, Barbara Rosenwein, and Peter Stearns." *History and Theory* 49 (May 2010): 237–65.

Poe, Harry L. "The History of the Anti-missionary Baptists." *Chronicle* 2, no. 2 (1939): 51–64.

Potter, Dorothy Williams, ed. *1820 Federal Census of North Carolina.* Vol. 19. Tullahoma, Tenn.: Dorothy Williams Potter, 1972.

Rabinowitz, Richard. *The Spiritual Self in Everyday Life: The Transformation of Personal Religious Experience in Nineteenth-Century New England.* Boston: Northeastern University Press, 1989.

Raboteau, Albert J. *Slave Religion: The "Invisible Institution" in the Antebellum South.* Updated ed. New York: Oxford University Press, 2004.

Reddy, William M. *The Navigation of Feeling: A Framework for the History of Emotions.* New York: Cambridge University Press, 2001.

Ritchie, Jean. *Folk Songs of the Southern Appalachians as Sung by Jean Ritchie.* 2nd ed. Lexington: University Press of Kentucky, 1997.

Rogers, Daniel T. *The Work Ethic in Industrial America: 1850-1920*. Chicago: University of Chicago Press, 1974.

Rosaldo, Michelle Z. *Knowledge and Passion: Ilongot Notions of Self and Social Life*. New York: Cambridge University Press, 1980.

Rosenbaum, Art. *Shout Because You're Free: The African American Ring Shout Tradition in Coastal Georgia*. Athens: University of Georgia Press, 1998.

Rosenberg, Neil V. *Bluegrass: A History*. Urbana: University of Illinois Press, 1985.

Rosenwein, Barbara H. *Emotional Communities in the Early Middle Ages*. Ithaca, N.Y.: Cornell University Press, 2006.

Russell, James A. "Is There Universal Recognition of Emotion from Facial Expressions? A Review of the Cross-Cultural Studies." *Psychological Bulletin* 115, no. 1 (1994): 102-41.

Ryan, Mary P. *Cradle of the Middle Class: The Family in Oneida County, New York, 1790-1865*. Cambridge: Cambridge University Press, 1981.

Schmidt, Leigh Eric. *Hearing Things: Religion, Illusion, and the American Enlightenment*. Cambridge, Mass.: Harvard University Press, 2000.

Schweiger, Beth Barton. *The Gospel Working Up: Progress and the Pulpit in Nineteenth Century Virginia*. New York: Oxford University Press, 2000.

———. "Max Weber in Mt. Airy, Or, Revivals and Social Theory in the Early South." In *Religion in the American South: Protestants and Others in History and Culture*, edited by Beth Barton Schweiger and Donald G. Mathews, 31-66. Chapel Hill: University of North Carolina Press, 2004.

Sellers, Charles. *The Market Revolution: Jacksonian America, 1815-1846*. New York: Oxford University Press, 1991.

Sherer, Robert. *Subordination or Liberation? The Development and Conflicting Theories of Black Education in Nineteenth Century Alabama*. Tuscaloosa: University of Alabama Press, 1977.

Sobel, Mechal. *Trabelin' On: The Slave Journey to an Afro-Baptist Faith*. Westport, Conn.: Greenwood Press, 1979.

Spangler, Jewel L. *Virginians Reborn: Anglican Monopoly, Evangelical Dissent, and the Rise of the Baptists in the Late Eighteenth Century*. Charlottesville: University of Virginia Press, 2008.

Sparks, Randy J. *On Jordan's Stormy Banks: Evangelicalism in Mississippi, 1773-1876*. Athens: University of Georgia Press, 1994.

Startup, Kenneth Moore. *The Root of All Evil: The Protestant Clergy and the Economic Mind of the Old South*. Athens: University of Georgia Press, 1997.

Stearns, Peter N. *American Cool: Constructing a Twentieth-Century Emotional Style*. New York: New York University Press, 1994.

———. "Emotions History in the United States: Goals, Methods, and Promise." In *Emotions in American History*, edited by Jessica C. E. Gienow-Hecht, 15-27. New York: Berghahn Books, 2010.

Stearns, Peter N., and Carol Z. Stearns. "Emotionology: Clarifying the History of Emotions and Emotional Standards." *American Historical Review* 90, no. 4 (October 1985): 813-36.

Stephens, Randall J. *The Fire Spreads: Holiness and Pentecostalism in the American South*. Cambridge, Mass.: Harvard University Press, 2008.

Stokes, Melvyn, and Stephen Conway, eds. *The Market Revolution in America: Social, Political, and Religious Expressions, 1800–1880*. Charlottesville: University Press of Virginia, 1996.

Stowell, Daniel W. *Rebuilding Zion: The Religious Reconstruction of the South, 1863–1877*. New York: Oxford University Press, 1998.

Stromberg, Peter G. *Language and Self-Transformation: A Study of the Christian Conversion Narrative*. New York: Cambridge University Press, 1993.

Stuckey, Sterling. *Slave Culture: Nationalist Theory and the Foundations of Black America*. New York: Oxford University Press, 1987.

Sweet, William Warren, ed. *The Baptists, 1783–1830: A Collection of Source Material*. New York: Cooper Square, 1964.

Tallmadge, William H. "Baptist Monophonic and Heterophonic Hymnody in Southern Appalachia." *Anuario Interamericano de Investigacion Musical* 11 (1975): 106–36.

Taves, Ann. *Religious Experience Reconsidered: A Building-Block Approach to the Study of Religion and Other Special Things*. Princeton, N.J.: Princeton University Press, 2009.

Taylor, Jeffrey W. *The Formation of the Primitive Baptist Movement*. Kitchener, ON: Pandora Press, 2004.

———. "'These Worms Will Cut the Root of Our Independence': Fears of a State Church among the Anti-mission Baptists of the Nineteenth Century." In *Fear Itself: Enemies Real and Imagined in American Culture*, edited by Nancy Lusignan Schultz, 83–92. West Lafayette, Ind.: Purdue University Press, 1999.

Temperley, Nicholas. "The Old Way of Singing." *Musical Times* 120, no. 1641 (1979): 943–47.

———. "The Old Way of Singing: Its Origins and Development." *Journal of the American Musicological Society* 34, no. 3 (1981): 511–44.

Thornton, Richard H., and Louise Hanley. *An American Glossary: Being an Attempt to Illustrate Certain Americanisms upon Historical Principles*. London: Francis, 1900.

Trilling, Lionel. *Sincerity and Authenticity*. Cambridge, Mass.: Harvard University Press, 1972.

Urban, Greg. "Ritual Wailing in Amerindian Brazil." *American Anthropologist* 90 (1988): 385–400.

Washington, James Melvin. *Frustrated Fellowship: The Black Baptist Quest for Social Power*. Macon, Ga.: Mercer University Press, 1986.

Weber, Max. *The Protestant Ethic and the Spirit of Capitalism*. Translated by Talcott Parsons. New York: Scribner, 1958.

Whisnant, David E. *All That Is Native and Fine: The Politics of Culture in an American Region*. Chapel Hill: University of North Carolina Press, 1983.

Wicks, Sammie Ann. "A Belated Salute to the 'Old Way' of 'Snaking' the Voice on Its (ca.) 345th Birthday." *Popular Music* 8, no. 1 (1989): 59–96.

———. "Life and Meaning: Singing, Praying, and the Word among the Old Regular Baptists of Eastern Kentucky." Ph.D. diss., University of Texas at Austin, 1983.

Wikan, Unni. "Managing the Heart to Brighten Face and Soul: Emotions in Balinese Morality and Health Care." *American Ethnologist* 16, no. 2 (1989): 294–312.

Williams, Heather Andrea. *Self-Taught: African American Education in Slavery and Freedom.* Chapel Hill: University of North Carolina Press, 2005.

Williams, Raymond. *The Country and the City.* New York: Oxford University Press, 1973.

Williams, Ruth Smith, ed. *Marriages of Early Edgecombe County, North Carolina, 1733–1868.* Rocky Mount, N.C.: Dixie Letter Service, 1958.

Wimberly, Dan B. *Frontier Religion: Elder Daniel Parker, His Religious and Political Life.* Austin, Tex.: Eakin Press, 2002.

Work, John W., III. "Untitled Manuscript." In *Lost Delta Found: Rediscovering the Fisk University–Library of Congress Coahoma County Study, 1941–1942,* edited by Robert Gordon and Bruce Nemerov, 51–126. Nashville, Tenn.: Vanderbilt University Press, 2005.

Wyatt-Brown, Bertram. "The Antimission Movement in the Jacksonian South: A Study in Regional Folk Culture." *Journal of Southern History* 36, no. 4 (1970): 501–29.

———. *The Shaping of Southern Culture: Honor, Grace, and War, 1760s–1890s.* Chapel Hill: University of North Carolina Press, 2001.

Acknowledgments

Without whom:

My friends and colleagues at Berea College and especially my comrades in the history department—Robert Foster, Rebecca Bates, Katherine Christensen, Dwayne Mack, and Richard Cahill—who so kindly and generously welcomed me to Berea and who make work atop our little Kentucky ridge a delight; my Berea students whose dogged questions and enlightening answers have made me a better teacher; Johnna Allen, who makes our building run; all the librarians and staff members at Berea's Hutchins Library but especially Patty Tarter, who works magic with interlibrary loan, the much-missed Jaime Bradley, who found me every book I ever asked for (and I asked for a lot of them), and Rachel Vagts, the Head of Special Collections and Archives, who swept in with some last-minute scanning expertise; Berea College's Office of the Academic Vice President, which several times provided generous and crucial support for this project; and Chad Berry, who plucked my name out of a stack of papers, breathed a sigh of relief in New York City, showed me around Appalachia, and somehow knew all along that Berea and I would be good for each other.

The Charlotte W. Newcombe Foundation, the Woodrow Wilson National Fellowship Foundation, the North Caroliniana Society, the American Psychoanalytic Association, the Filson Historical Society, and both the graduate school and the Department of History at the University of North Carolina at Chapel Hill—all of whose financial assistance helped defray, and in some cases outright eliminated, the costs of research, writing, and travel associated with this book.

Everyone at the University of North Carolina Press, but especially my editor, Elaine Maisner, who took an early interest in this project and then steadfastly guided it to publication; the anonymous readers whose keen counsel was indispensable; the press's ingenious design, production, and marketing teams; Alison Shay, who was exceedingly patient with my less-than-swift e-mail habits; Caitlin Bell-Butterfield, who cheerfully answered every question I had, including at least a dozen that emanated from the deeply neurotic recesses of an anxious writer's mind; and Julie Bush, whose copyediting eye is as sharp as an eagle's and whose line edits helped straighten my crooked prose.

The librarians, archivists, and staff members at the North Carolina State Archives; the University of North Carolina at Chapel Hill's Southern Historical Collection, Southern Folklife Collection, and North Carolina Collection; Wake Forest University's archives and National Baptist Historical Collection; Duke University's David M. Rubenstein Rare Book and Manuscript Library; the Special Collections division of the Southern Baptist Theological Seminary's James P. Boyce Centennial Library; the Madison County Records Center in Huntsville, Alabama; the Huntsville–Madison County Public Library; the Florida Collection at the State Library and Archives of Florida in

Tallahassee; the University of Kentucky's Special Collections Library; Berea College's Special Collections and Archives; and, especially, the Primitive Baptist Library, a treasure house planted in the middle of tobacco fields in Alamance County, North Carolina. Very special thanks to Susanna Leberman in Huntsville and Aaron Smithers at the Southern Folklife Collection.

Alan Wright, who generously shared his vintage postcards of old Huntsville; Alexia Smith, who graciously allowed me to reproduce photographs taken by her late husband, Mike Seeger; Mark Freeman, who kindly made available images from Rebel Records, the label—an American institution, really—he so skillfully captains; and the wonderful John Cohen, who patiently answered my pesky questions.

Kelly Baker, Charles Israel, Wayne Flynt, John Giggie, Ronald Walters, Loyal Jones, Bill Ferris, and Dan Patterson, whose comments on various conference papers sharpened my arguments and opened up new avenues of exploration; Philip Goff, Tom Davis, and the anonymous readers at *Religion and American Culture* for their helpful suggestions and criticisms on an early version of chapter 2; the members of the Dead Mule Writing Group—Susan Pearson, Ethan Kytle, and Matthew Brown—who bravely pushed their way through early fragments and showed me how I could make them better; colleagues at Guilford College—Anore Horton, Tim Kircher, and Sarah Malino—who gave me the opportunity to teach alongside them and learn from them; Mary Beth Averill, for practical and cheerful advice; friends near and far: Matthew Aron, Johanna Aron, Jason Cohen, Meghan Doherty, Andrea Woodward, Josh Woodward, Wendy Williams, Tyler Sergent, Kevin Gardner, Jill Bouma, Gary Mahoney, Adanma Barton, Shane Barton, Abby Nittle, Josh Nittle, Rob and Rebecca (once again), Lydia Wegman, April Leininger, Lauren Kaminsky, Chris Jones, Tasha Hawthorne, Geoff Tanner, and Latisha Walker Nelson; my dearest friends, Eric Hynes and Aaron Nelson; and my erstwhile running companions, Arlo and Homer.

Teachers who showed the way: Joan Willson, Joan Cox, Lorraine Meyer, and Eileen Tunick; Carl Smith, Jim Campbell, Terry Mulcaire, and John Kupetz; Joy Kasson, Jacquelyn Dowd Hall, Glenn Hinson, Charlie Capper, Lloyd Kramer, and Peter Wood.

John Kasson, whose loyalty has been inestimable, whose patience seemed never to flag, and whose writing and teaching taught me how to make connections; Robert Cantwell, whose book on the folk revival—stumbled upon more than a decade ago in a bookstore in Encino, California—was both revelation and confirmation and whose enthusiasm for my work has been a gift; Yaakov Ariel, who told me that I could make it when I needed that message most, who brought me over for Shabbat dinners, and whose class on American religious history opened up worlds within worlds; Don Mathews, whose kind words during this project's early days made me think I might be on to something, whose remarks over e-mail one day led me to think more clearly about Calvinism's strange career, and whose work proves that trenchant scholarship and arresting prose need not be at odds; and Harry Watson, who taught me many years ago how to read for the argument and whose incisive work on the South always set me straight.

The entire Michigan crew—Mimi and Don, John and Carolyn, Adrienne, Molly, Cory, Matt, Melissa, Felicity, Sophia, and Gabe—who welcomed me from the beginning.

My sister and brother, Emily and Alex, and their spouses, Craig and Lisa, who asked after me gently; my amazing nephews, Jonas and Eli, who take me on adventures to the gardens and the zoo; my tiny and lovely nieces, Rose and Reese; and, especially, my parents and first teachers, Caren and David Guthman.

Anne Bruder, whose impeccable timing changed my life in all the good ways and who traveled by me and stuck by me from beginning to end.

And then, always now, there is my son, Augie, who welcomed himself to the world before his too-slow father could finish his revisions, who giggles gloriously and chirrups like a lark, who holds my finger as we walk through the tall grass and stare at the sky: I've found in him an unexpected grace that I only now realize I had been searching for my whole life. With love and gratitude, I dedicate this book to him.

Index

Figures are indicated with page numbers in *italics*.

Aaron, 81
Abbotts Creek Missionary Baptist Church, 2, 3
Abbott's Creek Primitive Baptist Church, 2
"Across the Rocky Mountain" (Holcomb), 129
Adam, 61
Adams, Samuel, 112
African Americans: in African Baptist Church of Huntsville, 94–100, *96*, *97*, *98*; baptism of, by white churches, 92; Big Spring and, 94–100; breakaway of, 89–91, 174 (n. 6); Calvinism and, 107, 150–51, 159 (n. 33); education of, 101, 178 (n. 38); female, 110–11; in Georgia, 90; Methodists and, 95–96; as missionary Baptists, 94–95; National Primitive Baptist Convention and, 16, 88–89, 107–11, 158 (n. 29); as Primitive Baptists, 15–16; whites and, 91–92
African Baptist Church of Huntsville, 94–100, *96–98*, 106, 175 (n. 14)
Ahlstrom, Sydney, 45, 116–17
Alabaha River Association, 150
American Bible Society, 5
American Board of Commissioners for Foreign Missions, 32
American Sunday School Union, 5
American Tract Society, 41
Anglicans, 24, 25, 130
Aristocracy, 35, 40–41, 43
Arminianism, 65, 82; Calvinism vs., 157 (n. 27), 159 (n. 33); control in, 86; Hanks on, 59; Methodists and, 61; Primitive Baptists and, 13, 14, 15; Protestantism and, 86; salvation and, 7

Armstrong, Howard, 119
Assurance, in conversion, 47

Bank of the United States, 65, 70
Baptism(s): of African Americans by white churches, 92; at African Baptist Church of Huntsville, 94–100, *96*, *97*, 176 (n. 16); Baptists and, 25; at Big Spring, 94–100, 176 (n. 16); of Phillips, 50; of Purifoy, 54
Baptist Board of Foreign Missions, 5
Baptist Church at Abbott's Creek, 2–3
Baptists: as counterculture, 25; history of, 6–7; Landmark, 15; new ethos among, 28–34; numbers of, 154 (n. 10); persecution of, 26–27, 31; Separate, 16, 25–26, 28, 160 (n. 7); shared past among, 24–28; Sovereign Grace, 158 (n. 29); stereotypes of, in rhetoric, 42–43, 44–45; United, 28. *See also* Missionary Baptists; Old School Baptists; Primitive Baptists; Regular Baptists
Barnum, P. T., 173 (n. 46)
Beebe, Gilbert, 43–45
Beecher, Catherine, 117, 118
Beecher, Edward, 56
Benedict, David, 30, 31, 32–33, 34, 161 (n. 18)
Bennett, Mark, 56, 165 (n. 24)
Berry, Isaac, 91
Bethlehem Primitive Baptist Church, 92–93
Big Spring, 94–100, *96*, 176 (n. 16)
Black Rock Address, 154 (n. 5)
Blaikie, W. G., 69

213

Bluegrass, 120–33, 136–38.
  See also Holcomb, Roscoe
Blue Grass Boys, 126, 127, 139.
  See also Monroe, Bill
Blue Sky Boys, 135
Bolch, Arthur, 53
Boles, John, 29
Boykin, Samuel, 42
Bratt, James, 149
Bristow, Mary Beckley, 51, 118
Bureaucracy, missionary work and, 32
Burkitt, Lemuel, 22; Kehukee Association narrative in, 27–28; millennialism in, 28; optimism of, 23; persecution in, 26; revivalism of, 21, 36
Business, 73–77
Byrne, Frank J., 169 (n. 23)

Cainites, 69
Calvinism, 1, 8, 13, 14, 15, 16; African Americans and, 107, 150–51, 159 (n. 33); in Ahlstrom, 116–17; Arminianism and, 157 (n. 27); in Cash, 116; emotion and, 56; of Hassell, 71–79; in modern culture, 143–44; opposites in, 60; in origin rhetoric, 41; origin stories and, 40; in Primitive Baptism, 155 (n. 12); Stanley and, 142–43; turn from, 29, 117–18; in Weber, 168 (n. 11)
Cantwell, Robert, 127
Cartwright, Peter, 29
Carwardine, Richard, 157 (n. 27)
Cash, W. J., 116
"Celestial Railroad, The" (Hawthorne), 168 (n. 7)
Census, 158 (n. 28)
"Christian Perfection," 55
Chronicles. See Histories
Church of England, 25
Circle ritual, 111–15
Civil War, 77, 89, 91
Clack, Spencer, 58
Clay, Martha Mary Ellen, 105
Clay-Clopton, Virginia, 176 (n. 16)

Clinch Mountain Boys, 135, *135*, *136*
Cline, Curley Ray, *135*
Cohen, John, 119–25, 127, 128, 130–31
Colleges, sectarian, 5
Colored Primitive Baptist Association of Georgia, 90
Complexio oppositorum, 60
Confidence, 49
Congregationalists, 130
Control, 86
Conversion: assurance in, 47; conviction in, 46–47, 55; emotion and, 55; evangelicalism and, 29–31; in evangelicalism vs. Primitive Baptism, 46–48; mass, 79; missionaries and, 30–31; narratives, 46–47; normative emotional style and, 47–48; revivals and, 29–30; "Rock Daniel" and, 112; trials and, 54–55; uncertainty and, 48–51
Conviction, in conversion, 46–47, 55
Convulsions, 29
Corrigan, John, 11–12, 56
Council, William Hooper, 104–6
Counterculture, Baptists as, 25
Country Gentlemen, 125
Cox, Ida, 125
Cry from the Cross (Stanley), 139

Daisy, Ky., 121
Deception, 39–40, 53–54
Deism, 56
DeLand, Fla., 87, 173 (n. 2)
DeLand, Henry A., 173 (n. 2)
Delilah, 81
Dependence, of preachers, 83–85
Depravity, 58, 71, 110, 117, 148–49, 166 (n. 30)
Disciples of Christ, 15, 51
Discipline of the Primitive Baptist Church, 110
"Divine Plan of Organized Government, The" (Sams), 108–9
Doubt, 47, 48, 53, 59.
  See also Uncertainty

Dualism, 59–60, 62
Du Bois, W. E. B., 88, 90
Duffey, John, 125
Dylan, Bob, 118, 119

Education: African American, 100–107, 178 (n. 38); sectarian colleges in, 5
Emotion: belief and, 12; Calvinism and, 56; conversion and, 55; evangelicalism and, 11–12, 57–58, 64–65; failure and, 51–53; normative style of, 47–48; revivalism and, 38, 55–56; thought vs., 10–11; uncertainty and, 63–65
"Emotional communities," 11, 12, 64
Emotional exiles, Primitive Baptists as, 54–58
Enlightenment, 15, 56
Estrangement, 56–57
Eustace, Nicole, 11
Evangelicalism: accoutrements of, 13; conversion and, 29–31, 46–48; culture in, 6, 25; emotion and, 11–12, 57–58, 64–65; features of, 17–18; growth of, 7; millennialism and, 28, 63; missions movement and, 22, 79–80; money and, 67; normative emotional style in, 47–48; Primitive Baptists vs., 8, 14, 148–49; reinvention of, 7; "Rock Daniel" and, 112; Second Great Awakening and, 55; women and, 81–82, 85. *See also* Protestantism
Evans, Walker, 122, *123*, 182 (n. 36)

Failure, 50, 51–53
Fatalism, 35, 58, 116
Fields, Bud, *123*
Filene, Benjamin, 120
Finney, Charles, 58, 160 (n. 4)
First Great Awakening, 149
Fisher's River Association, 173 (n. 6)
Flint River Association, 94, 175 (n. 14)
Florida Baptist Association, 163 (n. 39)
Folk music, 123, 136, 138
Folk music revival, 1, 124

Folkways Records, 121
Foot washing, 88
Francis, Edward, 93
Franklin, Benjamin, 72
Fraud, 37
Frazier, Charles, 132–33
Freedmen's Aid Society, 177 (n. 27)
Freedmen's Bureau, 101, 177 (n. 23)
Friends of Old Time Music (FOTM), 122–24
Fristoe, William, 23, 26
Fuller, Andrew, 35

Garrard, William, 70–71
Gaston, William H., 101–4, 106
Gender, 80–82, 85, 171 (nn. 35–36)
General Baptists, 25, 28
General Convention of the Baptists Denomination, 32
God: covenant with, as contract, 71; as father, 80; gospel and, in salvation, 150, 185 (n. 4); preachers and, 83; suffering and, 34; in "Two-Seeds" doctrine, 60–63; as tyrant, 58
Goins, Melvin, *135*
Gospel, salvation and, 150, 185 (n. 4)
Graded and Industrial School, 106
Grant, Ulysses S., 101
Great Revival, 26, 27, 60
Grenell, Zelotes, 43–45
Griffin, Benjamin, 41
Group identity, 45
Guilt, 49, 52

Hale Creek, 178 (n. 34)
Hanks, Lee, 59, 118, 166 (n. 31)
Harris, Bartley, 94
Harris, William, 94
Hassell, Cushing Biggs, 18, 36–40, 66, 70, 71–79, 169 (nn. 17, 21)
Hassell, Sylvester, 36–40, 76–77, 174 (n. 8)
Hawthorne, Nathaniel, 168 (n. 7)
Hebrides, 129
Hell, 52, 117, 143
Heroes, 24

Index   215

Hervey, George, 31
Heyrman, Christine Leigh, 7, 55, 154 (n. 10), 156 (n. 17)
Higginson, Thomas Wentworth, 173 (n. 2)
"High Lonesome" (Country Gentlemen), 125
High Lonesome Sound, The (film), 131
High Lonesome Sound, The (Holcomb), 132
High Point, N.C., 1–2
Hill, Thomas, 46–47, 51–52, 54, 57–58, 64, 118
Hinton, James, 174 (n. 8)
Histories: narratives in, 27–28; in nineteenth century, 22–24; persecution in, 26–27; Rice in, 32–33
History of the Church of God (Hassell and Hassell), 36–41, 77
Holcomb, Ethel, 124
Holcomb, Roscoe, 20, 117, 118–33, *122*, *132*, 180 (n. 5)
Hollister, Sarah Ann, 48–50, 118
Howe, Daniel Walker, 155 (n. 16)
Howell, Robert, 30
Hudson River Association, 44
Huntsville, Ala., 94–102, *96*, *97*, *98*, 107–8, 176 (n. 16)
Huntsville Gazette, 104
Huntsville Primitive Baptist Graded and Industrial School, 100–107
Hussites, 27

"I Am a Man of Constant Sorrow" (Holcomb), 117, 131
"I Am a Stranger Here Below" (hymn), 8–9
Identity: formation, 43–44; group, 45; uncertainty and, 48–51, 53–54
Indiana Territory, 5
Indian Creek, 99–100, 102
Isaac, Rhys, 25, 160 (n. 7)

"Jerks," 29
Jones, Lewis, 112

Kehukee Association, 4–5; African Americans and, 174 (n. 7); historical narratives and, 27–28; *History of the Church of God* and, 36; Lawrence and, 172 (n. 44); missions and, 39–40; revivalism and, 159 (n. 2)
Key West, Fla., 90, 174 (n. 5)

Labor, 72–73
Landmark Baptists, 15
Lawrence, Joshua, 49, 52–53, 59–64, 68–70, 79–86, 170 (n. 29), 172–73 (nn. 43–46)
Led by a Way I Knew Not (Phillips), 50
Lee, H. C., 165 (n. 25)
Lewis, Joseph, 57
"Little Maggie" (Holcomb), 127
Lived religion, 10
Lomax, Alan, 112–13, 127, 136–37
London Confession of Faith, 108, 110
Loneliness, 57–58, 120, 126–28, 141–42
Lutz, Catherine, 11

MacLean, Annie Marion, 87–88, 111, 113
Macon, Dave, 125
Macon, Ga., 90
Mallett, John Frederick, 163 (n. 37)
Manichaeanism, 41, 61, 62, 69
Mark, Mary Ellen, 136, *137*
Marketplace, 66–71, 77–78, 86
Mason, Elder, 92
Mass conversion, 79. *See also* Conversion
Mathews, Donald, 170 (n. 32)
McCravy, Blount, 104–6
McIntosh County Shouters, 113–14
McLoughlin, William, 45
McReynolds, Jesse, 135
Men, 80–82, 171 (n. 35)
Methodist Episcopal Church (North) (Huntsville), 103
Methodists, 29, 59, 75–76, 78, 95–96
Millennialism, 28, 29, 30, 63
Millinder, Lucky, 114
Mind of the South, The (Cash), 116

Missionary Baptists: African American, 94–95; bureaucracy and, 32; conversion and, 30–31; deception and, 39–40; in *History of the Church of God*, 40–41; Kehukee Association and, 4, 39–40; money and, 38–39, 69–71, 170 (n. 32); Primitive Baptists vs., 3, 13, 22, 42–43, 63–64; rhetoric of, 41–42; rise of, 5–6, 30–31; in writings, 32–34
Money, 38–39, 63, 66–71, 74–76, 169 (nn. 17, 21), 170 (n. 32)
Monroe, Bill, 126–27, 136, 139
Mormons, 15
Mountain Music of Kentucky (Folkways Records), 121
Music: bluegrass, 120; Cainites and, 69; folk, 1, 123, 124, 136, 138; Holcomb and, 118–33; in Kentucky, 121; loneliness and, 120, 126–28; Old Baptists and, 130; "Rock Daniel" and, 112, 113–14; Stanley and, 133–43

Najar, Monica, 185 (n. 1)
Narratives, 27–28, 35, 46–47. *See also* Histories
Nasality, 142
Nashville, Tenn., 90
"National Hymn" (Sams), 109–10
National Industrial College, 100–107
National Primitive Baptist Convention (NPBC), 16, 88–89, 107–11, 158 (n. 29)
Nelson, Paul, 180 (n. 5)
New England, 40–41
New Jersey, 25
New Lost City Ramblers, 120
New School Presbyterians, 14–15
Niebuhr, H. Richard, 141
Niles, John Jacob, 124
Noll, Mark A., 118, 162 (n. 35)
Normative emotional style, 47–48

O Brother, Where Art Thou? (film), 133, 134
"O Death" (Stanley), 117, 133–34, 136, 144–45, 184 (n. 49)

Old Regular Baptists, 129, 130–32, 184 (n. 44)
Old School Baptists, 6, 15, 22, 49, 62, 154 (n. 7). *See also* Primitive Baptists
Old School Presbyterians, 14–15
Old-Time Baptist, 158 (n. 30)
"Old Way" singing, 129–30, 139, 140–41, 146
Opposites, 60, 61
Optimism, 23, 28–30
Orange County Baptist Society, 44
Original sin, 15, 61, 110, 117, 145
Origin stories, 35–36, 40
Orsi, Robert, 10

Palmer, Solomon, 105
Pankake, John, 119, 180 (n. 5)
Parker, Daniel, 60–62
"Parkerism," 62
Particular election, 58
Paternalism, 91, 103
Patriarchy, 79–86
Patterson, Beverly, 142
Paul, 32, 110
Peck, John Mason, 41–42
Perception, 47
Perfection, 55
Persecution: of Baptists, 26–27, 31; suffering and, 34–35
Petrobrusians, 27
Phebe, 110, 111
Philadelphia, 28
Phillips, Rebecca, 50, 64, 110–11
Pitch, 129
Poe, Harry L., 158 (n. 28)
Popular Front, 123
Practice, as concept, 10
Preachers: as dependent, 83–85; as historians, 22–23; as mothers, 82–83; pay of, 75, 78, 169 (n. 21); wealth of, 171 (n. 32)
Predestinarianism, 41, 58, 61, 71, 72, 74, 141
Presbyterians, 6, 14–15, 28, 61
"Priestcraft," 6, 40

Primitive Baptist (biweekly), 67, 71
Primitive Baptist Manual, 110, 111
Primitive Baptists: African American, 15-16; in American religious history, 9-16; Baptist Church at Abbott's Creek and, 2-3; beliefs of, 8, 9; as Calvinist, 8; conversion among, 46-48; as emotional exiles, 54-58; evangelicalism vs., 8, 14, 148-49; influence of, 1; Kehukee Association and, 4-5; legacy of, 148-49; missionary Baptists vs., 3, 13, 22, 42-43, 63-64; numbers of, 15, 158 (n. 29); origin stories of, 35-36, 40; rhetorical origins of, 40-45; rise of, 7-8, 14; as term, 6, 154 (n. 7). *See also* Old School Baptists
Protestantism: Arminianism and, 86; emotion and, 11-12, 47-48; in historiography, 149; republicanism and, 162 (n. 35). *See also* Evangelicalism
Purifoy, J. H., 53-54, 64, 118

Quantico, Va., 93

Rabinowitz, Richard, 165 (n. 23)
Racism, 88, 91-92. *See also* African Americans
Read, Jesse, 23, 26, 27-28
Rebel Records, 140
Reddy, William, 11
Reformation, 15, 28
Regular Baptists, 25-26, 28, 129, 154 (n. 10). *See also* Old Regular Baptists
Religion, lived, 10
Religious History of the American People, A (Ahlstrom), 45, 116-17
Republicanism, 13, 43, 162 (n. 35)
Republican Party, 101, 102
Revivalism: conversions and, 29-30; "dark age" and, 36-37; emotion and, 38, 55-56; fraud and, 37; Hassells and, 36-37; in historiography, 149; in Huntsville 1907, 107-8; Kehukee Association and, 159 (n. 2); Lawrence and, 172 (n. 44); millennialism and, 29; sincerity and, 37; skepticism over, 21-22; zeal in, 37, 38, 39-40
Rhetorical origins, 40-45
Rice, Luther, 32-33, 161 (n. 18)
Rinzler, Ralph, 122, 123
"Roane County Prison" (Monroe), 127
Roberson, Nelly, 92, 93
"Rock Daniel," 87, 111-15, 178 (n. 38)
Rosenberg, Neil, 125
Rosenwein, Barbara, 11, 12
Royall, Anne, 176 (n. 16)
Rust Normal Institute, 103

St. Annis Primitive Baptist Church, 88, 112, 114, 180 (n. 47)
St. Bartley's, 94-100, *96*, *97*, *98*, 106
Salvation, 23-24, 29, 37, 150, 185 (n. 4)
Sams, C. F., 108-12, 151
Samson, 81
Santayana, George, 150
Sarcasm, 23-24
Satan, 55, 60-61, 81, 145
Scarborough, Daniel, 164 (n. 13)
Scarborough, William, 164 (n. 13)
Schmidt, Leigh Eric, 55
School, 100-107, 178 (n. 38)
Schweiger, Beth Barton, 148, 185 (n. 1)
Scruggs, Earl, 136
Sea Islands, 173 (n. 2)
Second Great Awakening, 1, 13, 55, 149, 156 (n. 17), 157 (nn. 25, 27)
Seeger, Pete, 123
Sellers, Charles, 155 (n. 16)
Separate Baptists, 16, 25-26, 28, 160 (n. 7)
Sethites, 69
Shakers, 15
Sherwood, Adiel, 32
Shuffler, George, 182 (n. 34)
Signs of the Times (Beebe, ed.), 44, 82
Sin, original, 15, 61, 110, 117, 145
Sincerity, 37, 54
Singing, 138-39, 142, 144. *See also* "Old Way" singing; Voice

Skepticism, 21–22, 50, 60
Smith, Bessie, 125
Smith, Job E. W., 185 (n. 4)
Solomon, 81
Sons of Temperance, 76
Southern Baptist Convention, 3, 34, 42
Southern Folklife Collection, 147
Sovereign Grace Baptists, 158 (n. 29)
Sovereign Grace Recordings, 182 (n. 36)
Spangler, Jewel L., 160 (n. 7)
Sparks, Larry, 135
Sparks, Randy J., 159 (n. 33)
Stanley, Carter, 134–35, 141
Stanley, Ralph, 20, 117, 132, 133–43, 135–38, 144–45, 182 (n. 31), 184 (n. 44)
State Normal School (Huntsville), 105
Stereotype, 42–43, 44–45, 91–92
Suffering, 34–35
Sunday schools, 5, 7, 13, 16, 50, 88

Tallahassee, Fla., 109
Tanner, John, 26
Tarboro, N.C., 18, 41, 56
Tarboro Baptist Church, 67
Taylor, James, 161 (n. 18)
Taylor, John, 40–41
Temperance, 63
Temperley, Nicholas, 130, 145–46
Tharpe, Rosetta, 114
Thompson, Wilson, 59
Thought, emotion vs., 10–11
Tract societies, 5, 13, 41, 130
Tuskegee Institute, 107
"Two-Seeds" doctrine, 60–63, 166 (n. 35)
Tyrant, God as, 58

Uncertainty, 47, 48; anti-missionism and, 63–64; conversion and, 48–51; deception and, 53–54; emotion and, 63–65
Unitarianism, 5

United Baptist Association, 159 (n. 2). *See also* Kehukee Association
United Baptists, 28
Universalism, 16, 143, 184 (n. 44)
U.S. Census, 158 (n. 28)

"Village Church Yard" (Stanley), 140–41
Voice: of Holcomb, 120, 125, 126, 128–29, 130–31; of Monroe, 126, 127; of Stanley, 117, 138–40, 142, 182 (n. 31)

Waldenses, 27
"Wandering Boy" (Holcomb), 131
Ware, Charlie, 100–101
Ware, Georgia Ann, 100–101, 106
Washington, Booker T., 104, 106, 178 (n. 34)
Washington, D.C., 93
"Watching," 48–50, 164 (n. 6)
Watson, Doc, 125
Watson, John, 60
Weber, Max, 168 (n. 11)
Wesley, John, 55
Whites: African American separation and, 90–91, 174 (n. 6); baptism of African Americans and, 92; black churches and, 91–92
Williams, Roger, 27
Williamston, N.C., 66, 72–73, 77, 91
Women, 80–83, 85, 106, 110–11, 171 (nn. 35–36)
Work, John, 112
Worms, Primitive Baptists as, 58–59
Writings. *See* Histories
Wyatt-Brown, Bertram, 45, 166 (n. 30)

Young, Israel, 122
"You're Drifting On" (Stanley), 139

Zeal, 21–22, 37, 38, 39–40
Zion Primitive Baptist Church, 174 (n. 5)